PRAISE FOR THE WO

MW00936696

"Acclaimed author Randall Sil\ fiction…and leaves the reader guessing every step of the way." The Portobello Bookshop, Edinburgh, Scotland

"A soulful, deeply felt story." *Kirkus Reviews*

"DeMarco is a vividly realized, robust, and abundantly human character….a hard-edged, smartly plotted novel." *Booklist*

"*No Woods So Dark as These* has all the signs and qualities of another masterpiece by Randall Silvis." *Criminal Element*

"Powerful. Plot twists and tension come rapidly…but Silvis also writes a deeper set of questions into his novels. If you're not yet reading Randall Silvis, this is the moment to get going." *Kingdom Books*

"Gruesome, dark, heavy, suspenseful, and action-packed passages. Randall Silvis offers some powerful insights while his characters experience life at its most dangerous." *Criminal Element*

"Silvis is at it again, striving for a blend of crime story and literature, mutilated bodies and lapidary prose." *Booklist*

"The story is complex and intricately layered. The writing is beautifully descriptive and richly textured. A novel bursting with intrigue." *Blue Stocking Reviews*

"Randall Silvis is an author's author, critically acclaimed and recognized throughout the world…an author who never disappoints." *Book Reporter*

"Beautiful writing and a suspenseful pace that is simply spellbinding." *Dressed to Read*

"Dark, moody, and compelling. A powerful story of love and betrayal. Silvis possesses a rare talent." *JDCMustReadBooks*

"Randall raises the bar so high that after him it's difficult to read anything else." *BG Storyteller*

"This is a stellar work." *Indie Picks Magazine*

"A tour de force. Outstanding!" Karen Dionne, international bestselling author of *The Marsh King's Daughter*

"A gripping new literary thriller…literature posing as a mystery. One of the best reading investments you will make this year." *Book Page*

"A stunning, elegiac tale of love and loss." *Minneapolis Star Tribune*

"A masterpiece, a work of genius, a novel so filled with such immense imagery and strength as to make you catch your breath." *Over My Dead Body Magazine*

"Poetically written, finely-wrought, richly imagined. Randall Silvis gets to the hearts and souls of his characters like few other, if any, novelists." *New York Times* bestselling author John Lescroart

"Randall Silvis may be the last of a dying species, the creative genius." William Allen, author of *Starkweather* and *Fire in the Birdbath*

"A masterful storyteller, Silvis doesn't waste a word in this tale about 'the tart nectar of memory's flower.'" *Publishers Weekly*

"Silvis is a self-made master of fiction. His writing elicits visceral imagery, palpable conflict, and a core understanding of the human condition." Bestselling author Susan Wingate, host of *Dialogue: Between the Lines* radio podcast

"A gifted storyteller, a master of complicated human souls, Randall Silvis brings readers a remarkable blend of literary, drama, mystery, suspense, and psychological thriller." *LibraryThing*

"A powerful novel that deeply touches the reader emotionally and intellectually." *The Bloomsbury Review*

"The words fall as polished jewels." *The Agony Column Book Reviews*

"One of the best-written novels of the year." Jeff VanderMeer, editor of *Best American Fantasy*

"Masterful research, empathetic sensitivity, and skilled storytelling. A tantalizing adventure." *Booklist*

"*Heart So Hungry* is a complex love story but it is also a tragedy and an epic. The combination makes for a wonderful tale." *Quill & Quire*

"Atmospheric and cleverly researched, *Disquiet Heart* races to a sparkling denouement." *Publishers Weekly*

"Moody, emotionally tortured, and convincingly atmospheric, a graphically described descent into Poe's addictions." *Kirkus Reviews*

"A riveting tale of murder and betrayal...drips with descriptive power." *The New York Post*

"The writing is rich, fluid, packed with controlled energy – a page-turner that leaves the reader breathless with the force of its beauty." *Erie Times-News*

"The characters, real and fictional alike, are masterpieces of insight into the human experience." *Historical Novel Society*

"*Mysticus* is that rarest of rare books, the one that heaves the heart as much as it haunts the head." Lee K. Abbott, author of *Living After Midnight*

"Lyrical and parodic, philosophical and stylish and elegant. A tour de force." *Collages & Bricolages, An International Literary Magazine*

"A superbly written crime novel." *Booklist*

"A funny, engaging journey toward some pretty sweet truths." *The New York Times Book Review*

"One of the funniest books of the year. Highly recommended." *Library Journal*

"The storyline is riveting – complex, convoluted, and compelling. I couldn't put this novel down." *Los Angeles Reader*

"A stunning performance by a writer of exceptional talent." John W. Aldridge, author of *Talents and Technicians*

"Randall Silvis is a masterful storyteller." *New York Times Book Review*

BOOKS BY RANDALL SILVIS

RYAN DEMARCO MYSTERIES
Two Days Gone
Walking the Bones
A Long Way Down
No Woods So Dark as These
When All Light Fails

EDGAR ALLAN POE MYSTERIES
On Night's Shore
Disquiet Heart
(also published as *Doubly Dead*)

OTHER CRIME NOVELS
An Occasional Hell
Dead Man Falling
The Boy Who Shoots Crows
Blood & Ink
Only the Rain
First the Thunder
The Deepest Black

OTHER NOVELS
Excelsior
Under the Rainbow
Mysticus
Hangtime, A Confession
In a Town Called Mundomuerto
Flying Fish

SHORT STORY COLLECTIONS
The Luckiest Man in the World
Incident on Ten-Right Road

CREATIVE NONFICTION
Heart So Hungry
(also published as *North to Unknown*)
(cont)

THE LEGACY COLLECTION
(IN PROGRESS)

NOVELS
Marguerite & the Moon Man

STORY COLLECTIONS
My Secret Life
One Night in Jane Lew
Let's Keep the Children Out of This
Wicked World
The Ruin of Us All

CREATIVE NONFICTION
From the Mirror: Reflections on Living, Writing, and Dying Well
Ten Easy Steps to Becoming a Writer
I Was Born This Way, and You're Only Making It Worse
How to Die, and Other Ways to Improve Your Life
Trying Love
My Strange and Stranger Life

Ten Easy Steps
to Becoming a Writer

THE ART, CRAFT, BUSINESS, AND TEACHING
OF CREATIVE WRITING

RANDALL SILVIS

TwoSunsBooks
The Legacy Collection

Copyright © 2023 by Randall Silvis
Cover image by анна-рыжкова /Pexels
Cover design Two Suns Books
Internal design Two Suns Books

All rights reserved. No part of this book may be reproduced in any form or by any electronic or mechanical means including information storage and retrieval systems – except in the case of brief quotations embodied in critical articles and reviews – without permission in writing from the author.

Acknowledgements

The following essays were originally published, sometimes with other titles, in the following periodicals and books: "Ten Easy Steps to Becoming a Writer," "A Farewell to Adverbs," and "Why I Read" in the *Chronicle of Higher Education*; "Sentences, A Love Story," and "Cue the Music" in *Strand Magazine*; "Tough Love" in *Many Genres, One Craft*; "The Silence that Speaks" in *Suspense Magazine*; "The Writer's Obligation" and "Writing Out Loud" in *The Writer*; "Lost in Words" in *Clarion Magazine*; and "Books: What Are They Good For?" in *Tantalus*. The short pieces "Tell Me a Story," "When Less is More," "Writing the Devil" and "What's Your Colostomy Bag" were all composed for a column on Virtual Pitch Fest, a website devoted to professional screenwriting. "A Writer's Life" was presented as part of the Washabaugh Lecture series at Gannon University. The material in the What I've Been Reading and One Writer's Tips sections in this book are from my monthly newsletter; some of the tips also appeared in my first memoir *From the Mirror: Reflections on Living, Writing, and Dying Well*.

for my sons,
Bret and Nathan

Author's Disclaimer

You are going to find this out sooner or later, so I might as well tell you right now: Despite the title, this is not a how-to-write book. There is very little definitive writing advice in these pages. There is a lot of metaphorical advice and an equal measure of sarcastic advice. Most of these pieces were borne of what I learned over the past fifty years by writing thirty or so books, a couple dozen stage plays and screenplays, and at least two hundred novellas, stories, essays, and poems. I have had the pleasure, and not infrequently the frustration, of working with Big Five publishers as well as small literary presses and independent publishers, national and regional magazines, regional and off-off-Broadway theatre companies, plus a multitude of editors, agents, managers, actors, and Hollywood producers. I also spent most of forty years slipping in and out of academia. (I still have nightmares.)

Each and every manuscript and individual I worked with required a different approach, just as every puppy and every poisonous snake requires an individual approach based upon its temperament. So if you opened this book hoping to hear me say "you must always do this and you must never do that," you should probably close the cover now and grab a how-to-write-a-bestseller book. It doesn't matter which one you grab; they all say more or less the same thing, since each generation of how-to-write writers repeats what the previous generation repeated.

I suppose this book is as much a memoir as it is a loving consideration of the writing life and a not-so-loving critique of both the publishing world and academia. I have organized it into five sections, starting with an *Introduction*. The *Essays* section consists of thirty-three informal essays, most of them previously published between 1984 and 2023; they address the art, craft, business, and teaching of creative writing.

The third and fourth sections, *One Writer's Tips* and *What I've Been Reading,* were lifted out of four years of my monthly newsletter. The first of these two sections is self-explanatory; the next one lays out my opinion on each of the books I read in a particular month. More often than not, I chose to not finish a book, and I tell you why. In conclusion, there is *A Temporary Conclusion*. This book ends but the writing doesn't.

The material within all five sections is highly subjective, sometimes cynical, now and then contradictory, and infrequently complimentary, yet it does provide one writer's honest perspective on what constitutes good writing and what doesn't. Because each piece was written with a singular purpose in mind, you should not be surprised to find me repeating myself from time to time. But beware: what I believed at thirty might be a world apart from what I believe at seventy. I no longer teach the things I used to teach because none of those old chestnuts matter to the writer I am now.

And so, the material herein is not meant to be read as a prescription for success as a writer. There are no exercises to complete, no prompts, no formulas, no templates, no blueprints. My intent is not to preach or exhort but to offer up a lifetime of personal observations in regards to all facets of creative writing. There are no absolute truths in this book, just as there are no absolute truths in any field of the creative arts, despite what others might tell you.

And isn't life itself a creative art?

This collection, as well as all my other books, represents my experiences and practices as a writer and nothing more. If I knew more, I would have put it in this book.

TEN EASY STEPS TO BECOMING A WRITER

(cont.)

(CONTENTS *continued*)

Introduction: A Lamentable Truth

An unfortunate trend in academia – one of several unfortunate trends in academia – is the insistence on hiring, for faculty positions in creative writing, only individuals with an MFA or PhD degree in creative writing. To most in academia, a degree that requires little more than the completion of several pieces of unpublished writing is more important than years of actual success in the field that the degree allegedly prepares the student to enter. Those who make this decision do so because they are bearers of the same degrees, and to deny their importance is to invalidate their own degrees.

This is unfortunate on more than one count. First, individuals who have spent an extra three to six years in the classroom in order to get one of those degrees have spent those years *not* gaining the essential boots-on-the-ground life experience that all good writers must have, but instead with filling their heads with other professors' theories and dictums while having their own innate talent, if indeed they possessed any to begin with, shaved and grated and eroded by the criticisms of committees and workshops full of other unpublished writers.

How can this kind of education be healthy for any writer who aspires to create something more than mediocre work? Three to six years of pedagogy, during which the carrot of a degree is constantly dangled as the reward for compliance, is sure to do any original or visionary writer far more harm than good.

A second problem with the trend toward hiring only degreed writers whether they have published anything or not is that truly creative writers don't belong in an English department filled with academics. Academics are more like coroners of creative writing than creators of creative writing. The academics deconstruct literature in a futile attempt to understand how it came to be and how it accomplished the effects it had on them. They then impose their mostly clueless and useless opinions on students eager to learn the non-existent rules and formulas for successful writing.

In truth, career academics only admire dead writers, the ones who don't show up at their institutions to shame them with long lists of publications and literary prizes. Unfortunately, most writers, even those with major literary prizes and a bookshelf sagging with publications, will need to supplement their incomes from time to time, and the most likely way of doing that is by teaching or talking about writing. But I have yet to meet a single working writer who feels at home in an English department. (By "working writer" I mean the kind who does not teach fulltime but only when financially necessary, and who actually lives in the real world and is comfortable moving about in it, as opposed to the academics, who lose all semblance of authority and relevance when they venture beyond the campus and who will therefore cling all the more tenaciously to their courses and offices and committee appointments and titles in an attempt to bolster their egos.) In academia, the nearest specie to a creative writer can be found in the Theater or Film or Communication departments, but even there you will find more coroners than creators.

And this is the reason why an academic degree is more prized in academia than is actual literary experience and success. The presence of a real writer in their midst makes all the coroners look bad, for their CVs are noticeably short of publications that have garnered even the slightest degree of success. While academics will eagerly demean and denigrate creative writing that reaches a wider audience, literary success is precisely what most of them and their students covet. But because their heads have been stuffed with useless misinformation, few of them are capable of producing anything more than slim volumes of pretentious prose and poetry published by an academic press and read by almost no one.

I don't want this appraisal to be seen as an indictment against all academics or all English departments, for I, in nearly forty years of temporary visits to numerous institutions of so-called higher learning, have met several honest and fair individuals who will freely admit to their longing for literary achievements. But those individuals are few when compared to the others, most of whom wander from their offices to their classrooms grumbling and complaining, soured on the life they have chosen, the company they are forced to keep, and the achievements they have failed to achieve.

And yet creative writing programs proliferate. From what I have witnessed over my decades of hopscotching in and out of various programs, they are no longer the cash cows they were throughout the final decades of the previous century. Still, they continue to crank out several thousands of graduates each year. And that is precisely where the problem arises for gullible students who are led to believe that a terminal degree in creative writing will ensure them literary success and a plum job in a prestigious creative writing program.

Let's say that you are one of those hopeful candidates for a degree. Let's say you have just now taken a seat in your first workshop in a traditional MFA program – a program that will cost you thousands of hours of work and between $25,000 and $75,000 dollars over the next three or so years before you graduate. For that investment, you are expecting at least one of three things to happen: that you will learn how to become a successful writer and start publishing books right after graduation, and/or that your degree will win you a tenure-track teaching position, and/or that your degree will entitle you to a job in the publishing industry.

Only one of those expectations is realistic.

Consider the odds you face. I will start with the expectation that a creative writing MFA degree will secure you a job teaching creative writing in higher education:

According to the Academic Jobs Wiki page for Creative Writing 2023, there were 45 fulltime positions available for fiction writers, 27 in nonfiction, 23 in poetry, 8 in screenwriting and/or playwriting, and 15 in open genre. I will be generous and round that total off to 120. Those numbers fluctuate from year to year but are fairly typical of the number of positions available each year. There were also 24 visiting/limited term positions available.

Many but not all of the fulltime positions were tenure track positions, and most required that the candidate possessed not only an MFA or PhD degree but also at least one book traditionally published or under contract by a reputable publisher. Several of the visiting positions asked for professional writers with an impressive list of publications.

We can also assume that most of the MFA graduates who graduated in the spring of 2023 did not yet have a legitimate publication to their credit. Self-published works do not count. So most of that year's graduates did what unpublished graduates from all the previous years did, which was to get a job teaching in a high school or painting houses or walking dogs while trying to find the time and energy to write a publishable book.

Perhaps three out of every ten of 2023's graduates will be eligible to apply for one of the available jobs. Who is your competition? The Poets & Writers' database lists 217 universities that offer the MFA degree, and 23 that offer a PhD degree. So let's be conservative and assume that only twenty-five people per program will graduate each year, or about six thousand aspiring writers in all. Of that six thousand, 33%, or approximately 2000, will have at least one published book.

Therefore, if you too are a published writer, you are one in a pool of 2000 applicants hoping to land one of that year's 120 jobs. But wait! Don't forget those applicants who graduated in 2022, and 2021, and 2020, and so on back five or ten more years. They have all been scribbling away, writing book after book. Some of them have won literary prizes. Some have glowing reviews from the *New York Times* and *Publishers Weekly* and other influential review sources. And let us not forget that many if not most of the open positions are expressly aimed at a minority candidate. In this case, your chances might increase or decrease a bit more, or a lot more, depending on your skin color, gender, and/or lifestyle.

In every case, however, the pool of potential applicants for those positions grows exponentially, with a mere hundred or so successful applicants being skimmed off the total each year.

Are you getting the picture?

If your reason for pursuing a terminal degree is to land a cushy teaching job at a prestigious or even third-rate university, good luck, because your chances are abysmally low. In fact, I can think of few, if any, other terminal degrees whose placement rate sucks as much as the MFA in Creative Writing sucks.

Now let's look at the odds for and against your expensive degree turning you into a successful writer. For every Michael Chabon, whose master's thesis landed him a record-breaking advance and turned him instantly into a literary darling, there are tens of thousands of unpublished MFA degree holders who are grudgingly working jobs that have absolutely nothing to do with the publishing industry. For most of them, this will become not a temporary situation but their life's story. As Chuck Sambuchino points out in "The Pros and Cons of Getting a Creative Writing MFA," a *Writer's Digest* article, "Plenty of MFA grads never publish a book."

But how can that be? you ask. *Doesn't an MFA teach you how to be a successful writer?*

No, it doesn't.

Huh? Why not?

Because there is no formula to good writing. And because good writing is a subjective determination. And because talent cannot be taught. And because true and lasting discipline must be self-imposed. And because the road to publication is too arduous and frustrating and maddening for most to endure for the necessary years. And because what a student learns through their MFA workshops and seminars and lectures is too often not practicable instructions but abstract homilies, false encouragement, and mere opinions NOT founded upon experiential success.

Let's take a deeper look at the venerable writer's workshop, a standard fixture in nearly every American MFA program. One instructor and anywhere from eight to fifteen students.

Ask those students and professors how many of them hope to publish a critically-acclaimed bestselling novel, and every hand will fly into the air. Ask how many of them have already published a critically-acclaimed bestselling novel, and in most of those classrooms, not a single hand will rise. In most cases, only the top-tier universities can afford to hire a well-published author to serve as your mentor and professor.

All across this country and elsewhere, unpublished and unpublishable professors are presuming to teach eager but gullible young people to be better writers. What is happening, in fact, is that you, as one of those students, will be subjected regularly to the opinions of those who know as little about writing as you do. To take their advice on how you should write is akin to agreeing to heart surgery performed by a surgeon who has never actually performed surgery but has read a lot of books about it. Or, worse yet, who has performed several operations but whose patients always died.

Before signing up for any workshop, research your professors. If they have published nothing or are trying to peddle their self-published masterpieces as a viable credential, steer clear. In this case, an advanced degree means nothing. The only thing a writer who can't get published has to teach you is how to not get published.

But what if you can afford to attend one of the top-tier universities staffed by famous writers? Won't they have useful, priceless wisdom to impart?

That depends. Has your professor written several successful books in the genre in which you hope to find success? If the answer is yes, then okay, you might want to linger for a while and see how it works out for you. But if the answer is no, head for the exit.

Let me state this as simply as I can: why would you throw your time and money away by listening to what a roomful of failures and/or novices have to say about your work?

And know this: *No* instructor holds the key to your success. No instructor knows any secrets to success. All any instructor knows is what has worked for him or her. You should take this information for what it's worth, apply whichever elements work for you, and throw away the rest.

And now you ask, *Is that all the good that can come from an advanced degree in creative writing?*

No. There are hundreds of publishers here and abroad who require employees who can recognize good writing when they see it and who can express themselves clearly. However, these positions come with their own disadvantages: they are not easy to win and you probably won't get rich as an editor. According to Glass Door, the average salary for a book editor in 2023 is about $62,000.

In most cases you will first have to prove yourself as an assistant editor or a mere intern. It could take several years for you to work your way up to the average salary. And the plum editorial jobs are usually located in big cities where the cost of living is considerably higher than in a smaller city. For example, according to the Forbes Advisor cost of living calculator, what you can buy for $62,000 in Pittsburgh, Pennsylvania will cost $140,915 in New York City.

How about getting a job as an editor at a newspaper or a magazine? That's another possibility, but one that pays an average of 10K less than that of a book editor.

Well, maybe you would like to become a literary agent. Literary agents are essential for steering writers and publishers toward each other. Zip Recruiter reports that these agents earn an average of $53,000 a year. But bear in mind that this salary depends on the number of writers the agent represents, and the commercial success of those writers. If an agent's writers don't publish, the agent gets nothing.

Hollywood, on the other hand, is a meat grinder that never loses its hunger for more material. The same is true of TV and cable networks. The average length of a screenplay is that of a short novella, and the pay for a good screenplay can keep you in beer and pretzels for a couple of years. But after signing away your work of art, you will have zero control over it. The producer or other entity that purchases your script will own the story, the characters, and every word of the script *in perpetuity*. They can cast whomever they wish in the roles and they can turn your script into confetti if they feel like it. A great movie can make your career, but a bad one – and there are a lot of bad movies being made – can sink you into the mud of oblivion.

The corporate world also offers employment opportunities for good writers. You can write copy for a business magazine, newsletter, or website. In fact, writing for a large corporation can be very lucrative. But it can also gnaw away at your soul.

Good writers will always be in demand. That isn't in question. The question I'm posing concerns the value of an advanced degree in creative writing. And my point, in this Introduction and in this book as a whole, is that an advanced degree is in no way a requisite to your success as a creative writer, nor is it, in that case, a cost-effective expense.

Recently Flavorwrite interviewed several successful writers regarding their opinions of MFA writing programs for an article titled "27 Writers on Whether or Not to Get Your MFA." An overwhelming majority of those authors, nearly two-thirds, answered with a resounding "No!" Only five responded in the affirmative. The rest said some variation of "Maybe, depending on the program" or "Maybe, if it's free."

Writing guru Jane Friedman agrees with the majority of those writers. In an article on her webpage called "Three Myths about the MFA in Creative Writing," Friedman says this: "Most writers want an MFA for one of three reasons: They want to teach writing, they want to get published, or they want to make room in their life for writing. It turns out these reasons for doing an MFA are actually based on myths." She then proceeds to debunk those myths for the same reasons I have.

Friedman also brings up another pitfall endemic to the MFA industry: "Most MFA programs focus on literary fiction, creative nonfiction, and poetry. While these are noble areas of literature, they cover only a tiny slice of the wide and diverse world of writing. Heaven forbid a writer in a traditional MFA program produces something commercial – or worse, genre fiction."

How many successful writers, before the boom of MFA programs, held a degree in writing? Almost none. What they had was a natural talent and love for good writing, and the life experience that gave them something interesting to write about.

Good writing is, on every page, in every line, an individual experiment. A gamble. A roll of the dice. Nothing you learn in a classroom will ever make success more certain than that.

I know dozens of MFA degree holders who look back fondly on their time in the program, even if they have had no success in publishing a book. What they are remembering, however, is the camaraderie they experienced and now long for, the encouragement and sense of community. But camaraderie and community are not going to write a publishable book for you.

And do you really want to spend $25k or more to acquire a handful of friends who, after the program, will return to their homes hundreds or thousands of miles from your own? You can get the same love of books, the same input and criticism, and the same bad advice from a writing group at your local library.

Writing is a solitary art, and those who succeed in it learn to accept and embrace that solitude.

Yes, while in a program you will be forced to become a disciplined writer and a more critical reader. But the day the program ends, that external imperative will disappear. Who is going to instill discipline in you then? No one, that's who. The sad truth of the matter is that if you are not capable of adopting your own disciplined habits, an MFA program will not magically bestow them upon you.

Think of how many writers' conferences you can attend at $300 a crack instead of dumping the price of a compact car on a single MFA program. A few writers' conferences will expose you to far more expert opinions than you have access to from all but the biggest of MFA programs. Many conferences provide attendees the opportunity, for about $75, to submit one of their manuscripts in advance and then go over it with a well-published author. Lots of aspiring writers attend one or two conferences every year, and thereby gain far greater exposure to a diverse range of opinions and expertise while also enjoying the vacation-like atmosphere that pervades a writers' conference.

Don't want to travel for your advice? The internet offers up hundreds of possibilities for having your work appraised. However, you are even more likely to get bilked out of your hard-earned cash online. I almost never say never, but I will say it here: *Never* pay for a writing coach or a publicist or manuscript appraisal until you have taken a very deep dive into that individual's or business's credentials. Any substitute English teacher can throw up a fancy website and pepper it with bogus endorsements. Unless an individual has a long history of *successful* and fairly recent involvement in the industry as an editor, an agent, or a writer, keep your money in your pocket. Snake oil comes in a myriad of varieties.

My formal training as a writer is zero. When I was twenty, I signed up for a two-week workshop at a local college. On the first day, our instructor, who was only a few years older than the students, confessed that he knew nothing about teaching creative writing. He held a newly minted PhD in Elizabethan literature, but taking the job of teaching the workshop was a condition of his employment. Our workshop consisted of ten unpublished writers and one unpublished instructor reading and commenting on each other's work.

Before my first book won the Drue Heinz Literature Prize, everything I knew about writing was learned from reading the work of the masters. A couple of years later I was invited to teach creative writing at a local university, so, in order to have more to say to each class than "sit down and write," I read a couple of books. In one of them I learned about the Aristotelian pyramid of story structure, and in the other I saw a diagram of Syd Field's structure for writing a screenplay. On essence, they said the same thing: A good story needs a beginning that hooks the reader's attention, a middle through which the protagonist encounters obstacles that result in escalating tension and/or risk, and an end that shows the protagonist's success or failure. It didn't take two years of sitting in a classroom for me to learn that; it took two afternoons sitting in the library. And it certainly did not cost $20,000 or more; the library was three miles from home, and I rode there on a ten-speed bike.

When I teach creative writing, I always start out by making the MFA scam clear to every student I encounter. An MFA degree is a very expensive venture, and, for far too many degree holders, a wasted expense. You might love the camaraderie you experience during your years in the program, and you might thrive on all the false hope the program engenders in you and on the discipline it temporarily imposes, but the truth of the matter is this: Much of the encouragement you will receive in the program has no relevance to the real world of publishing, and the discipline imposed throughout those few years will no longer exist for you when the program ends.

In no way am I suggesting that those who teach in MFA programs do so to exploit gullible students. I have never met a single teaching writer with that agenda. To the contrary, they genuinely want to help young writers and are, in most cases, underpaid for the amount of attention they lavish on their students. Administrators of MFA Creative Writing programs, on the other hand, are paid to keep the program profitable, which frequently requires more attention on the bottom line and less on the program's practical value.

The points I want to drive home are these: an MFA creative writing degree is an unnecessary financial expense and expenditure of an aspiring writer's time, and the degree cannot guarantee publication or a teaching position. The best and most organic way to learn how to write better is to read good work and to read it critically, and to be just as critical about your own work, which you should be composing as ceaselessly as possible.

It is a life-long learning curve. There is not a single course of study on this planet to equal it.

In other words, creating a successful writer is a two-entity job; only God and you can turn you into a writer.

In short, here is the problem I have with writers' workshops, the heart and soul of every American creative writing program: Every writer writes out of his or her own imagination, which is a product of his or her own experiences. Every reader reads from a different set of experiences.

Let's say that you, as the writer, receive this comment from another member of the workshop: "Your portrait of this character is too harsh, too unforgiving. Readers will find it off-putting."

Oh yeah? Says who?

No reader can possibly know a character as well as the writer does. And no reader should assume to speak for the rest of the world. But that's what readers do in writers' workshops.

In these workshops, for any individual manuscript, there is one writer writing from his or her own perspective, and ten or twelve readers reading from their own perspectives and assuming that everyone else in the world will agree with them. Self-doubting writers are likely to cave under the pressure of two or three very vocal members of the workshop. This is why MFA programs produce such undistinguished prose.

One of two things will happen to every writer critiqued in a writers' workshop. She will either break the standard workshop rule that forbids the writer from defending her work, and in so doing will demean herself, or she will sit there stoically while thinking *what a bunch of asses these people are.*

A writers' workshop is a meat grinder, and every student writer the sausage.

I did my best, with every workshop I conducted, to ameliorate these negative effects by first stating my own aesthetic and editorial bias and by admonishing participants to take all criticism, including mine, with a grain of salt, and by advising each student that nobody but the individual willing to pay for the writer's work should be allowed to exercise an iota of authority over that work. Still, I regret all of the humiliation those workshops must have caused. Education should never be humiliating.

In my opinion, as one who has too often witnessed eight or nine unpublished readers ganging up on a single writer and urging her to soften or trim or disembowel her prose, this is precisely why MFA tutored prose is so anemic.

My advice to every writer considering joining a workshop is this: Don't. Instead, revise your piece until you can find nothing else to change. Then send it off to a dozen different editors. These are the people you need to please, not a dozen unpublished writers. You will spend far less money going this route than you will on an academic program, but if an editor to whom you have emailed a piece of fiction or nonfiction responds with an offer of publication, you will feel as if you hit the jackpot.

Bear in mind, however, that most literary journals are staffed by MFA students and former students. This presents a bleak scenario for those looking to get published, I know. But the profession of creative writing has always presented a bleak scenario. And, as always, writing a thoroughly compelling story that resonates with at least one influential reader is the only way to beat it.

So if not an MFA degree, what *will* help you become a writer? Here is a short list of the qualities you will need to possess and further develop:

- ✓ a basic understanding of story structure;
- ✓ a keen eye for concrete and sensory details;
- ✓ a keen ear for the way people speak;
- ✓ a keen understanding of human nature;
- ✓ the ability to analyze what you read for its effect on you and how that effect was created;
- ✓ an unrelenting discipline;
- ✓ a driving ambition to be a better writer than you are;
- ✓ a respect and love for the written word;
- ✓ a talent for expressing yourself with clarity and precision; and,
- ✓ patience and perseverance.

And now you should ask: *If that's what I need, why should I read this book?* Honestly, you needn't. If you have the drive and discipline to teach yourself, you should fill a backpack with notebooks, pens, and a camera and go tramping around the world. You will learn far more about yourself and the world from that experience than from any instructor or author, including me. And during your breaks in travel, you can find online, at no cost at all, the same information those creative writing professors would have fed you.

What you will not get through traveling and reading is the personal attention your professors might provide. Personally, I think this attention is far more important for the mediocre writer than for the naturally talented one. Disciplined talented writers usually find a way to get published sooner or later with or without personal attention, while also preserving their own distinctive ways of expressing themselves; mediocre writers seldom do. For me, when I was collecting one rejection slip after another, the only opinions I valued were those of the responding editors.

So get out there in the world instead of migrating into yet another bubble. Read as frequently as possible, analyze the masters and their methods, and dissect the works that move you and make you green with envy. This is a tried and true education that will always serve you well, and it is, frankly, the only education a disciplined writer needs.

What you will hear in the following pages are one writer's experiences, the methods and madnesses that have worked for me over the years – those that have allowed me to find some success in my novels, short stories, essays, plays, and screenplays without ever taking a course in creative writing; and those that have allowed me to indulge myself for a half-century in a career that makes me happy to crawl out of bed every morning. Despite its many frustrations, annoyances, and sometimes maddeningly small financial rewards, creative writing has provided me with the freedom to live my life as I see fit, to be nobody's employee, nobody's donkey, nobody's fool. It is an energizing and exhilarating way to live. I thank God every night and every morning that I have been blessed with the ability to survive and enjoy this profession.

ESSAYS

Why Write?

Nearly every time I am interviewed or engage in a public speaking event, I am asked, usually as the final question, for a tidbit of wisdom about how to become a writer. And my answer is always the same: Write.

Most people sit down to write. Hemingway stood up, at least during a certain period in his career; he used the top of his refrigerator as a desk. Or maybe that was Fitzgerald. It was one or the other. I really don't care enough to research it.

The top of my refrigerator has too much dust and too many old take-out menus atop it to be used as a desk. I have, from time to time, written in bed, but before long my neck and back start to ache and I have to crawl out of bed and go to my desk, so if I have a brilliant idea in bed that I want to preserve till morning, I will grab my cell phone and leave myself a voice memo.

I also write in my head frequently, as opposed to writing on paper or a screen. My head serves as my laptop when I am on my motorcycle, or hiking, or mowing the grass, or while pretending to listen to other people talking. Truth is, it really doesn't matter where you write. Write wherever you can. Just do it.

"But," the interviewer is likely to ask, "isn't there more to it than that?

Nope, that's it. Just write.

"What about a writing manual of some kind? Something that teaches the rules and so forth?"

Here I usually make the sound with my lips that is commonly referred to as a mouth fart.

"But," my befuddled interviewer asks, "what about some kind of formal training? Isn't that a requisite to becoming a writer?

The only rule is to read. A lot. If you aren't an avid reader, you can still write, but you probably won't be very good at it. If you read a lot but still aren't very good at writing your own stories, you either lack the talent for it or you haven't been paying attention to what you read or you don't have an innate sense of what a story is. For those students I usually recommend that they google three things: Aristotle's pyramid of story structure, the Syd Field Paradigm of Screenplay Structure, and the YouTube video of Kurt Vonnegut talking about the Shapes of Stories.

If you have been an avid reader all your life, you will read or view those sources and think, "Well, sure. Duh." If you haven't been an avid reader, you will think you have discovered the Holy Grail. In either case, a knowledge of basic story structure is all you need to get started. It is all I started with. All a lot of writers start with. Read everything you can get your hands on for the first couple decades of your life, then start writing, but also keep reading.

Here the interviewer will probably scratch his or her chin and say, "I was thinking more along the lines of getting an MFA degree in creative writing. That's a good idea, isn't it?"

Here I will usually roll my eyes and say, "Don't get me started on that."

When I was teaching myself to be a writer, it never occurred to me to read a how-to-write book or article. Instead, I read "In Another Country" a second and third and fourth time, and "Innocent Erendira," "The Shawl," and mountains of other short stories and novels. But instead of re-reading those books for entertainment, I read with my eyes and ears tuned to the structure, the syntax, the diction, the rhythm, actively alert for the footers and joists, the struts and the rafters.

I attempted to learn writing prescriptions only when I was invited to teach at a university, and then only because I was afraid that my opening lecture would last no more than thirty seconds or so, in which case the university might yank the regular-income rug right out from under me. But any aspiring writer who has been an avid reader since early childhood already knows how to make a story, already possesses an innate sense of story structure that governs the way they see the world.

My interviewer then asks, "But doesn't formal training help you become a *better* writer? The workshops and the lectures and all? It all helps to make the writer more focused and knowledgeable, right?"

If by focused and knowledgeable you mean more of a conformist and less original, less daring, more pasteurized and homogenized, more brainwashed into adopting one cockamamie formula or another, then yes, sure, those workshops and lectures can be the bee's knees. But if by focused and knowledgeable you mean more empathetic, more talented, more visionary, more despising of conventions and well-trodden paths, more of an independent thinker and idea machine, then no, it ain't going to happen.

There is only one way in which learning by classroom and workshop can gift you with that last set of qualities, and that is if you walk out of your first workshop in disgust and never go back. Use your tuition money to venture out into the real world where real people struggle and strive and love and fail and question the meaning of their lives. *That* will make you not only a better writer but a better person.

I make this assertion based on five decades of taking my own advice and four decades of "teaching" aspiring writers. I've put the word "teaching" in quotes because my experience has told me that writers are born but seldom made. A born writer, an individual with an affinity for the power of words and a natural knack for telling a good story, plus a keen eye for observing and isolating important details, and an ear with a gift for picking up interesting nuances in speech, can have her writing improved by being shown what is good and what is clunky or superfluous in her writing, but an individual born without those gifts has little chance of seeing her work traditionally published. Anybody can self-publish, of course, even the most atrocious of writers, and many of them do. But unless you stumble upon an audience of tone deaf readers who will gobble down your work like a blue whale wolfs down plankton, you will never have great success as a writer.

Oh, wait; there are a lot of tone-deaf readers out there already. And more every day, thanks to our country's rapidly deteriorating system of public education. So yes, lots of mediocre writers get published too. In fact, if you want to get rich as a writer, aim for the masses. Mediocrity is like caviar to them.

Okay, sorry, my animus is showing. But hey, if you are born with nothing more than an instinct for understanding human nature and the ability to craft interesting images with your words, yet have never been able to get a handle on grammar or story structure, you might become a very good poet. Poets, unfortunately, are the writers most sneered at by other writers and by society in general, because nobody but poets and wannabe poets read poetry these days.

Most screenwriters couldn't write a comprehensible novel to save their lives, but they do know how to build a story and create dynamic scenes. Their sentences are clunky and ungrammatical, but beautiful sentences are eschewed in screenwriting; it's all about the raw visuals, the images, and the dramatic power of the scene. I have counseled hundreds of aspiring novelists to switch to screenwriting because that is where their talents lie. I also warn those students that directors and actors and cinematographers will take their raw product and chew it up and spit it out so that it is unrecognizable as the original product, but that the screenwriter will be paid handsomely for that insult.

I have encountered students who couldn't tell a complete sentence from a fragment, but through lots of hard work and discipline learned to write unified paragraphs that built to a satisfactory conclusion – skills that could land them a job with a small town newspaper or an online gig. A lot of editors have failed at writing novels but can recognize a good story when they read one. There are also a lot of editors who cannot recognize a bad novel when they see one.

However, as Flannery O'Connor so astutely observed, university writing programs survive not because they attract so many brilliant young writers but because they accept and encourage too many who lack the innate skills to survive in the profession. If the objective of those writing programs is to produce traditionally published writers, there are few other degree-granting programs with such an abysmally low rate of success.

Over the course of my career as a teacher of creative writing, with students ranging from eighteen years old to seventy-five, I have encountered among those thousands only a few with sufficient talent and discipline to make a living as a writer. And those qualities were not bestowed on those individuals by the writing program but by birth and their first decade or so of conflict-riddled life.

As for the value of a master's degree in creative writing, two years of workshops and insults from unpublished writers with little or no literary sophistication can only erode natural talent. But even if a naturally gifted young writer does survive the humiliation of several writers' workshops, that individual, before giving birth to a book that is mature enough to be publishable, will still have to put in the necessary years of experiencing life's many travails and tribulations, heartbreaks and joys, in order to depict their characters and their conflicts with authenticity.

Creative writing, I tell my now thoroughly disparaged interviewer, is not a profession for the faint of heart, the easily offended or disappointed or discouraged. Far too many individuals waste years and thousands of dollars chasing a gossamer dream simply because they enjoy escaping into novels and stories. The pleasure of these escapes is so great for them, the immersion so easy, that they fail to recognize that the illusion of easy storytelling takes years and years and years of dedication and perseverance layered on top of an innate and multidimensional talent for telling a good story.

Here the interviewer will narrow his or her eyes at me and ask how I can suggest such things when I myself have spent more than a few years teaching in creative writing programs.

I assure him or her that I have cautioned every one of my students of every possible pitfall and shortcoming of entertaining an ambition to become a writer. And advised every individual who asked if they should enroll in a creative writing program to think twice about it, and then to think ten or twelve times more. With luck they will think long enough to miss the application deadline.

That an individual should even ask how to write, or how to become a writer, or any form of that question, is to presume that there is a prescribed way to gain entry into the profession, and that all one needs do is to memorize and follow the diagram, the rules, the dance moves. Lots of writers have come up with lists of rules, their do's and don'ts, in an attempt to assist the dazed and confused. But those writers are deluding themselves into thinking that they know the definitive way to write. At best, they understand how they and they alone write. But it would be the height of narcissism for a writer to believe that his way is the only way to write.

You might say that every writer has his or her own way of writing, and while that would be closer to the truth, it's not close enough for me. What I tell my students is that every story should be allowed to determine its own path, its own structure, its own voice. But students who come to a classroom expecting to be taught how to be a writer don't want to hear that answer. It's too amorphous for them. Too nebulous. And who wants to sit down at the desk every morning with no idea of what is about to happen or why or how it will happen.

I do! And so do lots of other writers.

You might say that a story is a kind of magic, but the writer is not the magician. The writer is the wand. The pen. The secretary. The vessel. The stooge. The victim. The ventriloquist's dummy. The sorcerer's apprentice.

Feel free to pick whichever of those nouns makes you happiest. The truth is that if a story is forced to follow a prescribed plot or formula, it will never come alive, it will never take a breath on its own. It will be a story on a respirator, and the reader will know it. If the writer isn't surprised and delighted by the sudden changes of direction her story takes, she's probably guilty of pumping air into a corpse.

At this point in the interview, my interviewer, or the young person from the audience who asked the original question, will usually slouch in his or her chair and regard me with a combination of confusion and seething contempt. They see me then as a traitor, a hoarder of secrets.

But the only secret to writing is not *how* to do it, but why so many of us want to do it. Only the best of interviewers ever asked me that question: *why do you write?* My standard answer, unless I am addressing a roomful of librarians or clergy, is: *Fuck if I know.*

Truth be told, I believe that I do know why I write. But I won't go into it all with an interviewer because he or she will reduce it to a sound bite. And it's a lot more complicated than that.

I didn't understand why I enjoy writing when I first started doing it, and most other beginning writers don't know either. I wrote for almost thirty years before I ever took the time to figure out why I willingly and even eagerly subject myself to the tedium of sitting at a desk for half a day seven days a week, and why I expose myself to constant public criticism for not writing what some miserable individual hiding behind a fake name wants me to write, and why I have to weekly if not daily employ social media in an almost always vain and relentlessly humiliating attempt to garner a little attention for my books, and why I willingly thumbed my nose at financial stability and corporate power and prestige and all of the other tasty accoutrements of our materialistic society.

Okay, let me start this essay over: Why did I choose to be a writer and not another cog in the wheel, another brick in the wall?

Because it thrills me. A beautiful sentence, with just the right cadence, the right image, the right subtext and music and magic, is every bit as exhilarating to me as an orgasm, plus it lasts longer. To build a story or even a whole novel out of those sentences, to take characters who are more real to me than my own neighbors and guide them through thicket after thicket of soul-ripping conflict so that they finally emerge into the clearing bloodied and sore and sorrowful yet quietly triumphant, it makes me feel godlike – like the god I hope the consciousness we call God really is, loving and paternal and maternal and doing everything possible to insure that his/her/its children will be happier and better in every way.

(Side note: I employed the triple pronouns above, with an implied emphasis on the *its*, not because the use of those pronouns is politically correct – a strategy to which I direct another mouth fart – but because I suspect that the divine consciousness is in no way human, not even corporeal, but does evince the finest and most life-affirming qualities of both a loving mother and father. That could be just wishful thinking, but what do I have to lose by thinking it? The misery of nihilism, that's what.)

Sorry; the introduction of God into this essay makes the wicket a good bit stickier. I can hear the seven-year-old me in

Sunday school asking why, if God loves us so much, life is such a shit-hole. That gets into a whole other discussion about the need for conflict in fiction *and* in our lives, but I don't want to wander off into a Taoist bramble bush right now. Suffice it to say that the more thorns we survive, as characters on paper or as characters in this illusion called life, the better off we are when we finally step into the clearing.

Let's turn our thoughts back now to the how and why of writing. How? By doing it. Why? Because we can. We are imaginative creatures, and we who become fiction writers are generally blessed with more capacious imaginations than most. We extrapolate. We think in scenes and speak in metaphors. We imagine, therefore we are. This is both a blessing and a curse – like life itself.

Imagination, said William Blake, is not only the first emanation from God but also the highest condition of an individual, the one that makes all other faculties possible. He was a pretty good thinker, that guy Blake. Without imagination, we'd be little more than drudges trudging through the muck and mire because nobody else exists with enough imagination to tell us what to do. Many of us still exist in that sorry condition, waiting for instructions. Don't end the sentence with a preposition! Use this trope, not that one! Don't think this, don't think that! Don't do that in public or you'll get arrested! Never use an adverb or you will surely die!

What an imagination does for we humans who possess one is to make all the muck and mire of life tolerable, because imagination tells us that there will be an end to the misery sooner or later. It is imagination that actually creates the sunny clearing we are aiming for.

Numerous non-writers and writers alike have pontificated on the why of writing. Most of them say the same thing: to impose order on a chaotic world; to impose meaning on a meaningless life. I used to say such things when I was much younger and didn't know any better. I am much older now and know a tiny bit more than I used to, so when I now hear such claims being made, I understand what the speaker is really saying: writers write because they can't bear living in a world that comes with an instruction manual and which is governed, more likely than not, by idiots.

Most of us write because we agree with William Blake; the imagination really *is* the highest condition of man, woman, boy, and girl. It is the closest we can come on this planet to understanding God.

Had we the instruments to make the necessary measurements, and somebody probably does, we might see that the gift of imagination is likely shared by every creature large and small right down to the single cell, which, by the way, possesses all the faculties we now recognize as consciousness. Knowing that, we writers enjoy our own imaginations more than almost anything else, and therefore, by God, we're going to use them!

Nobody on the planet really understands the imagination. No scientist can pinpoint exactly where the imagination is located, or how brain chemicals and electricity conspired to produce *Ulysses* or *The Sound and the Fury* or even the newest Superman comic book. Even if a writer is of the kind who meticulously outlines every plot point and reversal and bridge before beginning a project, and maybe does a storyboard and a spread sheet and sifts through the internet for character names with explicitly relevant meanings, the initial impetus for that project came from the imagination. Ditto a character, a scene, an overheard phrase. And I suspect that even during all the left-brained plotting et cetera, the imagination is *still* in charge, though an invisible hand at the wheel.

Me, I am happy to let my imagination drive me wherever it wishes. And don't tell me to buckle up, because I won't. My writing process is an exercise in trust and simplicity. I sit at my desk, have a sip of coffee, open up the laptop, and say without saying, "Take the con, imagination. Warp five!"

My imagination, throughout my pre-writing days, was comprised of a roomful of lunatic squirrels and monkeys that never stopped shrieking and chasing each other. I am fairly certain I came shooting out of the womb that way. And the menagerie only got bigger and more crowded as I grew taller. There were times as a teenager when I truly feared that my head was going to explode from all the chatter.

I thank God and my parents that I was never medicated. They allowed me to find my own path through the misery of adolescence. And the path I found, when I was nearly twenty-one and an accounting major, was to become a writer. Every time one of the squirrels or monkeys in my head shrieked something interesting, I wrote it down. And, through no fault of my own, because of some neurological tryst of chemical and electricity, I started thinking like a writer. *This would make a good story*, I'd think. And I would start writing. No teachers, no MFAs, no formulas, no secrets. I wrote. I still write the very same way.

I was speaking metaphorically just now, of course, when I said that my imagination consists of clamoring animals. That is just an image, the way I sometimes envision the action inside my skull. No animals actually speak to me. Instead, ideas come, almost always out of the blue (another metaphor), as images. My novel *In a Town Called Mundomuerto* took its first breath of life as the image of a beautiful dark-haired woman seated on a boulder and singing as fishermen came ashore in their skiffs.

The entire Ryan DeMarco mystery series leapt into being while I was driving over the Lake Wilhelm reservoir in western Pennsylvania. Out of the blue, I envisioned a state trooper standing on a bridge and gazing into the dark forest across the water, scrutinizing the shadows for some sign of a fugitive murderer.

Yep, the whole thing in a flash. It took you about a hundred times longer to read the sentence above than it took for that particular image to blink on and then out of my mind's eye. That's how imagination rolls.

Unless I'm a freak of some kind, and several people have not hesitated to tell me that I am, that's the basic modus operandi for imagination. One image after another. (Just in case you are too dull to have noticed this, note that nearly half of the word *image* is contained in the word *imagination*.) The image is there and then it's gone. No introductions, no fare-thee-wells, no explanations. *And no meanings.* No order out of chaos. My writing routine might be fairly rigid and disciplined, but the hand at the helm, the imagination? An undisciplined maniac.

The imagination will not tolerate a halter or bit. Just try to get a full night's sleep when you are midway through writing a novel. It has taken me decades of daily meditation to achieve ten seconds or so of no-thought.

Not all the images generated by my imagination generate a viable story idea; most don't. But when one does, I grab it. The act of grabbing it (sorry; another metaphor) seems to slow the spewing of ideas for a while. Maybe that is the purpose of the imagination after all, to make stories. Though for an architect, perhaps the imagination makes images of buildings. And so forth.

As for the story itself, it, like its mother, the idea, and its grandmother, the image, has no inherent meaning. I seldom intend a story to *mean* anything. If any of my work has a theme, don't blame me because I didn't put it there. All I ask of a story is that it carries me and my metaphorical canoe full of readers along on its current, through the whitewater and past hull-crushing rocks, maybe over a waterfall or two, and delivers us safely to shore, giddy with adrenalin.

You see what I just did? I turned an idea into an image. And I turned the image into a story with a beginning, middle, and end. I even gave it a happy ending! Because that's how things go re the imagination. It speaks in images so that writers like me can turn those images into stories.

And so we come back to the two questions posed by this essay. How does one become a writer? By writing and getting published. And why does one become a writer? Because he or she is possessed by an imagination that demands it, and because the writer can think of nothing else so exhilarating, and, despite the poverty and rejection and tedium and despair that often accompany the profession, because when your little canoe, battered and leaky and barely afloat, finally grinds ashore, and you step out with wobbly knees and are soaked to the skin and chilled to the bone, it just feels so damn good. You feel so damn liberated. You feel so *alive*.

Ten Easy Steps to Becoming a Writer

A student in an advanced fiction workshop at the Ohio State University once marched out of my classroom on the third day of instruction and straight into the program director's office, where the student charged me with malfeasance for refusing to share with him the secrets to getting published – secrets that all professional writers know, he claimed, but conspire to withhold from everybody else. To prove that I am no longer a part of that nefarious conspiracy, I am now prepared to reveal to you, in ten easy steps (two fewer steps than most addiction recovery programs!), every secret about becoming a published writer that I have been hoarding.

Step 1: *Be born strange, weird, abnormal, or any combination of the above.*

Or have an embarrassing physical flaw, or a big brother who beats you up every day, or a sexually enticing neighbor whose tantalizing ways fog and warp your prepubescent thoughts. The result of any such influence is that you will grow up with a cockeyed view of the world and your place in it, a perception that will cause you to disavow normally accepted values, maybe force you to seek solace in the amorphous notions of beauty and truth, or in the soothing music of language, or in the need to create and control your own imagined universes in rejection of the clearly demented universe you have been forced to inhabit. This will make your family seem strangers to you, will make you suspect you were adopted at birth, and will foster in you an indefinable longing, which you will attempt to assuage through shoplifting, sex, mood-altering drugs, and, eventually, creative writing.

Step 2: *Read everything you can get your hands on.*

The act of reading actually increases and expands your brain. More neurons, more synapses, more bridges between the two. You become a better speller, grow a bigger vocabulary, get higher SAT scores. Also, reading makes you a better writer without your having to work at it. You absorb the rhythms, you assimilate the syntax. Eventually Atwood and Dostoyevsky and Dickens and everyone else you read will infiltrate your blood, tweak your central nervous system, and restructure your DNA.

Consequently, this will turn you into a pompous ass for a while, especially during your high school and college years as you correct everybody else's grammar. But that, too, has a benefit: an occasional pummeling at the hands of a football player or even a pom-pom smackdown from a burly cheerleader will work nicely to enhance your sense of alienation and freakishness.

Step 3: *Live life.*

You might think this is an oxymoron. You might think I am an oxymoron. So let me say it another way: Get out there in the traffic. Get knocked down and run over a few times. Visit third world countries and drink the water. Fall desperately in love with somebody who, if you were the last other human being in the solar system, would prefer to mate with a rabid duck.

This, I believe, is what Vonnegut meant when he said that no writer under twenty-five is worth reading. (If, indeed, he ever said it.) Very few writers under twenty-five have ever lost a lover to a rabid duck. Few have experienced enough of true human tragedy and sorrow to have anything meaningful to write about. Better to emulate Hemingway and Peter Matthiessen and Isak Denison and their ilk than Emily Dickinson. Dickinson was a wonderful poet of the small, but I cannot help but wonder what the belle of Amherst might have written had her universe been larger than a bedroom.

So get out of the ivy tower and into the poison ivy. Learn something besides office envy and literary theory. Learn human nature. Learn nature's nature. Learn how those natures intersect and diverge. Flirt with danger. Confront your fears. Have children. Tattoo Henry Thoreau's aphorism on the inside of your wrist: *How vain it is to sit down to write when you have not stood up to live.*

And do all the above absent of any palliative. Too much painkiller of any kind will numb you to the soul-knitting potential of life's blows. So forget all that romantic bullshit about over-imbibing writers. Rehab is for actors, not writers.

Keep your senses raw and your third eye open.

Step 4: *Become a human tape recorder.*

Pilfer from overheard conversations, newspaper articles, social media, your neighbor's diary if it happens to fall open in your hands while your neighbor is busy stirring the spaghetti sauce. Collect gestures and mannerisms, idiosyncrasies and accents and speech impediments. Carry a notebook wherever you go. Record bits of description, the smell of a baby's hair, the way a tiny canary of sunlight falls on your neighbor's hand while she is stirring the sauce and you are stealing a peek at her diary ....

Good writers borrow, great writers steal. Fitzgerald said that, having stolen the observation from T. S. Eliot, who lifted it from Picasso, who probably pinched it from Flaubert.

Step 5: *Embrace poverty.*

Let's face it, nobody reads anymore. Not enough people, in any case, to adequately support all the writers in need of support – especially when J.K. Rowling, Stephen King, and R.L. Stine are sucking up nine-tenths of all the revenue generated from books.

The only practical escape from poverty for a writer is through another profession. Medicine is a good choice because it throws you smack-dab into the face of human frailty. And there is already something of the physician in a writer, in that we wield our craft in a desire to heal; and something of the psychologist in a writer, in that we write to plumb and know the human psyche; and something of the metaphysician in a writer, in that we write to probe and part the membrane between the knowable and the ineffable.

The legal profession can be advantageous in that it will grant you entrée into a class of individuals even more disrespected than writers. And there is already something of the lawyer in a writer, in that we aim to levy justice upon our characters and to make of our worlds an orderly place.

Perhaps the most suitable second job for a writer is that of a courtesan. Seduction is already our modus operandi as well as our raison d'être. Unfortunately, there are few job openings these days for courtesans, too few kings and queens to go around, too many writers and not enough fiefdoms.

The worst possible choice, academe, is the one most writers choose – which only goes to show that writers aren't all that bright to begin with, owing probably to the brain trauma sustained from correcting other people's grammar. While it might be true that a writer does not have to fear too much affluence as an academic, one *should* fear the sedating effects of tenure, the insistence on conformity, the insidious virus of political correctness, and the vocabulary devouring contagion of words such as pedagogy, discourse, multicultural, and gender-neutral. Teaching eager students can, in and of itself, be a joy, but as for acanemia as a whole, it is best approached with the standard guerrilla tactics of moving quickly and quietly, hitting and running, and, when necessary, hightailing it home through a tunnel.

Step 6: *Learn as much craft as you can, especially the craft of learning to ignore everything you were taught.*

Here I am tempted to quote Doctorow, who said that teachers and the taught are to be avoided, or Flannery O'Connor, who said that writing programs do not squash enough writers. But those are cynical sentiments and I am not cynical enough to repeat them even if I find them to be unequivocally true. Instead I will advise only that one should learn just enough but not too much. The few basic guidelines of what makes for a good story – namely a sympathetic character engaged in an interesting conflict that escalates in dramatic tension and personal risk until it culminates in a satisfyingly unpredictable resolution – is really the only thing a budding writer needs to know. And even that is just a suggestion.

Step 7: *Cultivate discipline.*

I am not sure why this is so important, but when I was twenty-one I read Hemingway's admonition about the necessity of discipline and I bought into it as divine gospel, and, subsequently, discipline has worked fairly well for me in terms of productivity, with the only negative side effects a divorce and the ruination of two serious relationships.

That aside, discipline is important. Discipline in any endeavor is a good thing. But don't overdo it. Don't sacrifice love for writing, for example. You want to be creative? There is nothing more creative than loving somebody. And nothing will make you a better writer. Or a better person.

Step 8: *Remain keenly aware of your own imperfection.*

Just because you have a knack for putting words together, that doesn't make you the oracle of Delphi. I think it was Nabokov who said that a writer's job is "to enchant," and I.B. Singer who observed that "a good writer is basically a storyteller, not a scholar or a redeemer of mankind." Learn to tell a story that holds a reader's attention from first page to last, maybe squeezes out a few tears and giggles, or else, as my steelworker daddy advised many times, and, alas, in vain, "learn a trade."

I might add that knowing you know almost nothing will make you a far superior writer than thinking you know anything at all. Writers, I was surprised to learn when I became one, are not the people with all the answers but the people with all the questions. There is absolutely nothing wrong with not being perfect. I've made a habit of falling short of perfection, and I see no reason to abandon that habit now.

So trust me on this: Ditch the ego. You have nothing to teach anybody. Just *move* me. Show me a heart in conflict with itself, as wise old Willie Faulkner said upon sobering up and finding himself in Sweden.

Step 9: *Wake Up and Dream.*

It was Samuel Johnson who said, "No man but a blockhead ever wrote, except for money." In other words, have a dream and go for it with all you are worth, but be realistic about your chances. Know what genres of books are being purchased out there in the shrinking literary marketplace. Know what you hope to achieve from your writing and that whatever your goal is, your chances are as slim as a matchstick.

Know that disciplined, persistent writers beat those odds every day.

Know that good writing is not as easy as you think it is, and that the more you learn, the harder it gets.

But know also, as you maybe already do, that there is nothing done in solitude that is more fulfilling than a beautifully wrought sentence.

And know that creativity, the exercise of your imagination, is not only a noble pursuit, it is the nearest we can come on this planet to understanding God.

Step 10: *Keep hope in your heart and ink in your pen.*

I was tempted to say, for the last half of that statement, "Keep lead in your pencil," but that's a strictly masculine connotation I don't want to imply. Ink in your pen has implications other than the merely sexual ones – not that I have any intention of excluding the sexual implications. The desire to create, in both male and female, is closely linked, I think, to the libido. All forms of desire, I think, are related.

The same hunger that drives us to search out new dishes in new restaurants, for example, is just another form of the hunger that has us struggling for new ways of depicting the old verities, the same hunger that sends us swooning over a waft of perfume or a smile from a stranger. It is the same inexpressible hunger we feel as we kneel over our lover and trace the miracle of her spine, or as we gaze in awe at the dizzying beauty in the rise and fall of flesh…the same ache of longing we intuit in mist over water, the grief we sense in the honking of geese heading south, the memory's warmth and scent of our mother's kitchen, the desperate longing to know, to experience, to understand and hold and write down and conjure up again, again, and again, all the images and sensations, all the collisions and collusions of human desire…all the frailness and fragility that shatters our hearts and makes us whole.

And that's it – everything I know and will probably ever know about writing. All the secret knowledge we writers possess. Use it at your own risk.

Ten Writers' Rules That Beg to Be Broken

I despise rules. Always have. Rules are for accountants and architects, assembly line workers and neurosurgeons. In order to be successful in those professions, there are procedures that must always be followed, variations that must never be employed. The word *creative*, however, as in the phrase *creative writing*, demands, at the very least, an imaginative interpretation of the rules.

I have held well over fifty different jobs in my life, and it was always the rules that made me leave. Writing is the only profession that has never made me long to do something else.

Unfortunately, young writers are frequently advised that they must do this or they must avoid that when writing. Sometimes such advice comes from veteran writers themselves, mainly because they have found commercial success by doing the same thing over and over again. What these writers have apparently forgotten is that they, in the beginning, were rule breakers themselves. Their own broken rules have become their personal rules to live by.

And that's the problem with rules; they create routine. Repetition. Redundancy. A lack of originality.

Admittedly, this is a much more complicated subject than I will go into here, since repetition in our current culture tends to be more richly rewarded than startlingly original work. So I will say only that there are *no* rules that will guarantee success for a writer. There are no formulas, no closely guarded secrets. There is only what works and what doesn't work to accomplish the writer's task of seizing and holding and rewarding the reader's emotional, intellectual, and financial investment in a piece of fiction.

Thanks to a degree of success over the years, I am asked again and again to lay out a prescription of rules for aspiring writers. This is one request I will not honor. I did publish one such list as a parody of such lists, but to compose a list of rules and intend them to be taken seriously is something I will not do. No writer living or dead has discovered a universally foolproof method of churning out successful fiction, and none ever will. How can you discover what does not exist? If success as a writer depended upon nothing but following a list of rules, why are there so many aspiring writers who can't get published?

The following are some of the so-called rules of writing fiction that I take a special delight in breaking. Creative writing is about possibilities, not about restrictions and limitations.

Never open a book with weather. Elmore Leonard

To his credit, Elmore Leonard makes it clear that he does not intend for his rule to be an absolute, though I have met too many editors and agents and teachers who remember only the rule and not the accompanying qualification. Leonard states in his preface to the rules that he had fashioned them out of a desire to "remain invisible when I'm writing a book," and added that, if one had no desire for invisibility, she should "skip the rules." If only the pedants who hold Leonard's rules inviolable had read more carefully.

Leonard also further qualifies this particular rule, explaining that it applies only to prolonged descriptions of weather rather than specifically to a character's reaction to the weather. But I disagree with this distinction. The writer's job is to coax and seduce the reader *into* the story, and a neatly-crafted though not over-long description of weather can often accomplish that task.

A few years ago I was searching for a new agent, and one of the many I interviewed said she would be happy to represent my new novel but that I had to delete the opening page and a half, which describe that season's weather and its effects. I declined her offer. The novel under question, *Two Day's Gone,* is now in its 10th printing and was an Amazon #1 bestseller, and with the opening pages exactly as I wrote them.

In general, the more specific and adamant the rule, the less trustworthy it is and the faster you should flee from those who preach it.

Never correct or rewrite until the whole thing is down. John Steinbeck

In 1962, in a letter to a young writer, John Steinbeck added six tips for writing well. The above was one of those tips. Its error lies again, as all rules do, with its use of the absolute *never.* I frequently will not, because I cannot, begin a story or novel until I have crafted the perfect first sentence.

Of course there is no such thing as a perfect sentence, but the temporary confidence instilled by thinking that I have crafted one is what allows me to tackle a project that will consume my waking and sleeping hours for the next year or more. For me, stopping now and then to polish a faulty phrase or image is like taking another hit of confidence. Five or six hits every morning keep me flying through the hours. But if I cannot fix a weakness within a minute or two, I will not allow my momentum to stall out with fretting and hand-wringing. Placing parentheses around the offending phrase, or highlighting the entire scene, will call my attention to it during the first rewrite.

I do not believe, as some practitioners apparently do, that a morning's work is like a fast-moving stream through which one must dare not stop paddling, not even for a moment. Go ahead and stop if you want to. Pull ashore. Have lunch. Creep up as close as you can to that egret in the tree. Take a nap if you feel like it. In short, do whatever works for you. The imagination is resilient and flexible, and your routine should be too. But *only* if that works for you. I am most productive when I adhere, albeit loosely, to the discipline of beginning the morning with a bit of meditation, followed by four to six hours at my desk, followed by a good workout or hike. That's *my* routine. It doesn't have to be yours.

Work on a computer that is disconnected from the internet. Zadie Smith

Apparently Ms. Smith finds the internet too seductive to avoid. I write with two laptops connected to the internet and my smart phone within reach. Why two? Because my older laptop has twenty years of my work on it, which leaves little memory space for other work. Some Van Morrison or Jackson Browne is usually playing on the second laptop, which also stands ready for some lickety-split research. When I am unsure that I have used the right word, or when I want some reinforcement to my understanding of history, or I need a few more details to describe a setting, I can swivel thirty degrees and have it there in front of me in a matter of seconds without bothering to go back and forth between screens on the same computer. The phone is handy for quick facts: Hey Google, how far is London from Miami? How tall was Benjamin Franklin?

Yes, sometimes writing is like a fever dream, sometimes it is like holding one's breath underwater, but sometimes it is like writing the alphabet for the very first time – slow and halting and difficult. Sometimes listening to Jackson Browne's "Sky Blue and Black" on a three-hour loop helps, and sometimes it puts me to sleep. Every morning is a new experiment. If it were all a matter of routine and repetition, I, for one, could not have kept writing for the past fifty years. That's approximately 75,000 hours spent on the job so far. Do the same routine that long and just *try* not to let it turn you into a zombie.

Even so, some people like and even need routine. Some of us look for ways to avoid it. My feeling is this: if you are so undisciplined as a writer that you will allow social media or the news crawl or anything else on the internet to keep you from writing, maybe you shouldn't be writing anyway.

Work on one thing at a time until finished. Henry Miller

This is rule #1 of Miller's eleven commandments for writers. I once finished the drafts of three books within the same week. And along the way took notes for three or four essays, stories, poems, or songs. Last month, while working on the copyedit of my fourth Ryan DeMarco mystery, *No Woods So Dark as These*, I also worked on the fifth novel in the series, and made notes for each of three stand-alone novels, a collection of new short stories, and a collection of personal essays.

Being a monomaniac as a writer might have worked well for Miller, but being a megalomaniac is better for me. You will most likely find your own most productive method somewhere between those extremes.

The first draft of a book – even a long one – should take no more than three months, the length of a season. Stephen King

Did you ever notice that the biggest egos have the most rules for how other people should live or work? The bit of nonsense above comes from King's *top* twenty rules for writers, with the implication that he has more than twenty rules to impose.

King's three-month rule allows for no consideration of the writer's other obligations. What about taking care of the children? What about holding down a fulltime job to pay the bills? What about maintaining the marriage and the house and the vehicles and a small semblance of a social life? What about getting enough exercise to keep your body healthy? Do you have pets and aging parents to take care of? Do you have ten acres to plow? Do you have a hundred freshman compositions to correct before next Monday?

Imposing a three-month deadline on the first draft of a novel (the hardest draft to write, by the way, since you are starting from scratch) is just plain silly. Anybody who spends most of the day and a good portion of the evening taking care of non-writing business has little energy left for writing or for thinking about anything other than those three loads of dirty laundry piling up in the corner.

Unless a writer is coasting through his day on a fat trust fund, with a maid and butler and a nanny, or otherwise wading through a steady stream of shekels, writing a couple thousand useable words each day is difficult to pull off. Especially until the writer has found her voice and her audience, which can take years.

A small handful of authors rake in enough money to buy themselves lots of time for writing or whatever else they wish to do, but midlist writers don't earn enough to buy a good used car let alone hire somebody else to drive the kids to soccer practice. And unpublished writers earn nothing. So, if you too have the luxury of several unfettered hours each day, and lots of unencumbered extra time for dreaming up interesting characters and compelling plots, then yes, you can write the first draft of a novel in three months.

For most of us, however, writing well is a demanding passion, and so is family, and it would be a mistake to indulge the first to the detriment of the second. Don't delude yourself into believing that ignoring your partner and children in favor of cranking out the words is for their own benefit because they will all have a better life when your bestseller is flying off the shelves. Children and marriages are important *now*, every day of now, and the damage you do by putting your writing before your family will stay with them forever.

Let me put it this way: do not allow any other writer's arbitrary writing schedule make you feel guilty about your own. The only deadline you have in regards to how quickly or slowly you produce creative work is the one you place on yourself. If it is your first book and you also have to feed yourself and maybe a family too, take your time. Watch your children grow. Take your spouse out on a date now and then. Have coffee with a friend. Get a decent night's sleep. And in whatever time is left, write something. Maybe it will be a paragraph, maybe a page, maybe a full scene. Word count matters far less than writing something that, even in first draft, makes you happy and proud of yourself. If you hurry through it, then reread it and find that it stinks, are you likely to try again? Rush jobs usually do stink. What's another few months? If you are so desperate to get a certain number of words on paper in a certain period of time, you will have no time to savor the joy of life, and living without that joy will short-circuit your career in no time at all.

Write without pay until somebody offers pay; if nobody offers within three years, sawing wood is what you were intended for. Mark Twain

First, let's have a closer look at Mr. Clemens's initial sentence: "Write without pay *until* somebody offers pay." Uh, Samuel, if nobody is offering pay, how would it be possible to be paid to write? And how many people are going to offer pay to a writer who has not written anything? Duh.

For the sake of clarity and accuracy, Mr. Clemens might have said: *Reconcile yourself to writing without pay until your writing is good enough that somebody will be happy to pay for it.*

As for the rest of his advice, had I heeded his time limit of three years, I would be a retired woodcutter now. I would have bigger muscles and calloused, probably arthritic hands. Instead I have two dozen books to my credit, plus a dozen plays and a handful of screenplays, and my only calluses are from playing the guitar. I wrote for nine years without making a penny from it.

Times change. Back in Clemens' day, not every person who could read wanted to be a writer. MFA programs were not even in existence then. Now there are hundreds of programs across the country handing out substantially useless degrees in creative writing to unpublished writers, most of whom will never be published except by themselves. In other words, the lines of aspiring writers queued up at the doors of agents and editors now stretch for miles in all directions. The competition is as stiff as lignum vitae and as tough to crack as a macadamia nut.

Let's face it: when you first start writing, you aren't as equipped as you will be years later to judge good writing from bad. You will write more of the latter than the first. However, if you keep writing and keep reading, over time – and I don't mean hours here, I mean years – your literary tastes will become more refined. The writer who publishes a first book is as rare as promethium.

Chances are, you will write three or four bad novels before you write one good enough to snag a publishing contract. I wrote my first short story at twenty, sold my first short story at thirty, and published my first book, a collection of stories, at thirty-three. Over the course of those thirteen years, I wrote nearly every day, hundreds of stories and poems and essays, and published only a small handful of them. My apprenticeship might have been shortened a few years if I hadn't been writing in total obscurity, with no teachers or mentors of any kind. On the other hand, formal instruction might have been, as it often is, detrimental.

So how long should you expect to wait (while writing nonstop, of course) before being discovered as the literary genius you are? That depends on a number of factors, including but not limited to your genre, your mastery of language, your market, your connections, your platform, your talent, and your output. If you don't receive encouragement from several educated strangers within a few years of when you start sending your work out, then yes, you might want to consider another vocation. There is not much call these days for woodcutters, but there seems to be no shortage of room available for yet another how-to-write book written by an otherwise unpublished writer.

The more circumspectly you delay writing down an idea, the more maturely developed it will be on surrendering itself. Walter Benjamin

Where do people come up with this stuff? Walter Benjamin was a prominent philosopher and literary critic in the first half of the twentieth century. His subjects included Proust, Kafka, Baudelaire, and many other literary luminaries. But did he really understand the nature of ideas? I don't think so. Most literary critics and other deconstructing left-brainers don't.

For creative right-brainers, ideas are ephemeral, fleeting creatures. Some can grow to be antiquarians, but most, in my experience, have the lifespan of a gnat. As a creative writer, your head is already infested with gnats. Now and then one will work its way into a Eustachian tube, where it will drive you half mad with its drill-like buzz.

When that happens, stop whatever you are doing and write it down before it stops buzzing and keels over dead. Another method is to employ your cell phone's voice memo app, but I urge caution here. Do not, like a writer I know too well, allow your voice memos to accumulate for a year or more without being transcribed. And don't assume they are safe on your hard drive either. Make copies on good old-fashioned paper. Phones die and hard drives crash, but paper abides, patiently yellowing in your Idea drawer or wherever else you shove the ideas you don't presently have time to expand into stories.

Someday you will have that time. Someday you will be as empty of good ideas as a politician. That is when your accumulation of yellowing brilliance will come in handy. Choose the most brilliant idea and start writing. The very act of writing will give that idea new life, and it is likely to grow and develop with every stroke of the pen or keyboard. Write until you can't think of anything more to say. Then shut up and take a walk, because now your subconscious mind will take over.

So always keep a tablet and pen handy – beside the bed, in the bathroom, in the car. The subconscious mind keeps odd hours. Don't tell yourself, "I'll write it down tomorrow," because in all likelihood you will wake up the next morning and that happy little gnat of an idea will be a dried out, withered corpse.

These next two rules are cited so frequently by high school teachers and other unpublished writers that whole generations of children have accepted them as holy gospel. I have heard both ascribed to Hemingway, and maybe he did articulate them while under pressure from an interviewer to do so, but I am confident he did not intend for them to be interpreted as simplistically as they usually are.

Write what you know. Ernest Hemingway

In the days of Thoreau and earlier, when it was necessary to walk several miles to consult with someone more knowledgeable than you, *write what you know* might have been sound advice. Hemingway also said that every writer needs a friend in every profession, someone whose expertise can be accessed – a statement that appears to contradict the earlier statement.

In order to do my research back in the 70s and 80s, I had to visit a small-town library every week to order another load of books on interlibrary loan, which made the librarian my best friend. Today, a writer's best friend is the internet.

I feel certain that Hemingway's *write what you know* admonition was not intended to be an absolute. A clearer rendition of that advice would be to write what you know after you've done a ton of research and before you forget it all.

And always remember that you are writing fiction. Fiction is stuff you make up. You can do that too. You can make stuff up.

Back at the turn of the millennium, I signed a contract, based on a single opening scene, to write two historical mysteries featuring Edgar Allan Poe for Thomas Dunne Books. I had never before written a historical novel and was not confident I could create a convincing New York City of 1840. In one scene it was necessary for me to get Poe across the East River in short order so that he could hotfoot it to Manhattan. I spent weeks trying to find a bridge he could cross or a ferry that would convey him in the allotted time. No such luck. I was stuck. I moaned about this impasse to a friend of mine who was also a writer, and he said, "It's fiction, Silvis. Make up a bridge."

Frequently it is the *not knowing* that brings a story alive, the writer's desire to know what he does not, which then leads to the character's discovery of what she did not know, and then the reader's delight in participating in that discovery.

Show, don't tell. A favorite admonition among unpublished high school teachers all over the world.

This admonition is only half-false. The true part is that good fiction is built on dramatic scenes comprised of action, dialogue, description, and conflict – i.e. showing through visual and other sensory details and strong, active verbs. But a certain amount of telling is necessary too. Summary and exposition hold the scenes together. Telling bridges the time gap between scenes and between relevant beats. A little bit of telling, even if it's something as simple as "Two weeks later," opens nearly every new scene and every chapter.

So, once again, the problem with the rule is not that it is wholly false but that it is stated too rigidly. Summarization complements dramatization in every novel. In some, it shoulders the narrative load. Sebastian Barry's *Days Without End*, for example, is a brilliant novel that is almost wholly told rather than shown.

In general, the more "literary" a novel is, the more it relies on reflection, speculation, and summaries of events. That is why a literary novel is so hard to adapt for the screen; so much of the momentum of the story is interior, taking place only in the characters' heads.

Screenwriter Charlie Kaufman ran into this very problem when attempting to adapt Susan Orlean's nonfiction *The Orchid Thief* for film. The problem was so infuriating that he finally seized upon introducing himself into the story as twins, one of whom was being driven mad by attempting to write the adaptation without sacrificing the book's artistic integrity, and the other as a hack only too ready to pander to Hollywood's lack of artistic integrity by changing the story willy-nilly.

"Show, don't tell" is fine advice if you are aiming for a quick sale of movie rights, or if you are fifteen years old and learning how to write in scenes, but the proper amendment of the phrase for the rest of us should be "show when you can, but tell whenever showing isn't necessary."

The writing life is mostly a lonely, miserable life. A common refrain among self-pitying writers.

This concept is a form of the romantic allure of the suffering artist. Trust me; there is nothing romantic about suffering. If you haven't done much suffering yet, you will after you have children, and then you will understand how unromantic it is to be a miserable wretch who can't stop worrying.

In David Foster Wallace's essay "The Nature of the Fun," he addresses the reader as *you* and delineates for her the psyche-strangling process she will undergo from aspiring writer to acclaimed author, except at the beginning. "In the beginning," he writes, "when you first start out trying to write fiction, the whole endeavor's about fun. You don't expect anybody else to read it. You're writing almost wholly to get yourself off."

I disagree. I expected all of my early stories to be published. (Only a few were.) Nearly every student I taught over a lifetime of teaching fully expected their early work to be published. So when Wallace says you don't expect anybody else to read it, he's speaking for himself.

Then comes success, Wallace says. What he should have said is, *If you work very hard and are very lucky and talented, then comes success, depending on how you define success, because in most cases it is a very minor success resulting in few readers and little money.*

After which, he says, "Things start to get complicated and confusing, not to mention scary. Now you feel like you're writing for other people," and the enjoyment you once found in writing "is offset by a terrible fear of rejection," until you soon discover that "90% of the stuff you're writing is motivated and informed by an overwhelming need to be liked. This results in shitty fiction."

Eventually, he says, you might somehow shovel your way back to the fun of writing and discover that writing fiction is "a weird way to countenance yourself and to tell the truth instead of being a way to escape yourself or present yourself in a way you figure you will be maximally likable. This process is complicated and confusing and scary, and also hard work, but it turns out to be the best fun there is."

Yeah, well, Mr. Wallace had himself some issues. It is a bleak journey he chronicles, no less so because it was one he was unable to see through to completion, which eventually led to his suicide. But it is not, despite the second-person address he employed, the journey *you* must take. It was *his* journey, the one he plotted for himself, but one tragically tainted by his need to be liked. There is absolutely no reason why any of that bleakness has to be part of your journey.

I have never thought of the writing life as fun or scary or complicated or as a way to be liked. It is sometimes easy, sometimes magical, sometimes maddening, demanding, and exhausting, yet frequently very satisfying. I do it principally for the magic and the mystery and the sense of satisfaction it can elicit. I love words and I love stories, and I take great pleasure from being able to indulge myself in those pleasures every single day. Storytelling is not a way to work out who I am or why I exist; being a father answered most of those questions for me. Storytelling allows me to share my passion with others and to get paid for it.

David Foster Wallace was a fine but very troubled writer who confused what he was with what he did. This is a common affliction. Do not fall prey to it, because it usually won't end pretty. If you don't believe me, have a séance and ask Hemingway, Virginia Wolfe, Hunter Thompson, Sylvia Plath, and John Kennedy Toole.

No matter how authoritative and confident a writer sounds, and no matter how much you admire that writer's work, he or she is capable of detailing only his or her truth, derived as it was from his or her own idiosyncratic journey. Your journey might be similar or it might be vastly different; it will never be exactly the same as any other writer's journey.

Yet many writers, in an attempt to be helpful, create lists of rules for aspiring writers. The honest writers speak only in generalities: *Write every day. Read voraciously. Write what you want to read.* The less honest, or merely less humble, get specific and adamantine: *Avoid all adverbs. Never start with the weather. Write short sentences.* The more specific a writer's rule, the less trustworthy it is, and the sooner you should find the nearest exit.

By all means go ahead and read the rules, if you wish. Give them a try. And if one of them works for you, use it until it stops working, then dump it in the trash heap with all the other useless rules that have been crammed down your throat since your first hour in daycare. Writing is *creative*, so don't look to prescriptions or those who preach them. Sit down and create. Stick with it, and you will figure out the rest along the way. That has always been and will always be the only true way to learn.

My favorite piece of writing advice comes from Margaret Atwood: *Nobody is making you do this: you chose it, so don't whine.*

That is the only rule you will ever need to post over your desk: *Stop whining and write!*

A Writer's Life

When I was invited to speak here this evening, I asked, quite naturally, "What should I talk about?" The suggestion was made that I talk about the writer's life. People would be interested, I was told, to know how a fulltime writer lives these days.

I understand that curiosity. I share it. Writers have always fascinated me, and I often take more pleasure from reading about their lives than from reading their work. As the written word, especially as it pertains to fiction and poetry and other creative genres, becomes less and less relevant to an age of information and images, the writer has become more of a curiosity. We now occupy a place in society akin to the place in paleontology occupied by a creature called the Ediacaran biota, the first known complex multicellular organism.

The Ediacaran died off in a mass extinction about 500 million years ago, but they left a lot of fossils behind, just as we writers will when we all finally give up the ghost. And ever since the first Ediacaran fossil was discovered, they have puzzled and intrigued scientists, because here was a creature that seems impossible to classify. They had no heads, no tails, no mouths, no eyes, no teeth, no internal organs, no insides or outsides. Paleontologists don't even know if Ediacaran were animal or vegetable. The only fact about Ediacaran that scientists can agree on is that there were so many different kinds that nobody knows how many kinds there actually were.

That's sort of what writers are like. We are so different from one another that not even writers understand writers. But, like all freaks, we do tend to flock together when possible, just as The Bearded Lady might hook up with the Rubber Man, or the Tattooed Wonder with the Monkey Boy. We have little in common with one another really, except that in our solitary habits we are each conspicuously different from what we perceive as the rest of the world.

If you put any stock in a personality classification system called the Enneagram – first developed by the ancient Greeks and refined by modern pseudo-psychologists – you learn that most writers fall under the classification of *The Individualist*, which corresponds, more or less, with the Myers-Briggs *Apollonian Temperament* category. We tend toward introversion and value intuition, perceiving, and feeling above thinking. Apollonians comprise about 12% of the entire human population, while only about 1% of all Apollonians are writers. Infer from that what you will.

All this is my way of apologizing to you in advance for not talking about "The Writer's Life." I cannot speak with any authority except about *this* writer's life. How, or maybe why, did I become a writer? Is this proclivity something that could have been detected at birth? Something that could have been prevented with early treatment?

These questions have always intrigued me, because to ask them is not at all like asking, "Why does one become a lawyer, or a doctor, or a stock broker?" Those professions are defensible. Being a writer, in our culture, isn't.

And when I use the term *writer* tonight, I mean specifically the kind of writer I am, the kind who makes his living from writing – a living that includes no subsidized pension plan, no 401K, no benefits package, no tenure or seniority, no parachute, and no safety net.

The truth is, what I like best about the writing life, what I most cherish, is that it is such a risky and indefensible venture. It is fit only for a certain kind of entrepreneur – not the ones who hope to make a quick killing, but those satisfied to make a slow killing – over the next twenty or thirty years or so. Over the next lifetime.

To choose to spend your life fiddling with words has always been a choice difficult to justify, but never so much as in this materialistic, celebrity-awed culture of ours, never so difficult as now when success in every endeavor – including, since the mid-seventies or so, the arts – has been measured not by the degree of creativity or originality or courage involved but by the revenue it generates.

By today's standards a book that receives a six-figure advance is at least twenty times more important than one that garners a four-figure advance. It has to be; numbers don't lie. The truth is in the digits.

But I have never been able to subscribe to that philosophy. And I actually enjoy being out there on the tip of that skinny limb all by myself, with no poles of affiliation to prop me up. I like being forced to cling to my perch by tooth and claw through every thunderstorm and blizzard. I like having to fly off every morning in search of my daily worm.

A week or so ago I ran into an acquaintance of mine; it was around ten or eleven in the morning. He was on his way to repair the heating and air conditioning component for one of his customers, and I was on my way to the golf course. He gave me one of those long, jaundiced looks and said, his voice dripping with sarcasm, "It must be hard to have your life, Silvis."

My response was, "It isn't hard at all. The hard part was in getting here."

It took me nearly twenty years to get here. It probably shouldn't have taken that long, but I suffer, as Poe did, from a kind of contrariness that will sometimes make me do exactly the opposite of what I should do at any given moment. My mother would have called it "cutting off your nose to spite your face." I have made a lot of mistakes along the way, a lot of dumb choices.

And, unlike Frank Sinatra, I have a lot of regrets. But a clear conscience is usually the sign of a bad memory. I, at least, can still remember the things I did wrong, which might help me to not do them wrong twice.

In any case, I deliberately burned a lot of bridges simply because I knew that, in a moment of weakness, I would be tempted to cross those bridges again. And I didn't want that opportunity to exist; I didn't want to have the chance to abandon my principals. In other words, I was offered good, solid, reliable jobs in various businesses, but I turned them all down because I knew they would be the kiss of death for an incipient career as a writer.

What matters most in life to me, and to other Apollonians, is not security or financial success or fame, but individual freedom. I come from blue collar, anti-authoritarian stock, and the anti-authoritarian chromosome in my DNA is a mile wide. Growing up, I watched my father leave for his job at the steel mill every morning at 5:30, and I watched him come dragging home every evening at 5:30. He did that, without complaint, for forty-five years. And for most of those years, I kept asking myself, "This is the American Dream?"

My high school football coach once came upon me playing tennis in the middle of a weekday – this was when I was in my early twenties and in possession of a bachelor's degree in education – and chastised me rather sternly for "playing" instead of working. "Life isn't meant to be fun, Silvis," he told me. "Life is supposed to be hard."

I disagreed then and I disagree now. I think that though life is, quite frequently, hard, it can also bring enduring fulfillment. What my football coach did not know about me when he made that comment is that I had already put in six hours of writing before heading off to the courts that day. He came upon me mid-match while he was out walking his cocker spaniel, so he had no idea that I was living in a drafty little cabin in the woods that was suffocating in the summer and an icebox in the winter, or that I was subsisting on a box of Kraft macaroni and cheese per day. (You could buy six boxes for a dollar back then, and had only to add a bit of water to the powdered cheese.) In other words, I *was* working hard, but I was also loving every minute of my self-deprivation because I was doing self-chosen work, doing what I found relevant and significant even if others did not.

I have held at least four dozen different jobs since the age of fifteen, and to sit at a desk day in and day out with no resources other than my own imagination, and to come up with something on a regular basis that people will pay for, is the most demanding job I have ever held, and also the most exhilarating.

But how, you might ask, does one *become* a writer? To attempt to answer that question, I have to take you back to when I was twenty years old and a rather unenthusiastic accounting major in college. The notion that I, a backward boy from the coalfields of western Pennsylvania, could aspire to be a writer had not yet seized my mind. Writers were people who knew things, who had all the answers. Only later would I realize that writers are people who *ache* to know and understand things; they have far more questions than answers. But I didn't know that yet. All I knew was that my brother had been a business major and had gotten a good job, so I should be a business major too.

Then, out of the blue, two of my professors, literally within days of one another, took me aside to compliment my writing and storytelling ability, and to ask if I had ever considered becoming a writer.

And it was like – *wham!* All the lights came on. A writer. Of course! Why hadn't I ever thought of that?

At the end of the semester I became an English major, and that was the start of an ambition, something I had been sorely lacking until that day. Everything since then has been one long roller coaster ride.

And why not? I asked myself back then. *Why not become a writer?* I had always loved to read, always loved to make up stories. But those two passions never gelled into an ambition until a couple of kindly professors suggested that I give it some thought. And from that moment on, there was no turning back for me. From that moment on, I knew that I not only wanted to be a writer, but, being cursed with contrariness, I wanted to make my living from writing.

Furthermore, I was going to be a serious writer, damn it. I was going to be literary. And my first two books were. Great reviews all across the country, a couple of awards, enough literary acclaim to make a reasonable man dizzy. Unfortunately, the total revenue earned for those two books and maybe five years of toil was a grand total of approximately $15,000. Fifteen thousand divided by five. Well, I did the math, and I had an epiphany: This job don't pay the rent.

It was true then and it's even truer today. Literary fiction has a very small audience. Publishers almost always lose money on literary fiction. That's why nearly all so-called serious writers also teach or practice medicine or do something practical to pay the bills.

It came like a sucker punch to me to realize that good writing does not pay well. I staggered around for a while trying to catch my breath. After those first two books, I gave playwriting a shot, because, after all, plays are serious business too – just look at O'Neill and Beckett and Arthur Miller – all very serious guys. And I had considerable luck in getting my plays produced. Everything I wrote for the next ten years or so won a prize of some kind. Once again, good reviews and a fistful of awards. But when I went to New York City to see one of my plays in production, I ended up spending more money parking my car for a week than I made in royalties.

That was another sucker punch, and it left me reeling. But besides being a dreamer, as all writers are, I have a very practical side, and I finally had to admit to myself that my two ambitions – of being a serious, literary novelist and/or playwright, and of making my living from writing – appeared to be mutually exclusive.

It was at about this time that I read a book review in the *New York Times* – I was still reading the *New York Times* in those days – in which the reviewer lambasted the author for, and I quote from memory, "spending far more time worrying about plot than any serious writer should."

And I thought *What? What did he just say?*

All I ever did as a writer was to worry about plot. It was the one thing I did worry about. Because good plotting is hard. For me, plot is the hardest thing to get right. Dialogue and characterization and description and cadence, that's all a breeze for me. Plotting is what keeps me awake at night.

And here was this guy, this *New York Times Book reviewer* – whom you would think should know what he's talking about – saying that plot is not only not important but that a serious writer should treat it like hair lice.

This was more than a sucker punch. This was like growing up believing you're next in line for the crown of England only to be told a week before coronation that, sorry, you're really the illegitimate bastard of the scullery maid.

It left me devastated and confused. My second reaction, though, was to get angry. Because I knew in my heart that this reviewer and anybody else who denigrates plot is dead wrong. Plot is important, and a lot more of our so-called serious writers should be worrying about it. I know this for two reasons: first, because anything so difficult to do well must be important. And secondly, because plot, hand-in-hand with character, is an essential element of story, and story, my friends, provides the thing we come to literature for. Please excuse the sloppy construction but I really don't know how else to say it. Story provides what we come to literature to get.

Plot is conflict, and conflict is the window through which character is revealed, and, as such, it is what invokes our fear, our enmity, our compassion, our empathy, our sense of justice. It is what makes us weep and laugh and clutch at our hearts. Plot is what pulls us into a book and keeps us there. Plot is what fulfills that ancient and primal need in us for closure and resolution, the reassurance we require to face each day with renewed strength.

But back in the early 80s, when I was mulling these things over, the literary movement called minimalism had swept through town with its spare, bleak prose and plotless stories and had, to my way of thinking, sucked all the lifeblood out of American literature. Unfortunately, I seemed to be the only person complaining. By all appearances, I was so far out of step with the rest of the literary world that I wasn't even marching in the same parade.

I felt, in fact, that the parade had passed me by, that I had turned east when everybody else marched west. And I was simply not willing to go chasing after them in an attempt to jump onto their bandwagon. So, what to do?

What I did was to take a good hard look at the marketplace. What soon became obvious to me is that it isn't an innovative style or lyrical prose that draws massive audiences to writers such as Rowling and Clancy and Grisham, any one of whom sells more books than all the world's literary writers combined. It is the presence of interesting characters caught up in a satisfying plot. Good old-fashioned storytelling.

My choices were clear. I could continue to read a hundred or so freshmen compositions every week, struggling not to let my own writing be affected by a steady diet of clumsy prose, and write plotless, anemic literary novels on the side that might earn me more literary acclaim but precious few dollars. Or I could become the best damn storyteller I knew how.

To make this long story shorter, I wrote a mystery. Had I ever written a mystery before this? No. Did I even read mystery novels? I did not. But I love a good challenge. So I wrote a mystery novel, but I deliberately, and a bit defiantly, created an investigator void of all the typical characteristics of the typical hardboiled investigator.

I sent the novel to my agent, and, after a few days, he called to tell me that the novel was too well-written to market as a mystery and the plot was too strong to market the book as a literary novel.

I told him "It's a literary mystery."

"There's no such thing," he said.

"That's why I wrote it," I said.

Unfortunately, he wasn't in the business of representing books he could not sell.

I sent the novel, *An Occasional Hell*, to a small independent publisher in New York City, who, fortunately, did not share my former agent's qualms. The book was published in hardcover to excellent reviews – the *Washington Post* called it "an extraordinarily literate mystery." The paperback rights quickly sold, the movie rights sold, and I finagled my way into being hired as the screenwriter.

Those two incidents, my first commercially successful book and my first screenplay commission, turned the tide for me. In my case, it wasn't the early bird that got the worm; it was the second mouse that got the cheese.

Not that it's been all beer and gorgonzola since then. My choice cost me one of the things I most craved – namely, a reputation as a serious writer. Only half of my eight books to date have had a mystery plotline, and I paid no less attention to style and characterization in them than I did with my "literary" novels, but each one of the "mysteries" has sold more copies than my other four books combined. Therefore, I am a mystery writer. It must be so; the truth is in the numbers.

I would be remiss here, for those of you who desire more practical information than I have given thus far (or am likely to give), if I fail to mention that a significant portion of my fulltime writing income derives from non-book projects. I worked for several years as a feature writer for the Discovery Channel magazines, a gig that not only paid me very well but sent me off to Europe and the Arctic Circle and other far-flung places at their expense. Lately I have been doing more and more work for Hollywood, an experience that could be the focus of a talk in and of itself, including but not limited to the day I was banned from the set of my own movie.

Like all novelists, I have mixed feelings about Hollywood. I love the size of the checks they send; Hollywood money allows me to relax from what would otherwise be a day to day hustle of trying to make ends meet. But I hate the disregard with which Hollywood treats the written word, and, consequently, the screenwriter.

Whenever I think of Hollywood, I am reminded of the story about the woman who was out walking one morning in late September. It was a fine bright morning but there had been an early frost the night before and the ground was still wet. As this woman walked along the road, she came upon a snake that hadn't made it back to its den before sunset the previous night and, being cold-blooded, it had been paralyzed by the cold.

So this woman, who was a very kind and well-meaning woman, picked up the snake and took it home and laid it out in front of her fireplace. She massaged it and kept it warm and, lo and behold, the snake thawed out and came back to life. The woman didn't want this snake to have go back out into the cold again, so she made a little den for it there in her house and she fed it pieces of hamburger and she massaged it daily, and the snake really seemed to enjoy being stroked and handled by her.

One day, out of the blue, for no reason at all, the snake drew back and struck her, right in the neck. As the venom coursed through her veins, she begged to know, "Why? After all I've done for you – why would you bite me?"

The snake looked at her and said, "What? You didn't know that I'm a snake?"

That's a good story for a writer to keep in mind when he goes to work in Hollywood. The nature of a snake is to bite, and the nature of Hollywood is to wring every drop of lifeblood it can get from the writer and then to turn on him. The filmmaking industry is home to a lot of massive and yet strangely fragile egos, and if a writer allows himself to get too close to this environment, the consequences can be toxic.

Now don't get me wrong; I'm not saying that all movie people are screwed up. It's just that first 95% of them that gives the rest a bad name.

The second reason why writers have so many bitter experiences in the film business has to do with the process by which a movie is made. Another story:

A screenwriter once wrote a screenplay and submitted it to a producer. The writer waited an appropriate amount of time and then telephoned the producer and asked, "So? Did you like my script?" To which the producer replied, "I don't know. I'm the only one who's read it so far."

Producers are essentially business people. Many of them are not terribly creative, not especially language-oriented, and certainly not inclined to take risks with the huge sums of money required to make a movie. So they really don't know if they like a script until several other people have told them to like it. And that's only the first hurdle a writer in Hollywood has to get past.

A script is never finished. Everyone who touches it – agent, producer, director, actor – is going to ask for changes, many of them arbitrary, many having nothing at all to do with the storyline. But the writer in Hollywood is low man on the totem pole and he is somehow expected to satisfy everybody at the same time. If he doesn't, and the person he failed to satisfy has enough power, the writer is fired and another writer is brought in.

Lots of deliciously nasty lines have been uttered by dyspeptic writers who bellied up to the Hollywood feedbag only to have their stomach soured. Some of my favorite lines came from Raymond Chandler, who observed, among other things, that the process of moviemaking is "an endless contention of tawdry egos," and that in Hollywood "nearly every sleeve conceals a knife," and that if movies were made as they should be, "the director – heaven help his strutting soul – would be reduced to the ignominious task of making pictures as they are conceived and written, and not as the director would try to write them, if only he knew how to write."

And that, in a nutshell, and with a great deal of over-simplification, is what it is like, for me anyway, to live the writing life. It is a tenuous and unstable and depressing and maddening and exhilarating business. It is even, at times, a quietly satisfying life. That last part, the part that keeps me doing it, begins and ends with the work itself, with an individual sitting alone in a room and struggling to find a story and the best words with which to tell it.

The Writer and the Oyster

I won't presume to know why other people read, but I read for one of two reasons: to gain information and/or knowledge, or to be immersed in a world other than my own. To fulfill the first need, a book requires no special prose style other than a trustworthy voice. To fulfill the second need, however, the author has to work harder. The voice must be not only trustworthy (except in the case of an unreliable narrator) but must also be, in a manner of speaking, hypnotic. It must pull me into the story and hold me there.

It is easy to walk away from a factual book for a day or so because you know that the facts will still be there when you return to your reading. But a good novelist will make it difficult for the reader to lay down a book that has held you entranced; you are not walking away from facts in this case but from people who have become real to you, people who have laid claim to your attention and emotions. A good author of this type of book will create a fully imaginable world, complete with settings and scents and sounds and tastes: a world that lies parallel to the reader's own, and only a few steps away.

The distinction between these two types of books is not simply a matter of fiction versus nonfiction. Certain types of creative nonfiction, such as the personal essay, memoir, travel writing, nature writing, and biography all have characters too; frequently, but not always, that character is the author. In any type of book in which a character, real or fictional, holds the stage, a voice rendered through prose that is somewhat denser, pithier, more evocative than mere journalism is a requisite for me. Without it, I have a difficult time paying attention. It would be like watching a movie without a soundtrack.

In order to invoke trust, a book of facts and information requires a succinct and objective journalistic voice. In a book whose principal aim is to convey information, any attempt at lyrical or manipulative prose can make the reader suspicious of bias and pretention in the writer. But a book that provides entre into another world, whether that world is wholly realistic, futuristic, historic, or fantastical, seduces the reader not through facts but through voice. To create that voice, good grammar is not enough, and sometimes isn't necessary.

From this kind of book and this kind of effect, I expect to discover on the very first page two things: an interesting individual as the main character and a voice that, like a pretty smile from across the room, or like a song from a well-played piano sounding from somewhere down the hall, always urges me closer.

What makes a character interesting? Risk. The tangible prospect of loss or danger. A desperate need. A barely controllable rage. A mystery. The threat of violence. A tantalizing tease of something craved or feared or about to be granted or denied. One or more compelling dramatic questions that a curious reader will follow to its end.

It helps if the character is also likable, and that we, as readers, want him or her to succeed. But a wholly unlikable character can keep us reading too.

The reader's compelling desire to know the answer to the dramatic questions can supersede, for many readers, the need for graceful prose. I could name numerous bestselling authors who have made their fortunes from compelling stories rendered in bland, homogenous, and even awkward prose. For most readers, a solidly sunk hook, with escalating tension applied to that hook throughout the story, will be hard for the average reader to shake.

Still, for me to feel wholly satisfied at the end of a book, both of my needs must have been fulfilled, though the second need (for distinctive prose) is often mediated by my own expectations. For example, I don't expect such prose from Grisham or Dan Brown or several other popular writers of plot-driven books. I do expect it in literary fiction, which, by definition, has less developed plots, if any at all. But a book whose only virtue is either skillful prose or a propulsive plot will likely find itself in my Give Away stack.

I am more likely to toss an inelegantly written literary novel aside after fifty pages wherein nothing of import happens than I am to toss aside an inelegantly written novel in which the plot has wrapped its hands around my throat. I will read to the very last word of such a novel, but will then feel as guilty as if I have devoured a whole bag of potato chips.

But that's me. My preferences are neither right nor wrong. Different strokes for different yokes.

As a writer, I aim for a reader whose literary aesthetics match my own, i.e. a reader who appreciates skillful prose but also wants to be dragged through the pages by an irresistible plot. There will always be readers who, craving either more external plot or more internal cerebration, dislike, mildly or vehemently, what I have written. Their dislike causes me no loss of sleep.

My point here is that any writer who attempts to sustain a career without identifying his or her own literary aesthetic and that of the audience he or she wishes to reach is destined for disappointment. If you write like Marcel Proust, don't expect a glowing blurb from Stephen King. If you write like Stephen King, don't expect an invitation to lunch from Philip Roth.

Likewise, you can't go through life blaming readers for not loving what you write. For example, the sight of raw oysters triggers my gag reflex, but that doesn't mean the oysters should be offended by my reaction. It's not them, it's me.

Sentences, a Love Story

When it comes to sentences, I am polyamorous. Yes, I am a philanderer of sentences, a syntax satyr, a serial sentencer. And I have no intention of ever changing my ways, no twelve-step program for me – even though, with each passing year, I become more of an oddball, more of a freak. I've seen the looks some of you give me, you Jersey Shore couch riders, you Real Housewives, you chuggers of graphic novels, you internet surfers, you *typers*. I've heard the mutters and giggles. And I just don't care. My lovers are true.

Roosters wear out if you stare at them too much.

I had already been bedazzled by García Márquez's *One Hundred Years of Solitude* when I picked up the story collection, *Nobody Writes to the Colonel*. But even when you expect a writer to bedazzle you, and maybe because you expect it, the bedazzling sentence, like this one from the title story, still comes out of nowhere and slaps you cross-eyed.

I remember reading that sentence and chuckling out loud. But then the chuckles seized in my chest, because I just had to know: In what *way* does a rooster wear out?

Márquez, for all his genius, doesn't tell us. Fortunately, I have known several roosters in my time, and I even bear the scar tissue signature of one particularly petulant cock that nearly tore my eye out. So I know for a fact that roosters have only three jobs in life. The first is to call the populace to arms at the break of every day. The second is to service the ladies of the coop and to keep one's rate of begetting running a digit or two ahead of the omelet maker's. A rooster's third job is to fight, to risk wing and comb keeping all other roosters away from the harem, including a seven-year-old human rooster who is obviously up to no good.

So when García Márquez has the old Colonel – a human rooster himself, though retired from fighting and not much interested in crowing at the sun – admonish his wife, the Colonel is saying, in effect, "Stop staring at my comrade or he won't be able to take care of his girls. You ever hear of erectile dysfunction, woman? You keep staring at him with that critical, disappointed look on your face, what do you expect to happen? Viagra hasn't even been invented yet. Look at the way his comb is drooping. Show a little simpatico, why don't you."

Yes, in that one sentence, Márquez's naked genius reveals itself. What makes a writer truly unique is not vocabulary or plot or the size of her latest advance, but that uncommon way of seeing the world, of reacting to the mundane. Take these two phrases, for example, from Márquez's "The Handsomest Drowned Man in the World": *Even though they were looking at him there was no room for him in their imagination.... They wanted to tie the anchor from a cargo ship to him so that he would sink easily into the deepest waters, where fish are blind and divers die of nostalgia.*

Show me a story by García Márquez and I will show you a sentence where a simple twist has been applied, a tiny knot or bow of words, and the sentence has been transformed, lifted out of the ordinary and into the sublime.

In the fall the war was always there, but we did not go to it anymore.

Did ever a story start out more beguilingly, yet with such a ponderous sigh of resignation, as Hemingway's "In Another Country"? I first read this story perhaps forty years ago, and its hook is still embedded in my neck. If any single sentence can lay claim to my addiction, to giving me that first blue rush of intoxication, that first frisson of syntactic sexuality, it is this one. I was a young man then, my brain swamped with testosterone and sloshing in fear while I waited, viscera trembling, for the long arm of Vietnam to yank me out of the meadow and into the jungle. I felt certain that my country had earmarked me for death, had already inscribed my fatality on Walter Cronkite's nightly death count.

And then along came this sentence from off the Italian front of the first World War, written by a young man with his genitals full of shrapnel. *In the fall the war was always there, but we did not go to it anymore.* Why such sadness in that sentence? Why not a more celebratory tone?

I was nineteen when I first read that sentence. And not only did I feel, as all nineteen-year-old boys probably do, that my testicles were full of hot metal, but I had already seen the glassy look in the eyes of former classmates home on leave, and I had viewed the closed casket of one sent home in a body bag, and I had shaken the hand of another who had left part of his leg in another country. So I had to read only that one sentence to know why Hemingway's mustered-out narrator would always be sad, would always shoulder that rucksack of sorrow through every day of his life. The rest of the story merely confirmed what my aching viscera already knew, that even if you are lucky enough to survive war and never have to go to it again, it will never leave you, it will always live inside.

That sentence, more than *Apocalypse Now*, more than the wrenching *The Things They Carried* or *The Naked and the Dead* or *From Here To Eternity*, more than *Platoon* or *Full Metal Jacket* or *Bat 21* or *Blackhawk Down*, more than a thousand other glaring images of war, marked and defined me, stabbed and cauterized and embedded itself in my soul.

Mother died today. Or, maybe yesterday; I can't be sure.

Deep in London's rumbling tube, searching for enough light to read by, I am hungry, so hungry, but I will not eat for a while because I have spent three times my daily ration on this slender little volume, *The Outsider*, by Albert Camus. I bought it at a Farringdon Road bookstall because of the title, handed over the £4.55 while again cursing the stranger who, while I had been enjoying my weekly shower in the dollar-a-night hostel, had plundered my backpack and left me with only the money in my pocket. Over the past week I had punched two extra holes in my belt but I was not ready yet to go home. There was still Stonehenge to visit, Salisbury Cathedral, the White Horse, the Royal Botanic Gardens…. I would sleep in the bushes again if necessary. I would eat words and drink the moor's gray air. Isn't that what an Outsider would do, and isn't that precisely what I was and always had been?

All this I was thinking when I purchased the book and as I entered down into the darkness with no intention of climbing on a train, no money to do so, just hoping to get out of the sun for a while, hoping to find a bench from which the Bobbies would not chase me.

Mother died today, I read. The pang, the pinch, the ache for a mother's love – it all flew back to me with those three words. The succulence of my mother's bread pudding, the cinnamon rolls warm from the oven.

And oh, the punctuation of those two sentences – how exquisite it was! How precise! Camus might have written, *Or maybe yesterday, I can't be sure.* But there is a nonchalance to that punctuation, an implied indifference. And Camus' narrator is anything but indifferent. Because of the pause after *Or*, I can hear the man thinking. *Or*, he thinks, and looks up from the telegram, gazes squinting into a sun-bleached sky, *maybe yesterday*. And then the even longer pause after *yesterday*, the slow, grating stop of a semi-colon. It is a surprise to him, this post-semi-colon revelation. No, he can't be sure. How can one ever be sure?

I adore Camus because of that comma and that semi-colon. Because of his punctuation, I know that Camus was an outsider just like me, a thinker, a ponderer, a scrutinizer of angles.

There in the stale cool dimness in the belly of the Tube, I fell in love again. Screw the money. Who needed food? In my hands I held a perfect feast of words, all perfectly seasoned with just the right blend of punctuation.

My mother is a fish.

Ah, metaphor! How do I love thee? I love thee to the depth and breadth and length the sentence can reach.

I love when writers say something by saying something else. For my money, Faulkner was usually guilty of saying too much to say too little, but in this sentence from *As I Lay Dying* – this *complete chapter* from *As I Lay Dying* – he proves his mettle. Who in American literature (which leaves out the author of "Jesus wept") has said more in fewer words?

We have the much heralded *Call me Ishmael*, of course, but those words have never thrilled me, never walked me down the lane where lovers will be, will be…. No, Melville's lauded opening has no resonance unless the reader reads the name and thinks *Hmm, sounds Biblical, better look it up*, only to discover that Ishmael was the son of Abraham and banished to the wilderness by his father, and there aided by God, and ho-hum several hundred pages into the whale book later the reader might remember this and think *Yep, I guess that sort of applies to this Ishmael too.*

But *My mother is a fish*!

Is it any wonder that Hemingway was always jealous of Faulkner?

Where I am, I don't know, I'll never know, in the silence you don't know, you must go on, I can't go on, I'll go on.

This is the last line from Beckett's *Unnamable*, so hopeless yet so life affirming, so full of surrender yet so resolute. I could say that this line sums up the totality of a writer's existence, but if you are the wealthy writer of an unscripted reality TV series you would disagree. So let me say instead that this line perfectly sums up the existence of every thinking and feeling human being except for the writers and producers and viewers of reality TV shows.

Howsoever, I do have a bone to pick with Beckett. Or, rather, a comma to pick. Plus a period or two. As much as I love that little Irishman, he could take a lesson from Camus. Maybe it was the Irish whiskey in him, maybe the Guinness, but if he had just slowed down a bit, stopped running his words together, his beautiful sentence might have buzzed with annihilating electricity like the Ark of the Covenant.

Where I am, I don't know. I'll never know. In the silence, you don't know, you must go on. I can't go on. I'll go on.

That's how I would write it. Fear. Realization. Resignation. Surrender. Perseverance.

You say no? You say my punctuation destroys the rhythm and frackles the harmony? You say how dare I presume to rewrite the maestro himself? I can answer only this: "Why I presume, I don't know. I'll never know. In the silence, you never know, yet you must presume. I can't presume. Fuck it, I'll presume."

Today I write. I will kill myself tomorrow.

I have no idea who said this. I seem to remember reading it in a short essay, but written by whom, I do not know. I have googled the phrase in every configuration conceivable and I am still batting zero. So maybe I said it. Maybe I only thought it to myself. Maybe I was sitting there on the edge of my bed one afternoon, looking fondly at the revolver, or turning the bottle of aspirin in my hands, and along came that string of simple words, that alchemical juxtaposition of letters and syllables. A chant. A mantra. Whatever gets you through the night.

How is it that words, mere words, mere plebian, pedestrian, mere commonplace words – words of which we all are capable – how can mere words exert such power? How can they throw off such sparks, such scintillation and suggestion?

For an increasingly few of us – fortunate or unfortunate, nobody yet knows – no other palliative will suffice. But would it be so bad, would the world be a less endurable place, if the addiction to well-chosen words were to spread? What if, in the back alleys and taverns of America, in the mean streets and abandoned houses, wherever minds erode and bodies whither, where spirits flag and souls turn to dust, what if, in such places, a simple fix were available, a quick, inexpensive hit whispered into your ear, enough to sustain you through another day, through another night of dripping rain?

Let us go then, you and I, when the evening is spread out against the sky like a patient etherized upon a table....

Magda flopped onward with her little pencil legs scribbling this way and that, in search of the shawl....

It was love at first sight. The first time Yossarian saw the chaplain he fell madly in love with him.

"She would of been a good woman," the Misfit said, "if it had been somebody there to shoot her every minute of her life."

A Farewell to Adverbs

Yesterday I was reading social media posts from a writing group I belong to by virtue of teaching at that university, and I read of one young writer's excitement about a new online digital editor, called the Hemingway app. The app promises to prune and shape one's writing so that it can shine "bold and clear" like Hemingway's. Since I have read and learned (or so I thought) from virtually every one of Hemingway's novels and stories and have credited him as one of my most influential mentors (nevermore!), and have consistently discouraged my students from expecting an electronic anything to turn them into better writers (shame on me), I thought it wise to take the Hemingway app around the block once or twice.

I opened my first edition copy of Hemingway's *For Whom the Bell Tolls* at random and copied this from the bottom of page 85 into the Hemingway app:

> *We made love there, the room dark in the day time*
> *from the hanging blinds, and from the streets there*
> *was the scent of the flower market and the smell of*
> *burned powder from the firecrackers of the traca that*
> *ran through the streets exploding each noon during*
> *the Feria. It was a line of fireworks that ran through*
> *all the city, the fireworks linked together and the*
> *explosions running along on poles and wires of the*
> *tramways, exploding with great noise and a jumping*

from pole to pole with a sharpness and a cracking of
explosion you could not believe.

The Hemingway app rated the readability of that paragraph "poor" and said "2 of 2 sentences are very hard to read."

So okay, maybe I hadn't given the Hemingway app sufficient time to warm up. Maybe it needed to adapt to Hemingway's innovative style. I turned the page in *For Whom the Bell Tolls* and picked out another paragraph:

Just then three Heinkel fighters in V formation came
low over the clearing coming toward them, just over
the tree tops, like clattering, wing-tilting, pinch-nosed
ugly toys, to enlarge suddenly, fearfully to their actual
size; pouring past in a whining roar. They were so low
that from the cave mouth all of them could see the
pilots, helmeted, goggled, a scarf blowing back from
behind the patrol leader's head.

Once again, the Hemingway app rated the readability of that paragraph "poor" and said that not only were 2 of 2 sentences hard to read, but 2 of 2 sentences were very hard to read. The app pointed out two adverbs that should be removed, and suggested that Hemingway "aim for 0 or fewer" adverbs. It did not explain, however, how to achieve fewer than zero.

I gave the app one more shot at appraising its namesake's prose. Surely it would recognize the virtues of the Nobel Laureate's distinctive and influential style. I turned the page again, then typed in this paragraph:

It was a clear, bright day and warm now in the sun.
Robert Jordan looked at the big, brown-faced woman
with her kind, widely set eyes and her square, heavy
face, lined and pleasantly ugly, the eyes merry, but the

face sad until the lips moved. He looked at her and then at the man, heavy and stolid, moving off through the trees toward the corral. The woman, too, was looking after him.

Finally the app found something to approve. The general readability was rated good, but the sentence beginning with "Robert Jordan" was rated "very hard to read." And, again, two nasty adverbs had reared their ugly, unnecessary heads. Once again, Hemingway was admonished to "aim for 0 or fewer" adverbs.

In general, it seems that even Hemingway's prose was not sufficiently Hemingwayesque for the Hemingway app. I found myself feeling glad that Papa was no longer around to suffer such criticism. Had he and previous reviewers of his work known that his prose was, at best, "good," but more usually "poor," would J. Donald Adams, for example, writing in the *New York Times* in 1961, have proclaimed him "the Byron of our time" and "the greatest descriptive writer of our time"?

Would Gabriel García Márquez, writing in the *Times* twenty years later, have so publicly admitted that "Hemingway is the one who had the most to do with my craft – not simply for his books, but for his astounding knowledge of the aspect of craftsmanship in the science of writing"?

By the standards of the Hemingway app, Hemingway's craftsmanship could have used a good bit of tweaking.

In 1992, Frederick Busch observed that Hemingway "listened and watched and invented the language…with which we could name ourselves."

Hmmm. How could Busch, Márquez, and Adams be so wrong? And what about that misguided, ill-informed Nobel committee that had awarded both Hemingway and Márquez the Big Prize? I began to wonder if perhaps Márquez's tribute to Hemingway was little more than lip service; had the maestro learned his craft from Hemingway not by emulating Papa but by stylistically repudiating him? There was only one way to find out.

I plugged in these two sentences from the middle of page one of Gabriel García Márquez's masterful (I used to think) *One Hundred Years of Solitude*:

> *A heavy gypsy with an untamed beard and sparrow hands, who introduced himself as Melquiades, put on a bold public demonstration of what he himself called the eighth wonder of the learned alchemists of Macedonia. He went from house to house dragging two metal ingots and everybody was amazed to see pots, pans, tongs and braziers tumble down from their places and beams creak from the desperation of nails and screws trying to emerge, and even objects that had been lost for a long time appeared from where they had been searched for most and went dragging along in turbulent confusion behind Melquiade's magical irons.*

The Hemingway app rated the readability of those two sentences poor, suitable only for post-collegiate readers (which seems to imply that only highly educated people should read poor writing). Two of the two sentences were "very hard to understand" and contained three uses of passive voice. "Remove them," the app scolded. The only thing Márquez had done correctly, according to the app, was to use zero adverbs. For that he received a conciliatory "Well done."

It was now becoming clear to me that Busch, Adams, García Márquez, and millions of other readers who, like my former deluded self, had found in Hemingway's poor to good prose sensitively rendered representations of action, violence, poignancy, love, loss, betrayal, despair, grief, truth, and even beauty, had done so only because we were not as well-educated, or our literary tastes as refined, as those of the Hemingway app inventors and the multitudes of aspiring writers who now wisely embrace the digital editors that guarantee literary success.

But now that I, too, finally understand what it takes to be a good writer, I, too, have embraced the new standards. After struggling for at least fifteen seconds, I composed the following paragraph and plugged it into the Hemingway app:

> Hemingway was a writer. He wrote fiction and nonfiction. I used to like the way he wrote. I used to think I had learned a lot from reading his work. But he is dead now. Times have changed. Phooey on Hemingway. Phooey on Márquez. We don't need hard to understand great literature to teach us how to write. Now we can learn to write better from brainless and heartless and talentless machines. Now the brilliant inventors who invent these machines are our heroes. Now multitudes of writers can write brilliant machine-generated prose like this. So I will use the Hemingway app. I will aim for zero or fewer adverbs.

The result? I was rewarded with the Hemingway app's equivalent of a gold star: no suggestions for improvement!

Hey, Nobel Prize committee: What do you think of that?

Choosing a Book

Choosing a book to take home from the bookstore, to welcome into your home, is not appreciably different from choosing a puppy from the Humane Society kennels. You are going to spend some time with this puppy or this book, intimate time, just the two of you alone, so it is not a choice to make lightly. You do not want to take either one home only to discover that it is a biter or a barker or a furniture chewer or a pisser that cannot be trained. There is no regret quite like that of laying down mucho dinero for a puppy or book that soon reveals itself as unsavory, a waster of your time, shallow, even stupid, a taker who gives nothing but dissatisfaction in return.

Libraries, however, which seldom sell puppies, are a haven for the impetuous. Pull a book off the shelf, take it home, read a few pages, and, if so inclined, toss it in the back seat of the car until your next trip to the library. That's something you can't do with a bad puppy. Though you can take the bad puppy back to the Humane Society. When it comes to returning puppies, the Society is more humane that most libraries.

The book purchase, on the other hand, is a commitment. A temporary marriage. So much so that I have developed a ritual of sorts, a catechism for bookstores. Here is the routine I follow when deciding whether or not to purchase a book. It is not for the harried.

First off, ignore the cover. The cover art means nothing to you as a reader. There is an entire science behind the design of cover art, the single provocative image, the genre implication, and so forth. The cover is designed by a marketing team (that hasn't read the book) so as to hook the impulse consumer. And you, discriminating reader that you are, would never buy on impulse.

So ignore the cover. Ignore the title page and the acknowledgements. Ignore the blurbs whether they are on the back cover or inside the book. Blurbs, as we all surely know by now, are gross exaggerations penned by a friend of the author or by somebody hoping to be a friend of the author and therefore someone for whom the author will someday write an equally effusive blurb.

Ignore all those crudités and go straight for the meat, page one of the text, which is usually an unnumbered page 3 even though it is the ninth or eleventh page in the book. Read the first paragraph. If during those sixty seconds you do not detect a certain suavity of language, a music, an intimation of wondrous things to come, lay the book aside and choose another.

But if you do hear music and feel that warm hand of companionship upon your shoulder, now close the book and flip it over. But not to read those incestuous endorsements from fellow writers. What you are looking for here is the author's photo and bio notes, sometimes on the back jacket, sometimes on the inside rear flap or the last page of the book. What you see and hear in the photo and bio will determine whether, in the end, to carry this book to the check-out counter or to shelve it.

I look to see how old the author is. This is sometimes tricky, because authors are no more immune to vanity than the rest of mankind and are often even more insecure. So it is not uncommon for a writer to use a photo ten years younger than her first-born child, who will enter Stanford in September. But before I can proceed I must convince myself that the author is not a child. Not an MFA prodigy, narcissistic and chic, raised on television and Hollywood, weaned on *The New Yorker*, lost her virginity in the back seat of the minimalism bus, or, worse yet, in a sloppy postmodernist orgy of storyless narrative.

Kurt Vonnegut once said that no writer under twenty-five is worth reading. When I first read that statement, at twenty-three or so, I took great umbrage. Now, at fifty-plus, I view my own age as a good middle ground and will gladly read books by writers whose age falls within ten years short or twenty years long of mine. Just as I avoid writers too young to have acquired the necessary layers of experience in their lives, writers who have not yet suffered sufficiently to render their perceptions relevant to we who are older, I avoid dodderers as well, those who have surrendered their anger and their angst for serenity. I cannot bear serene writers, safe writers, writers whose work pleases everybody, takes no risks, offends no one.

No, I am scrutinizing the author's photo for evidence of pain, wounds, scars, the way the mouth, even in smile, pulls down; the way the eyes, though uplifted, gaze into the distance, peer into the dark.

If not discouraged by the photo, I move to the bio. This paragraph, by the way, is almost always composed by the author. So if the writer prominently and proudly mentions an MFA degree, it is not inconceivable that I will fling the book away as if I have turned the page to find a used condom there. Nor do I care to read a book by somebody who "lives in a Victorian farmhouse in Connecticut, which he shares with his poet wife and two spoiled felines named Tigger and Winnifred." Such facts of life do not necessarily disqualify a writer from writing well, but, as bio notes, they suggest that the writing has emerged from a life so superficial as to elevate cats and whimsy to a point of personal pride.

What I would prefer to read here is that this writer once sold life insurance, or, better yet, still does. This tells me that he has peddled his sad wares from door to door, made cold calls, been hung up on, been treated like last week's uncooked Spam. He has pulled up a chair in the ashes of a burned-out home, has handed a check to a suicide's widow. In short, this writer has lived. This writer has suffered. This writer has lain awake long nights, has railed at God, has in the four AM of his soul cradled a Smith and Wesson in his hands and wondered which way to point it.

Here is a writer who has something to say and who does his or her best to say it with beauty and grace. That's all it takes for me. A book by this kind of writer is worth twenty-five dollars every time, because what you are paying for is not the paper and ink, not the mere product of imagination, but the warm hand on the shoulder, the knowing whisper in the ear, the strangely haunting music that beckons you come hither to the unlit room at the top of the stair.

Profit and Loss

I sometimes wonder if I might be an archeologist today, or maybe an accountant or a forest ranger, if, just once during those years when I was studying how to read and write stories and how to teach others to do the same, somebody had whispered a word of caution that if I wasn't careful I might catch what I was pursuing. But one thing nobody ever told me was that my chosen métier would all too soon result in the erosion of the joy that had driven me to it in the first place, the joy of reading and the sweet transcendence it provided out of mundane Pennsylvania and into sublime Paris or Pamplona or Macado or Yoknapatawpa or a thousand other landscapes so much more vivid than my own.

It used to be – in the early days of writing, before I had published enough to be asked to teach writing and consequently had to investigate the mechanics of what I was doing – that I would sit on my front porch in the misty light of a bucolic dawn, armed with nothing but a yellow legal pad, a pen, a cup of coffee, and the notion of a story, and soon the magic would descend from the ether, and the real world would blur around the edges, fade to gray, be swallowed whole by the colors and squawks of a clamorous Tijuana, the strangely serene but frenetic finger work of a tiny lace maker at her table beside a canal in Bruges, or just a twilight valley a ridge or two away – imagined landscapes one and all, corporeal only in the parietal to the occipital lobes of my brain.

And when I would look up from this world after what seemed only a few minutes immersion in it, the magic broken by the *beep*

beep! of the mailman's horn, I would realize, blinking like a dreamer dragged out of his bed, that three or four hours had passed and I was in Pennsylvania after all, and that a dozen pages blank only a few minutes earlier were now filled with inky squiggles, and the funky scent of the Rio Grande still peppered the air, or the heat of a crunchy *frite* still lingered on my tongue.

This was how I wrote my stories in the early days and how I read the stories of other writers. I had no idea back then how a story was made or where stories came from, I only knew that some of them came through me, and I was blissful in my ignorance.

After ten years or so of this and a couple of published books, I was offered a teaching position. Artistic creation is a jubilant way to pass the day just so long as you can keep yourself from peeking at the checkbook, but I peeked once too often. So, when the offer came, I said yes, even though I had had no instruction in either teaching or composing fiction, no MFA degree, no secret *gnosis*. How, then, to teach what I did not know? How to deconstruct instinct and explicate the amorphous?

For no other reason but so as not to appear a fool in the classroom, I studied that which I had so assiduously avoided studying – avoided because writing from the gut was plenty productive and effective for me, so why fix what wasn't broken? But now I had to teach what I was doing without knowing how I was doing it.

I studied the craft of narrative, the elements of form. I read and analyzed and slipped one story after another under the microscope. And eventually I learned to spot the wiring and plumbing, the load-bearing walls and the nails that held those walls together.

Then on to playwriting, then screenwriting, and before long their innards too became visible to me. The story, those transporting stories, were all sliced into pieces, reduced to plot points, bridges, reversals, and so forth. I could spot a denouement coming from a mile away.

I became a good teacher, filled to the brim with practical information. But although I can still be thrilled occasionally by a svelte turn of phrase, can still be startled and flooded with gratitude when one slips out of my own pen and onto yellow paper, when I am reading or writing these days, the real world almost never blurs around the edges anymore, almost never fades to gray. I pound too many nails now, snap too many chalk lines. The joy of artistic levitation requires a weightlessness born of innocence, and I carry too many tools to float away into the ether of imagination.

I miss the magic buoyancy of story in my daily work. Oh, it still pops up now and then, but never frequently enough. Mostly I rely on craft and life itself, neither as numinous as unfettered imagination. A good teacher cannot afford to be an ignorant one, but I miss my ignorance. And that is why I always warn my students: Be careful what you wish for; you just might get it.

Or, as poet and painter William Blake warned, "The fool who persists in his folly will become wise."

Better to remain a fool than to lose the magic.

Cue the Music

Before I wrote fiction and creative nonfiction, I wrote poetry. And before that, I wrote songs. A couple hundred of them. From the age of thirteen to twenty or so, I wanted to be the next Paul Simon, John Lennon, Van Morrison, and Brian Wilson. Over those years I made a few tapes on my little Radio Shack recorder, printed up the lyric sheets, and sang, badly, while accompanying myself (more badly) on piano or guitar. A few A&R directors said, "Hey kid, these songs ain't awful. Come drop by the office and let us hear what all you've got."

The thought of traveling alone to Nashville or Muscle Shoals caused me no distress. But the notion of sitting at a piano or standing with a guitar in my hands and performing for a professionally discerning audience nauseated me. I had barely enough confidence to play my songs for the dog, who opened her eyes only on the high notes. So I didn't go anywhere, and I stopped sending out demo tapes.

During my sophomore year in college, a couple of English professors said, "Hey Silvis, your stuff ain't awful. Have you ever thought about being a writer?"

The good thing about writing short stories and novels, I realized, was that I could do it alone in my room and didn't have to perform them for anybody. Stick them in the mail and wait for the rejection letter: my kind of human interaction. So I became a writer of fictions and kept my songwriting identity in the closet.

Music, however, is still essential to my life. I might have flamed out as a singer/songwriter, but I still try to get as much music into my prose as possible, and I often listen to music to help surround myself with the appropriate mood for a particular scene or story. I seem to need music the way others need caffeine, just to get the juices flowing, and to make me care enough to pull the chair up to the desk yet one more time.

Music in prose is closely tied to cadence, the rise and fall of language, and to rhythm, the variations of stress. Writers use cadence and rhythm to increase or decrease the pace, to slow or speed up the reading. The effect on the reader is subliminal; readers are eased into a mood, just as a lullaby can soothe, and just as a lively Sousa march, hip hop or heavy metal song can rouse the reader to action.

Cadence and rhythm are experienced aurally, urged into a sentence via syntax and diction, commas and the absence of commas, half-stops and full stops and no stops at all. This is the melody line. But the other senses must be massaged as well, textures and scents and images conjured out of mere words colored for weight or buoyancy. These are the bass lines and the harmonies of prose.

By carefully piecing together music and story, writers move their readers to tears or laughter, bittersweet smiles, shivers of fear, or to that deep acknowledgement of aloneness that precipitates a terrible ache of longing. Every scene a song, every chapter a movement, every book a symphony.

Over the years I have compiled a list of songs I find particularly inspirational. It's a very subjective list, as all lists are. I make no apologies for my bias toward aging balladeers. I, too, am an aging balladeer, and I have a particular fondness for those minstrels with whom I have wailed and wept and raged throughout the years. Boisterous, exuberant songs seldom find their way onto my list. Solitude is a writer's milieu, and, therefore, almost universally, melancholic is his temperament. Besides, my ancestors were Portuguese and Irish; *suadade* floods my veins while tiny Irish leprechauns bedevil my neurons.

This list of twenty-five songs is, of course, a partial list. If I had the time and were getting paid for it, I could enumerate powerful, inspirational songs until the day the music dies.

The best *Dump Him and Come to Me* song: Sting's "When We Dance"

The best *Dead Wife* song: Springsteen's "Missing"

The best *Go Away and Leave Me Alone* song: Brian Wilson's "In My Room"

The best *I've Squeezed All the Juice I Can Out of This Place Teen Angst* song: Springsteen's "Fourth of July"

The best *I Can't Figure Out Why I Still Want an Asshole Like You* song: Patsy Cline's cover of Willie Nelson's "Crazy."

The best *Better Luck Next Life* song: George Harrison's "Within You Without You"

The best *Pick-Up Song to Play in a Crowded Bar* song: Springsteen's "Let's be Friends"

The best *Let's Blow This Party and Have Sex Out in the Field* song: Van Morrison's "Moondance"

The best *You Made Some Money and Now You're A Dick* song: Sinead O'Conner's "Success Has Made a Failure of Our Love"

The best *This World Is So Screwed Up that I'm Just Going to Sit Here and Play My Guitar* song: George Harrison's "While My Guitar Gently Weeps"

The best *Love Me or I'm Going to Off Myself* song: Harry Nilsson's cover of "Without You"

The best *This World Is So Messed Up I'm Going to Jump Off this Stupid Dock and Drown* song: Otis Redding's "Sittin' on the Dock of the Bay"

The best *Mom Died, Dad Died, and You Left Me Standing at the Altar Looking Like A Dork So I'm Going to Jump Off this Tower and Go Splat* song: Gilbert O'Sullivan's "Alone Again"

The best *I'm Just an SOB Who Loves the Sea More Than I Love You* song: Tom Wait's "Shiver Me Timbers"

The best *I'm Just an SOB Who Loves My Truck More Than I Love You* song: Tom Wait's "Ol' 55"

The best *I'm an Asshole Please Forgive Me* song: Tom Wait's "San Diego Serenade"

The best *Self-Pitying Blubbering Idiot* song: Eric Carmen's "All By Myself"

The best *Where's My Dealer, I'm Freaking Out Here* song: Rodriquez's "Sugarman"

The best *Am I the Only Sane Person in this Nuthouse* song: 4 Non Blondes' "What's Up?"

The best *Life Sucks Sometimes but I Still Love It* song: Edie Brickell's "Good Times, Bad Times"

The best *Maybe a Bus Ride Will Shake This Depression but I Seriously Doubt It* song: Paul Simon's "America"

The best *Fuck You I Don't Need You Please Come Back* song: Sinead O'Connor's "Nothing Compares to You"

The best *You Treat Me Like Shit but I Can't Let You Go* song: The Rolling Stones' "Wild Horses"

The best *I'm Drunk and Alone but I Have a Fear of Commitment and I Don't Have the Balls to Say Hello* song: Tom Waits' "I Hope That I Don't Fall in Love with You"

The best *I'm Pretty Damn Special and Nobody Understands Me but That Doesn't Make Me Any Less Special* song: Van Morrison's "Philosopher's Stone"

Creative writing, like music, is an act of seduction. And if the seduction is successful…well, you know what happens next.

A Writer to Live By

Every writer can point to an older writer who somehow influenced the younger writer's work. The two probably never met except through the older writer's words – words that subtly echo through the younger writer's work and, though he might not always be aware of it, through his life.

In my life as a writer there have been two such influences. I read *The Sun Also Rises* when I was twenty-one, the summer after I discovered that I wanted to be a writer. (There were other influences before I began thinking of myself as a writer, but I will save them for another essay.) Many years later, after the posthumous publications of *The Garden of Eden* and *True At First Light*, the last of Hemingway's novels to be published, I grieved as though he had just then died of a long illness and not at his own hand nearly four decades earlier, back when instead of reading I was listening to the Pittsburgh Pirate's broadcaster Bob Prince on my Radio Shack transistor radio and trying to perfect my Roberto Clemente basket catch.

Lots of other writers have moved me since then, but I sensed long ago that few, if any, would ever fill me with awe and envy as Hemingway had with his spare but elegant prose, so understated yet so keenly observant, so simple yet so layered with the nuances of what was left unsaid. Hemingway provided to all writers who came after him a model of literary style and discipline.

For many years after reading *The Sun Also Rises*, I patterned my work habits after his. I disciplined myself to write every morning whether I felt like it or not. I never wrote myself dry but always stopped when I could still see ahead to the next few lines, the next scene. And when, during a pilgrimage to Key West and Sloppy Joe's Bar, while walking through the Hemingway House on Whitehead Street, I seized the opportunity, when my tour guide looked away for a moment, to slip one of Papa's shot glasses into my pocket. It sat on my desk for many years after that, a daily reminder to keep the glass empty until the work was done. Unfortunately, the little glass was lost in one of the mopping up periods that followed one of many domestic storms. I still miss it; still feel its absence.

But as much as I admired and tried to approximate Hemingway's talent, his personal life troubled me. I longed, of course, for Africa and Pamplona and Paris and Squaw Valley and Michigan's Upper Peninsula, but Hemingway's posturing and bravado always made me wince. Unfortunately, Papa had felt the need to create a public persona that belied the pain and sensitivity of his private life, a caricature of toughness that, to some of his critics, diminished his talent.

Then I happened upon Peter Matthiessen's *At Play in the Fields of the Lord*. With the first pages, I felt that frisson of awe and envy I had thought I would never enjoy again. But because I was poor and unpublished – which is a far greater destitution for a writer than the equally common one of being poor and published – there was only one way I could own that book. And ownership, which promised a continued proximity and study and intimacy, was the only way I might, through some miracle of absorption, acquire a portion of the novel's beauty for myself. So instead of taking the book to the librarian so that she could write my name on the index card, allowing me to possess the book for a mere two weeks, I slipped the book under my waistband and covered it with my shirt.

What I loved about Hemingway's work I found again in Peter Matthiessen's. The exquisite sensory images. The knife-sharp attention to detail. The beguilingly exotic locales. But more. Where Hemingway had given me a style to model, Matthiessen would give me not only the beauty and power of his words but also the model of a writer's life.

His nonfiction *The Snow Leopard*, for example, not only added Tibet to the list of places I absolutely must visit before I die, but it turned me into a dilettante of Buddhism for a few years, got me doing transcendental meditation, made me feel better about being a person with more questions than answers. Book by book Matthiessen instructed me – *The Tree Where Man Was Born. Far Tortuga. In the Spirit of Crazy Horse. Killing Mister Watson. Baikal: Sacred Sea of Siberia. Bone by Bone. Tigers in the Snow.* And all the others. The mystical wonder, the moral outrage, the compassion, the abiding ache of wanting to know more, to be better, to reach for the ineffable. I learned from Hemingway how a writer should work but I learned from Matthiessen how a writer should live.

Once when I was swooping between peaks of the Brooks Range at the Arctic Circle on assignment for the Discovery Channel, white-knuckled in a bush plane held together by duct tape and my mumbled prayers, with nothing to guide me but a vague notion that the caribou were off to the east somewhere and a desire to not die here, not now, my nerves were steeled by the thought of Matthiessen flying over, I think, West Africa with nothing but a *National Geographic* map to guide him. Had he, as I seemed to remember, described his flight in similar terms, a sputtering dance through the high white death? And had he come to an acceptance of whatever fate awaited him by thinking fondly of Hemingway's flights over the African plains, maybe even of one of the skull-banging crashes? I seemed to remember that he had, but maybe that's just what I needed to remember at the time.

What I know for certain is that I am still trying – usually failing but not yet a failure – to model this writer's life after Matthiessen's. Has there been another American writer we can point to who better embodied the kind of writers and readers and citizens we all should be in this time of global crisis: a craftsman of incandescent beauty, whether imagined or experienced; a seeker of truth and reason, of purpose and spiritual fulfillment; a tireless environmental activist; a lyrical but never sentimental champion of the natural world; an adventurer; a risk-taker; a committed and graceful artist who longs for a time when all mankind will live more gracefully upon this earth?

In *Tigers in the Snow* Matthiessen wrote: "That winter afternoon in the Kunalaika, the low sunlight in the south glancing off black silhouetted ridges and shattered into frozen blades by the black trees, the ringing clarity of the great cat tracks on the snowy ice, the blood trace and stark signs of the elk's passage – that was pure joy." Peter Matthiessen's words transcend the page because his life transcended, as much as is humanly possible, the ego. He saw and wrote and thought with enviable clarity. I strive to be more like him in every way, as a writer and as a man.

I will always be grateful to Hemingway for what he taught me about writing. But all of us are indebted to Peter Matthiessen for what he showed us about the world and our place in it.

Tough Love: Make Your Protagonist Suffer

*I would never write about anyone who is not
at the end of his rope.* Stanley Elkin

Elkin, the winner of two National Book Critics Circle Awards for the novels *George Mills* and *Mrs. Ted Bliss*, was a consummate stylist, and, like most literary writers, more concerned with language and character than with plots. The darkly comic conflicts that drove his characters tended to be more internal than external. But in no way did that diminish his resolve (nor should it diminish yours) to create characters who are *at risk*.

Conflict is the heart and soul of story. This is true of every form of narrative, whether short fiction, long fiction, screenplay, stage play, narrative nonfiction, or even narrative poem. Without conflict, there is no story.

In a *Paris Review* interview, Elkin, speaking of Leo Feldman, the protagonist of his novel *A Bad Man*, also said, "I believe in the big things, the traumas that…change all preexisting alternatives for the character…. He is going to a place where Feldman cannot be Feldman anymore."

Conflict is what turns *character* into *story*. And conflict is no less essential to make the reader truly care about your protagonist. The more your character suffers, the more the reader cares. Elkin didn't mean that every protagonist must face physical death, but that something significant to the character's essence at the story's beginning – her view of herself or the world, her spiritual values, her physical or psychological well-being – must be tested. The specter of imminent loss must haunt your protagonist's actions. Only then will the resolution of that test, the protagonist's success or failure, result in a significant change, a different perspective on the world or her place in it. Feldman will no longer be Feldman.

Consider, for example, the tenacious heroine portrayed by Julia Roberts in the movie *Erin Brockovich*. Her initial struggle, as the story opens, is against poverty. A single mother, she tries again and again to find a job, only to have her efforts thwarted by her lack of marketable skills and her less-than-professional demeanor. But she is so earnest and intent on preserving her children's well-being that we can forgive even her attempt to defraud an insurance company. Finally, near the end of Act 1, she successfully bullies and wheedles a lawyer into giving her a job.

We wonder for a while if her lack of social refinement will sabotage her new success, but soon a bigger problem surfaces, and now she finds herself no longer struggling to feed her family but struggling to find justice for an entire town. And because we are so sympathetic to the plight of the people who have been trampled under the hooves of corporate greed, we can't help but to care about their champion. If Brockovich loses, all of working class America loses. So we applaud her efforts while watching with fascination as she gradually transforms. For as Brockovich painstakingly gathers her evidence against Pacific Gas and Electric, then goes head-to-head against the megabeast's lawyers, she is also constructing a new self, a woman whose brash, foul-mouthed surface, now tempered, belies the depth of character and compassion within.

In other words, as Brockovich confronts her obstacles, she confronts her own weaknesses and flaws, her own passions and fears, and, in doing so, she discovers new strengths as well as new truths about herself and the world. She develops as a character. She grows. Between Act 1 and Act 3, she transforms from a *character* into a fully developed and self-driven *person*.

The more duress your character is under, the more the actions he takes while under that pressure will reveal character.
Laura Rennert, author and literary agent

Such characters are not indigenous only to movies or literary fiction. In plot-driven stories, a fully rounded and complex protagonist who undergoes a character arc can lift a story above the level of mere escapist fiction.

In some genre fiction, the protagonist is the same individual at the end of the story as at the beginning. He is still hardboiled and cynical, or she is still loving and tolerant. We read escapist fiction for the thrill of the plot, the roller-coaster ups and downs of suspense. But the writing that stays with us, the characters who imprint themselves on our memory, are the ones who struggle, as we do, with guilt and desire, with greed and generosity, with selfish and altruistic impulses. And who, consequently, are transformed by those struggles. Characters who, in Faulkner's words, embody "the heart in conflict with itself."

In Thomas Lipinski's *Death in the Steel City*, for example, Pittsburgh investigator Carroll Dorsey is hired by a Jewish mobster to track down a once-beautiful African-American girl. That is the external plot. And of course the investigation puts Dorsey's physical safety in greater and greater jeopardy. But midway through the novel, some unpalatable truths about Dorsey's politico father emerge. Consequently, Dorsey's version of personal history, his sense of honor and his sense of self all hang in the balance. That is the internal plot.

The action scenes with druggies and mobsters keep us flipping the pages, but it's Dorsey's internal struggle that makes him such a compelling protagonist (and that sends satisfied readers in search of the other Carroll Dorsey mysteries.)

In summary, if you want the reader to love your protagonist as much as you do, place her at risk, whether physical, psychological, emotional, spiritual, or any combination thereof. Start out with one kind of threat, then add to it. Tighten the noose, keep turning the screws, ratchet up the pain. Make her squirm, make her suffer, make her question all she holds dear. And in the end, show that she is a better person for it.

The Idea: Getting and Using

The first essential for any piece of creative writing is the idea. But ideas can be temperamental; they seldom yield to insistence or force. You cannot coax one out of hiding by staring at a white screen or a blank sheet of paper. Ideas are rebellious. Ideas are obdurate. Ideas live by the motto, "You ain't no boss of me."

At the same time, ideas want to be wanted. They know how special they are, and they long to be appreciated as such. They are a lot like fireflies on a warm summer night. "Here I am. Missed me, ha ha! I'm over here now. Missed me again, ha ha ha!"

The question for writers, then, or for anyone in need of a good idea, is how to bring one of these impish little blinkers close enough that we can seize and bottle it and make it our own. I have found this first of five steps to be a two-part process: first, we desire it, and then we ignore it.

Desiring an idea is like raising the window and looking out, hoping to see something relevant and exciting. It is a state of openness, of watching and listening, of capturing stray scents and exploring their sources. It is a matter of being present and open to all that surrounds you, and of allowing even the banal to whisper its suggestions to you.

For example, once upon a time, I decided it was time to write another novel. I had already written some fifteen books; the most recent had been published the previous summer. Problem was, I had no new ideas, no characters, no story. But instead of fretting about that, I knew enough to know that sooner or later the idea would come. It you desire one, it will come.

Then one frosty morning, on my way to teach four more classes at the university, I glanced across the Lake Wilhelm reservoir into the fog-enshrouded woods beyond and thought, *That would be a great place to hide a body.* I.e., I had opened the window and looked out and saw something interesting. Something vague and undeveloped, yes, but something interesting. That setting. The dark, tannic water. The naked, jagged spears of dead trees sticking up out of the water.

Then I drove on, continuing to the university, where I taught my classes, put in my office hour, drove home and read a few of my students' papers while the frozen pizza was baking, and completely forgot about that body I wanted to hide.

A few days later I repeated that same trip, though it was a bright autumn morning that time, with a tangerine sun just beginning to show above the distant horizon of the reservoir. And suddenly, out of nowhere, the image of a Pennsylvania State Police sergeant flashed before my eyes.

It is possible that this flash of – what shall I call it? A flash of insight? Of association? Of illumination? It is possible that this unbeckoned image, so pertinent to my thought on the previous commute, is an entirely different step in the process. All I know is that it always takes place for me after a period of time spent being open and attentive and desirous of a new idea. I see a young sassafras tree turning into a boy, pulling his pink feet out of the soil. I see a raven-haired beauty sitting atop a boulder while watching a dolphin leap high above the water. I see a baby being thrown out of a high window and into the river.

Sometimes the image will figure in at the beginning of a story, sometimes in the middle or at the end. It strikes me as a kind of introduction, a way for an important character to announce his or her presence and say, "I heard you're looking for a story. I'll be your huckleberry."

In the case of my first Ryan DeMarco novel, the trooper I saw in my mind's eye looked suspiciously like a young Tommy Lee Jones as he stood alone on the bridge that crosses the reservoir. And in that moment a character was born. Sgt. Ryan DeMarco of the Pennsylvania State Police.

Unfortunately, a character is not a fully developed idea. A character is a firefly of an idea.

And that brings me to step two of turning the beginning of an idea into a story: Let it be.

Don't rush your fragile little firefly. Don't shake the jar, don't scream at it to blink, don't even bother to look at it for a while. In fact, this is a good place to switch metaphors to one more appropriate. The caterpillar. Leave the darn thing alone while it builds the chrysalis and disappears inside it. And keep your greedy hands off that chrysalis. Something very special, even magical, is happening inside that shell. The caterpillar is busy turning itself into a soupy mess of cells, all but a few of which it devours. That's not something you want to see; you're not a biologist or a scientist, you are a fiction writer, and a fiction writer is a creature that, like a caterpillar, creates something beautiful out of next to nothing.

Those few remaining cells of the caterpillar are called imaginal cells, by the way. Imaginal – isn't that wonderful? It's as if the caterpillar soup is imagining itself into a butterfly.

For the writer, this period of deliberate non-attention is essential. The act of self-cannibalism is something you can't see even if you want to. It is taking place in some dark sub-cellar of your mind. You don't want to go there. The place is filled with all kinds of slimy and slithering things you don't want to know about. So just go on about your business and let the alchemy do what alchemy does.

Sooner or later, step three is going to kick into gear. This is when those few imaginal cells start multiplying. This was when Sgt. Ryan DeMarco became a man ridden with guilt over the death of his infant son. A man who turned to the bottle every night as a way of smothering that guilt for a few hours. A man whose wife left him. A friendless man. A man who hated himself so much that he wanted no friends.

And so forth. I took notes. I took a lot of notes, every time some new detail came to me. Eventually I learned who the suspected murderer was. A writer. A newly successful writer. A writer with the perfect life, the perfect family. But one now suspected of wiping out his entire perfect family.

Oh, it was gruesome. It was the absolute worst crime I could imagine.

A lot of these details came to me during my hour-long commute three times a week. Others came while I was riding my motorcycle, or showering, or shaving, or raking the leaves. There was nothing linear or chronological about their arrival. Each was a single imaginal cell floating freely in the caterpillar broth.

All of them materialized out of the blue, not out of any rumination on my part. The blue is just another name for the subconscious mind, that same sub-cellar from which the original notion arose. But in this stage the brew is percolating, one new detail after another bubbling up, sometimes so many at once that I have a hard time scribbling all of them down on paper, so I leave myself dozens of phone memos to transcribe later.

This third step in the process is the most exciting time for me. I am so eager to start writing, to start piecing all the random pieces together in a unified story, but, like a sprinter at the starting line, I have to hold myself back and wait for the gun. The time isn't right just yet to jump into the book. I will know when the time is right. Somehow I will know. I will feel it in my bones.

Until then I wait. I bide my time. The ideas accumulate, the random scenes, the snatches of dialogue, the obstacles, the characters. I rake them in like fallen leaves, and the pile grows.

And then, at last, step four. I am ready to write. I am ready to commit myself to several months of sustained work. The marathon begins.

If I haven't done so already, I will first spend some time rolling an opening sentence or two around in my mouth, smoothing off the jagged edges. I'm aiming for music here, in the case of the DeMarco novel something foreboding, something that will give the reader shivers. In truth, what I'm doing is easing myself into the voice of the story, feeling my way in. I have to find that voice before I can dive in headfirst. I have to keep trying, one sentence after another, before I can put my opening to paper.

And all this time, though I feel as if I know my two primary characters fairly well and I know the crime and how it was committed, I know almost nothing else about the plot. I don't want to know anything else. At this point, I don't want to know too much. I could take notes for two or three days and do a scene breakdown of the entire novel if I wanted to, but I won't let myself do that. I need to discover the story as it writes itself. I want to experience the story as the characters experience it. Were I to do a full breakdown first, I would already know every beat in the story before I start to write it, and then the actual writing of it would have no surprises for me, no excitement, no sense of discovery. And I would lose interest in writing that story.

I don't want to write a story that I have already written, whether in outline or narrative breakdown form. My urge to write it as a novel will sputter out. In order to sit at my desk morning after morning for three or four months while I write the story, I *need* that sense of discovery. Without it, the writing feels stale and safe, and I don't want to live or work in such a place.

The late, great David Bowie was also an advocate of the creativity that comes from inhabiting the unknown. He said, "If you feel safe in the area that you're working in, you're not working in the right area...and when you *don't* feel that your feet are quite touching the bottom, you're just about in the right place to do something exciting."

I agree.

Will this process work for you? Who knows? Some writers prefer to pave a path for themselves to follow. I avoid trails already laid, whether made by myself or somebody else. I live to discover what I don't already know. For me, the known is boring, the unknown is exciting. That, and that alone, is what makes every work session exhilarating. I know a little bit about what is going to happen that day, but not too much.

I want to walk alongside the protagonist every inch of his or her journey, not to stand at the endpoint of the journey waiting for the protagonist to arrive. How anticlimactic would that be?

My only focus for a while are those opening sentences. Then the opening chapter. I revise both until I can almost recite them from memory. That opening chapter has to make me shiver. It has to fill me with dread. If that doesn't happen to me, it won't happen to the reader. That first chapter has to make me wince and squirm.

And the journey continues. My sub-cellar is brimming with more information – so much information that it has climbed the basement stairs and is oozing out over the kitchen floor. I wade through it every day. I'm writing chapter three but a scene from the last third of the book is pooling under the table. I'm writing chapter five but another of three possible endings laps against my ankles. It's wondrous, it's enlivening, it's exhausting, it's magical.

And all but the physical writing of it is happening down in that mysterious sub-cellar of my consciousness. That is where it forms, not in the left-hemisphere of my brain, not in the neo-cortex. A scene bubbles up out of that sub-cellar, I see it and hear it and write it down. Each scene begets the next. I don't even have to choose which ending to use; the story itself will make that decision when the proper time comes. The story decides, and I write it down.

Creativity obeys no rules of logic. Creativity flips rational thought the bird. Creativity is a firefly, a caterpillar, an idea, a novel. There is no way to explain it, no way to measure it, no way to capture it in a hundred metaphors or more. It can't be forced. But there are ways to adapt to it and recognize it and use it. I have been doing that now for fifty years. If you survive the first five years without going crazy, and you learn to embrace the fickle, fiendish, whimsical nature of creativity, you too can do it every single day.

Tell Me a Story

Thanks to my overpriced cable provider's attempt (successful, alas) to retain me as a customer, I spent the past week indulging in a gluttony of movies from my two new (and free for twelve months!) premium movie channels. I watched everything from hundred-million dollar space spectacles with stilted acting and dialogue as crisp as petrified wood to micro-budget indie films that broke my heart with their wit, warmth, and authentic recreations of this dramedy we call life. I compared my enjoyment quotient to the box office successes (relative to the films' budgets) of each of these movies, and here, in a nutshell, is what I learned:

Story is everything.

The success of a film begins and ends with the story. Not with the size of the budget. Not the dazzling CGI. Not the marquee value of the actors. Not the gimmicky cinematography. (Does anybody actually enjoy having their eyeballs rattled while watching movies that look as if they've been filmed by somebody in the throes of St. Vitus Dance? Isn't it time we put that annoying trick called cinéma vérité out of its misery?)

There is only one thing that will keep this viewer in his seat for ninety minutes, and that's the story. Writers, of course, have always known this. But every time I find myself dozing off to another zillion dollar bow-wow, I have to wonder (when I wake up again) why the rest of Hollywood doesn't seem to get it. (Raymond Chandler, by the way, provided a very entertaining answer to this mystery nearly seventy years ago. If you haven't yet read his famous *Atlantic* essay "Writers in Hollywood," you must read it at the earliest opportunity or consider yourself not properly educated.)

My point (since this is supposed to be a screenwriting advice column and not a rant about dubious filmmaking choices) is this: Tell an engaging story with a beginning, middle, and end. Create a couple of engaging characters, disrupt the equilibrium of at least one of their lives, and have them struggle to the best of their abilities to recover that equilibrium. And have them grow through the course of that struggle.

Forget about trying to be outrageously clever. Forget about trying to find a place in the story for the biggest explosions ever seen on screen. Be a storyteller. Probe the vicissitudes of the human heart. Think *Juno. Napoleon Dynamite. Seeking a Friend for the End of the World. Silver Linings Playbook. The Blind Side. Elegy. Titanic. The English Patient. Punch-Drunk Love. Sideways.* Even the space spectacular *Gravity* is, first and foremost, a story about the convolutions of the human heart and the struggle of the human spirit.

Expensive and exotic settings, special effects, and quirky storytelling devices should all grow out of and be essential to the story. If you try to graft a story onto a series of gimmicks, the movie might get made (far too many do), but it will quickly fade into obscurity like a winter's breath.

When Less Is More

Historically, the novella has seldom been highly regarded in this country, despite the esteem earned by such novellas as Hemingway's "The Old Man and the Sea," Camus' "The Stranger," Conrad's "Heart of Darkness," Steinbeck's "Of Mice and Men," and a handful of others. In general, "fewer pages" has translated to "of lesser importance" to American publishers, both in terms of potential revenues and literary significance. This sentiment persists among mainstream publishers but is being steadily eroded by the boom in indie, aka electronic, publishing, where readers are delighted to snap up a novella for one-third the cost of a paperback.

And that, I suggest, is a good thing not only for readers and writers but also for the film industry.

A film cannot authentically recreate a novel in its entirety, not unless the film is ten hours long and filled with interior monologues. But a film can recreate a portion of a novel in exquisite detail, and in fact with an all-ensconcing level of detail that surpasses even the visual and auditory capabilities of a reader's vivid imagination.

A novella, containing anywhere between one-sixth to one-half as many pages as a novel, has a more condensed storyline – often the perfect length for an authentic yet exquisitely detailed recreation on film. Novellas, like films but unlike full-length books, are all about compression and distillation.

The only thing I don't love about novellas is that not enough of them are published to satisfy my reading habit. I love writing them even more than I love reading them. In fact my imagination seems to be more suited to the conception of novellas than to the conception of novels.

Until a year or so ago, I resisted the urge to write the novellas I wanted to write. No more. A new synergy is looming between Hollywood, indie publishing, and the novella, and I intend to slip my board into that wave. During the last year and a half, the only fiction I wrote was in the form of novellas. Five of them so far, each of the North American magic realism sub-genre called slipstream, each written with an eye toward adaptation into a visual medium.

Word counts in full-length screenplays and novellas are roughly equivalent. Screenplays contain 40-60 scenes; most of my novellas, especially the longer ones, fall on the low end of that range. Scenes are composed with regard to their cinematic potential and storylines are kept tight enough that they can be enjoyed from beginning to end in two to three hours of reading, or in a hundred minutes or so of viewing.

More important from a writing perspective, a novella, written with the same attention to dynamic scene creation as one must give a screenplay, is so much easier than a novel to turn into a screenplay. Adapting a novel requires a lot of winnowing and whittling and disembowelment, each of which too often destroys the very soul of the story.

Writing novellas provides me with the best of both worlds: I can indulge my love of language and deep characterization, and I can also lay the foundation for indulging my passion for movies. A tight, well-written novella is a more immersive reading experience than a treatment, and, when published, can be an effective marketing tool.

As a source for movie stories, the novel isn't dead but its legs are often wobbly. In the meantime, the novel's little sister is ready-made for adaptation. Long live the novella!

Writing the Devil

Many of us were first drawn to writing because it provided a patient ear, a way of listening to what we did not know we needed to say. As a teacher of writing, I was treated to hundreds of those necessary stories from my students. Here are a few of them:

Emily: tall and elegant and bright, pretty and freckled, green-eyed and sad, raised by neglectful welfare parents, recently diagnosed with lupus, working two part-time jobs, no health insurance, no money for tuition, but with a desperate need to stay in college.

Marie: abusive first husband, zero self-esteem, fifty-five and with no marketable skills, only son dead by suicide, and her struggling to find a reason to keep from joining her son.

Alex: a young soldier home from the war in Iraq, breaking down in class while reading aloud about being caught up in the desire to shoot, to kill, and then despising that newly discovered part of himself, afraid that he is about to unleash a rage he cannot control.

These and the hundreds of other such stories are what I cherish most from my years of teaching, the essays and stories shared with me, the words as startling as X-rays of shattered bones, the wounds that still bled, the hearts full of bullets.

Most of these young writers had no interest in parading their pain in public as a way of making a career. All they really wanted was to be heard, to be granted permission to speak, to try to put themselves back together again by turning the broken pieces into words, words into sentences, a few pages of brutal and healing honesty. All they really wanted was to open the valve on the pain in their souls and release the poisonous gas. All they really wanted was to command that demon to *Come out, come out*, and then to trap it on paper, bound there by ink, disarmed, *expressed*.

To express: to show, manifest, or reveal. From the Latin *exprimere*: to squeeze out.

For writers like these, and for many of us who have chosen writing not as a profession but as a way of life, a way to keep living, writing is never about theory. Theory and theme and symbolism are what teachers choose to talk about so they don't have to talk about the pain, because they cannot convincingly discuss others' pain without facing their own, and this they are unwilling to do, it's too messy, too ugly, why probe what already hurts?

But probing is cathartic. It is good for the writer, and it is good for the audience that shares that catharsis.

It was through teaching writing that I learned a sad truth: Everyone is broken.

That recognition led to a revelation about writing: The best stories, the most compelling ones, are about broken people putting themselves together again. That attempt to repair what is broken is at the heart of every story worth telling.

What's Your Colostomy Bag?

Recently I was having a conversation with my good friend and fellow writer John to discuss a possible collaboration. At one point the conversation came around to dissecting the requirements of a memorable character. John asked how I had come up with Ernest DeWalt, the protagonist of my first literary mystery, and a character who might have been the first colostomy bag-wearing detective in American fiction.

My answer was simple: I wanted to create a character who evinced none of the detective clichés; in other words, a detective who was not hard-drinking, hard-fighting, and womanizing.

A lot of research was required before I found a condition that made all the above impossible for my hero. If I saddled him with a shot-up kidney, which now required continuous ambulatory peritoneal dialysis (i.e. wearing a bag), drinking alcohol would be an absolute no-no. The bag, along with a fairly sedentary lifestyle, would prevent him from engaging in recreational martial arts or any other physically demanding activity. The bag provided the added bonus (for the writer, though not for the character) of being a debilitating psychological impediment to getting naked with a sexy woman. Psychological impotency is not an uncommon side-effect of his condition.

And presto! I had a former hardcore cop whose self-image and every action as a private detective would now be influenced by the very thing that kept him alive.

Besides being a finalist for the Hammett Prize for Literary Excellence in Crime Writing, that novel won a Nevermore

Award "for inadvertent achievement" in a category "neither dreamt nor dared by Mystery Writers of America."

The novel also prompted a book contract from another publisher. The film version, unfortunately, suffered from the common Hollywood malady of too many cooks tastelessly tweaking the recipe. Still, the checks for film rights and screenwriting were very nice indeed.

So what's the lesson in this – other than Faulkner's advice to novelists to take the Hollywood money and run? Simply this: Saddle your main character with a physical or psychological burden that will transform him or her from a stereotype into an original.

The Greeks called this burden the character's fatal flaw. For the Greeks, that flaw was typically *hubris*, an overweening pride that would eventually bring the mighty down.

Frequently in movies, but not always, a physical flaw is employed as a visual metaphor for the character flaw. You can see this principle at work in film characters such as Orson Welles' Charles Foster Kane, Jack Nicholson's Col. Jessup, Michael Douglas's Gordon Gecko, Al Pacino's Scarface, Leonardo DiCaprio's Jordan Belfort, and a multitude of others.

For *An Occasional Hell*, I chose to go in the opposite direction by giving poor Ernie a very humble and uncertain sense of self, precipitated by a physical condition that made him physically weaker and sexually impotent. That character trait, plus the physical cross he bore, made him endearing to a lot of readers.

My friend John's succinct advice, then, is this: When creating a protagonist, always remember to ask yourself this question: "What is his or her colostomy bag?"

Why I Read

It is not for the reasons I recite to my students:

Reading will increase your vocabulary, I tell them, without you even realizing it.

Reading will make you more informed and more aware of the world around you.

Reading builds neurons and synapses and actually increases your brain power.

Reading will enhance your knowledge and your understanding of the world, and will give you something to talk about at parties. This, in turn, will make you sound more intelligent and less egocentric and will help you get laid.

Reading will make you a better writer. And being a good writer, I tell them, will help you get better grades in all of your subjects.

Later, reading will make you stand out from the hundreds of others applying for the same job you want, and will increase your likelihood of getting that job.

Reading, I tell them, by virtue of making you more intelligent and more aware and informed, and a better writer and communicator, will help you, after you get that job you want, to be promoted faster and to climb the ladder of success more quickly than your non-reading colleagues.

Being a reader, I tell them, will help you earn more money.

The person who can read but doesn't, I tell them, quoting Mark Twain – because Twain might be the only writer some of them have heard of – has no advantage over the person who can't read.

In other words, I tell them, if you can read but don't, you might as well be illiterate.

That's something they can chew on for a while.

I don't bother to tell them the old cliché that reading will sensitize them to the human condition, because they haven't lived long enough to know what is meant by the human condition. Plus, they all believe that they are plenty sensitive already, and that in their whopping nineteen or twenty years, they have already amassed an entire universe of empathy. Each of them believes he or she may be the most sensitive person alive.

A few of them don't want to be made to care about the plights of others. Either they have been raised to believe that they, by being born, became the center of the universe, or else they have been so battered by life that they are desensitized to all pain but their own. These are the hardest ones to reach. But I do not tell them that sooner or later their bubble of self-absorption will be popped and the gravity of the real world will swoop in to crush them if they do not first develop a greater understanding of that real world; I tell them they will not pass the course if their reading and writing skills do not improve.

There are other things I don't tell them too, because if I did, they would sit there at their desks and stare at me in bewilderment, or they would look at each other and roll their eyes, or they would just gaze into the middle distance and tune me out.

I don't tell them, for example, that reading a good novel, like watching a good movie, takes me to places I have never been and might never go. And although watching a movie – say, *The English Patient* – does allow me to experience the harsh beauty of the North African desert or the hushed tragedy of the Villa San Girolamo hospital room, it does so in only two dimensions, and so keeps me outside of those places, a spectator looking at a flat picture that moves.

Reading Michael Ondaatje's novel, on the other hand, puts me deep inside that world as my imagination allows me to feel the desert's desiccating heat, the sand fleas and gritty sand in my socks. Reading drops me down into the hospital room where Almásy lies bandaged, grotesquely burned. Reading fills my nose and mouth with the putrefying scent of decaying flesh. It puts me so close to beautiful Hana's tears that I can very nearly reach out and wipe them from her cheek.

Reading, I do not tell my students, will startle their senses alive again by throwing open the world when their small, cluttered rooms have grown tight and stale.

Reading will lay a hand on their shoulders when they are homesick, or when their hearts have been broken, or when that C-minus seems like the greatest tragedy in the world.

Reading, I do not tell them, because they would not believe me, can keep you from cutting yourself, can keep you from suffocating in the quicksand of your self-absorbed despair.

Reading, I do not tell them, can turn on the lights in your darkness, can help you see yourself more clearly, can help you find yourself when you are lost.

Reading, I do not tell them, because this is something that cannot be taught but must be learned, can make you feel like not one lone cell stranded in the desolation of the world, but as one of eight billion cells conjoined by the world, all hearts echoing the others in the song of one enormous heart.

I do not tell my students that being a human is a lonely, lonely business and that only a couple of things can assuage that loneliness. Loving someone is the best remedy, I do not tell them. Making music is good medicine too. And so is reading, another form of love – an act of faith and trust and surrender, an act of reaching out and of coming together.

My job is not to ease their loneliness. My job is to give them the skills to help them land a job. So I tell them what I know will keep them from staring at me in bewilderment, will keep them from rolling their eyes or gazing at the wall.

Being a reader can help you get laid, I tell them.

Being a reader can help you make more money.

Some of them will listen. A few will take heed.

And every once in a while, one of them will come striding toward me with a light in her eyes that has never shone before, and with a look on her face of inexpressible surprise, to tell me, "Professor! I read the most fantastic book last night!" And I will know that she, this one out of many, is on her way now to learning all of the rest.

The Writer's Obligation

I still remember the first hardcover book I was ever given. I was six or seven years old, maybe younger, and my babysitter, the old maid who lived next door, gave me an illustrated edition of *Swiss Family Robinson*. Within minutes that book transported me to a place I had never imagined, and I have been in love with the power and the magic of words ever since. To me that is what good writing does, no matter what genre a marketing department might assign it to. Good writing is like Marley's ghost; it takes us to what is, what was, or what might yet be.

This is what makes writing meaningful; it gives us a memorable experience.

I do not believe, as some writers and critics do, that in order to be meaningful a piece of fiction must address timely social concerns or be intellectually challenging or provide us with startling insights into the latest zeitgeist. When was the last time you read something and thought, *Gee, I didn't know that about the human condition?* This might happen to us when we're children, in that first dizzying flush of discovery that there's a complicated world going on wholly independent of our own needs and feelings, but for any reader with a few books under her belt and access to social media, there is little left in this world that can surprise us.

Yet the notion persists that serious fiction must be edifying, must make us think, reconsider, adopt the trendiest theory or ideology. My Tom Swift novels might have accomplished all that for me when I was in grade school, but now?

Most adult readers will resent any kind of mini-lecture from their fiction. Fiction should make us *feel*. Isn't that what we really want when we pick up a novel or short story?

Teachers like to say that good fiction should sensitize us to the human condition, and it can certainly do that for children. But the rest of us really don't need to be sensitized to the human condition; we are already acutely sensitive to it. We are readers, after all, a fairly elite group nowadays. And because of our sensitivity, good fiction will move us. That emotional response might or might not give rise to contemplation, but ultimately our reaction to fiction is seldom based on how much it makes our brain hurt but on how it makes our heart feel. And considering the state of the world today, which is more or less the same turmoil-filled state it has always been in, I do believe that compassion is more relevant than cogitation.

In nearly every workshop I have taught, at least one student has attempted to defend writing that is pedantic, sententious, or murky with contrived symbolism. "I want the reader to have to put some effort into understanding my work."

My usual response is, "Why should I, as a reader, bother? Why should any reader bother?" Because it is not the reader's job to work hard, it is the writer's job to work hard to provide the reader with a satisfying reading experience.

Working hard to unravel a writer's meaning is a task best reserved for the classroom. The rest of us read for the pleasure of it, for a sense of connection with other lives. Spending $25 for a book is onerous enough. After that, all we want and expect is to be engaged and moved. Experienced writers know that this is the best we have to offer. If a piece of fiction we've written ends up being discussed in literature class, that's terrific. But any writer who makes that his destination, his motivation for writing, is doomed to fall on his face right out of the gate. Many do, and rightfully so.

Writing that demands too much of the reader without providing any kind of emotional pay-off is often labeled as experimental or avant-garde by people who don't want to admit that they don't understand it. This kind of writing, if it ever gets published, will end up in a literary journal with a circulation of a hundred or so readers, only five of whom, all friends of the writer, will put any effort into trying to decipher what the hell the writer is saying.

Such writing shows little regard for the reader, and I have no patience with it. Here's what Raymond Carver, a consciously artful writer, had to say on that subject: "Too often 'experimentation' is a license to be careless, silly, or imitative in the writing. Even worse, a license to try to brutalize or alienate the reader."

That brings me to another type of egotistical writer: the one who believes it is his job to shock or offend the reader with graphic images or phrases. Unless you have had the raw experiences of a Stephen Crane, unless you have felt your soul being drawn out of your body like a silk handkerchief as Hemingway did – in other words, unless *you* have been shocked and brutalized into enlightenment by life itself, and instead of retreating into a wallow of self-pity have transformed your experiences into an embrace of life in all its staggering beauty and pain – then any shock you offer is gratuitous and is best avoided by both reader and writer.

I read an interview with a young writer a while back in which the writer said that the reading experience implies a contract between the reader and writer, that the reader must agree to come to the piece with trust and a willingness to give herself over to the story.

I think this is nonsense, the product of a young writer's ego. The reader has no obligation to agree to anything. The writer bears the sole burden of responsibility. If I as a writer fail to draw you in, if I don't seduce you into giving yourself over to the story, you have every right to toss that story aside after twenty pages, five pages, or even, as I frequently do, after the first page.

The notion that the reader is in any way responsible for a story's effectiveness simply cannot be justified except on a purely egotistical level. Because the truth is, we read fiction primarily for enjoyment – whether it is the delight we take in a writer's use of language, the vicarious pleasure of watching a new world unfold, or the titillation of being perched on the edge of our seats and leaning forward with all senses cocked. So why should we as readers be forced to struggle to comprehend a story when we can be quite confident that the writer, unless she has spent the last thirty years in a cave in Tibet learning how to levitate, is probably not going to reward our labors with some startling insight?

The best that any of us can hope to do with our writing is to present to the reader a piece of the world, and to do so with honesty and clarity and gratitude. The best we can hope to do is to extend an invitation to the reader to see and feel the worlds we create inside our heads. The irony of writing is that, although conducted in solitude, it is an act of communion between the writer and her readers. Not a contract that implies a conscious mutual agreement, but an inexplicable connection between hearts that will probably never meet.

If our writing has to be deconstructed to be understood, whether because of its difficult syntax, its murky symbolism or its preachy arrogance, the story has failed. In fiction, understanding should emanate not from the brain but from the heart. And in that case, any interpretation of the story that satisfies the reader is the right interpretation.

Faulkner was once asked by a critic if readers ascribed too much symbolism to his work, and he answered, "Not nearly enough." To me, this answer shows Faulkner's realization that writing is not really about the writer, it's about the reader. The story might come from the writer, but all meaning originates within the reader.

As writers, our obligation to readers is intimately bound up with the reason we write in the first place. Why do writers write? Why do we willingly, even enthusiastically, subject ourselves to such an uncertain, solitary, tenuous, rejection-filled existence?

What was it Lord Byron said? *Who would write if he could do otherwise?*

The world is not the way we want it to be. That's the dilemma we wake up to every morning. And once we become reconciled to the impossibility of making the world a little more like the way we think it should be, we lose the need to recreate the world through fiction. We lose the need to write stories that impart some kind of emotional resonance, and as readers we lose the need to lose ourselves, and maybe find ourselves again, inside that resonance.

Stories feed and sustain us. They help us to go on.

The writer's only concern should be in finding the best words, images, and rhythms to portray, as Faulkner put it, "the heart in conflict with itself."

Has anyone ever said it more succinctly? *That* is what good writing is all about. Forget symbolism, forget literary theory, put aside your desire to be anthologized. Tell the most authentic story you can, with as much attention and sensitivity to life as you can muster. Put your *heart* into it. That, in the end, is all the reader wants from you. Withhold that, and the reader will abandon you.

Writing Out Loud

The greatest pleasure of writing is not what it's about, but the music the words make. Truman Capote

Most people would probably tell you that reading is a visual experience. But they are wrong. Reading is an aural experience. While it is true that good creative writing must always be a full sensory experience – images, sounds, tastes, smells, and textures must all come alive – that isn't what I'm talking about here. When we read, we first see the words on the page or screen, but we then hear the words inside our own head. We hear the cadence, the inflection, the pauses and full stops. We hear the lilt of prancing language and we hear the ponderous trudge of heavy-footed syntax.

Writing falls upon the reader's ears like a kind of soundtrack, the pitch and timbre of which will, like all music, have a visceral effect. Just as the background music in a film can deepen the mood of a scene, so will the subliminal soundtrack of your prose enhance your narrative.

> *In conversation you can use timing, a look, an inflection. But on the page all you have is commas, dashes, the amount of syllables in a word. When I write, I read everything out loud to get the right rhythm.* Fran Lebowitz

The words that form our soundtracks should be composed for the ear. But how can you know if your composition sings or stinks?

Read it aloud. Better yet, have somebody else read it aloud to you, or else read it into a voice recorder and listen to the playback. This accomplishes two things: You will experience the words as your readers will – aurally. And you will identify, by the stumbles and hitches in the reading, where the phrasings are awkward or unclear, and where the dialogue rings false.

Early in my novel-writing career, I also wrote plays. And every time I attended a read-through, I heard lines that made me wince. I learned to welcome those winces. By them I knew which lines needed to be rewritten. The same applies to all poetry and prose. One reading out loud can help you identify problems that might remain hidden through a dozen silent read-throughs.

Listen to your work. *Hear* it.

Become aware of the effect that certain stylistic choices will have on the reader. For example, a series of short declarative sentences will increase the pace and dramatic tension. James Lee Burke has written some of the most melodious and evocative description in print, but this excerpt from *A Stained White Radiance* shows that he clearly understands the value of short, unadorned sentences too:

> *I returned to the bar and asked the barmaid for a pencil and a piece of paper. She tore a page from a notepad by the telephone and handed it to me. I scribbled two or three sentences on the back and folded it once, then twice.*

Did you notice the pattern at work in the construction of those sentences? Subject, verb; subject, verb; subject, verb. You probably didn't notice it on a conscious level, but you *heard* it, and the sound of that repetition, like the barely audible thump of a pumped-up bass line pulsing from a teenager's car, had its effect on you.

Longer, more fluid sentences will slow the reader down. Hemingway is known for his short, journalistic sentences but his cumulative phrasings are no less masterful. Listen to the way this brief passage from *Death in the Afternoon* captures both the breathless tension and the physical fluidity of the action described:

> *The bull was watching the man and the triangle of red cloth, his ears pointed, his eyes fixed, and Hernandorena kneed himself a yard closer and shook the cloth. The bull's tail rose, his head lowered and he charged and, as he reached the man, Hernandorena rose solidly from his knees into the air, swung over like a bundle, his legs in all directions now, and then dropped to the ground.*

Words create images, yes. They bring characters and settings and actions to life. They give voice to speech and thoughts and feelings. And all the while, the soundtrack plays in the background. So compose your soundtrack as deliberately as you craft your narrative.

Everything that moves us has its music. Sometimes the music in our lives occurs spontaneously, like the rumble of distant thunder you hear while lying in your lover's arms. But the music of words most often requires effort, or at the least a close attention to syllables and emphasis, to pauses and consonants and images and endnotes. Harnessing such energy is an achievement every writer should seek, to find the harmony inside every word and to arrange those harmonies into a symphony.

Act Like a Professional Writer Now

(if you hope to ever be one)

Over the past many years, I have served as a writing coach and mentor to hundreds of aspiring writers, in and out of academic writing programs. And I have observed a slow erosion of the degree of professionalism these students bring to their craft (an erosion now endemic to nearly every profession). I won't even attempt to account for that erosion. Besides, the reason for it is irrelevant. The relevant fact is this: No busy editor or agent is likely to be swayed by any of the excuses I have heard for behavior unbefitting *any* profession, let alone one in which the chances of success are so slim to begin with. Nor am *I* likely to be swayed, or are the other writers who do what they can to help aspiring writers advance their careers.

And so, in hopes of doing my bit to promote the cause of professionalism in the business and art of writing, I have prepared this White Paper. I still feel a great deal of empathy for apprentice writers; the desperation for knowledge I felt throughout my twenties is still fresh in me. The realities of traditional publishing were brutal back then and are even more brutal now. That is why I refuse to sugarcoat the truth for my students. If I can save them a year or more of form rejections by inciting a bit of painful self-analysis now, I will have done my job.

Professionalism as a writer: What does that mean?

Embodying a professional attitude as a writer is not dissimilar from doing so as a teacher, a lawyer, a doctor, or in any other profession. The difference is in the personalities people bring to those professions. Writers, studies have shown, tend to test higher on the eccentricity scale than other professions, especially the left-brain ones. We tend toward brooding, rumination, depression, self-absorption. Some of us lean precipitously toward the anarchic. These are traits that might be fertile ground for ideas that eventually become stories and novels and screenplays, but they are traits that offer little sustenance to one's career as a writer. Talent is not rare. But the self-discipline necessary to convert raw talent into shining gold is rare. Yet it is essential for success as a writer.

This self-discipline applies not only to one's writing habits but also to the ways we present ourselves and our work to individuals who can be instrumental in our careers. It's important for apprentice writers to remember that there are no entry-level positions in the writing business; in order to break into this tough, tight industry, a writer must be functioning, creatively and personally, on a level as high as that of the published writers whose ranks she hopes to join.

The following strategies for an aspiring writer will go a long way toward branding you as a professional, and will create a first impression that no editor, agent, or mentor will be quick to dismiss.

Educate yourself.

If you come to a workshop or enter into a conversation with a publishing professional before you understand such terms as character arc, point of view, syntax, subtext, and so forth, if you don't know the difference between summarization and dramatization, if you don't understand the purpose of dialogue in fiction and what a scene must accomplish in order to be a scene, if you don't know standard manuscript format, if you don't know basic story structure and what distinguishes a story from an anecdote, if you don't know all this and more, you need to educate yourself. MFA workshops are not designed for beginners. Neither are the publishers through whose gates you hope to pass.

There is absolutely no excuse for a writer remaining ignorant of writing terms and the requirements of contemporary fiction. A few hours online will tell you all you need to know. In fact, a disciplined and determined writer can uncover an MFA degree's worth of information and instruction online for free. There are even free workshops to join so that you can get the benefit of other readers. This is all good preparation for the more intensive scrutiny you will receive from a mentor, agent, or editor.

Provide clean manuscripts!

Never show your work to anybody until you are convinced that it is the most polished and complete you can make it. You get one shot with an agent or editor. And if your manuscript contains more than one or two misspellings, typos, faulty sentence constructions, misplaced modifiers, inappropriate tense or point of view shifts or other errors, you have blown that one shot. A writer with a professional attitude would never, ever let a manuscript out of her hands unless it has been written, revised, and proofread *meticulously*.

Basic grammar skills should have been mastered well before you left the auditorium on your last day of high school. If they weren't, you must either resolve to become your own very demanding copy-editor, or to pay somebody else to fill that role. But don't make the mistake of thinking that just anybody can copy-edit. It takes a very close and critical eye to copy-edit something that will pass professional muster. And good copy-editing is not inexpensive. So you are much further ahead learning to do it yourself. Learn it before you apply for that MFA, before you attend your first workshop, and before you send out your first query letter. Otherwise, you are wasting your time and the time of every agent and editor you query.

Understand that a "rough" or "first" draft in a workshop setting is a misnomer. It refers only to the first time the workshop participants have read it, and not the original rough draft you dashed off at the bus stop while waiting for your ride home. If you come to a workshop thinking you can use the mentor and other participants to do your copy-editing, or if you make a submission thinking the agent or editor will tell you what's wrong with your work, you are not only being unprofessional, you're being lazy.

Gird your loins and check your ego at the door.

As screenwriting guru John Truby observed, the mark of an amateur is the inability to take criticism.

Do not come to a writing workshop – in fact, don't even entertain the notion of becoming a published writer – if you are not ready, even eager, for constructive criticism. We mentors do you no good at all unless we can pinpoint weaknesses in the work. We will give you all the pats on the back your work deserves, but if you come to a workshop expecting universal praise, you are going to be sorely disappointed. Nobody, not even grizzled veterans, will turn out a manuscript adored in every word and line. This is not to say that all criticism is valid, but that all criticism should be considered.

Criticism, given publicly and frequently, is part and parcel of the workshop process. In my opinion, it is the primary benefit of an MFA degree. As I have already mentioned, anybody who really wants to write can find all of the same writing instruction and wisdom for free on the Internet. But what you don't get from your laptop (or, sadly, from some MFA programs), are the experienced eyes and ears of a successful working writer.

The advice of an individual who has not been in the business long enough to have experienced both failure and success, and to have weathered the changes of the industry not as a spectator but as an active participant, is of small value to you. Would you allow a surgeon who has never successfully removed an appendix to remove yours? Would you hire a carpenter whose only previous constructions were made with Legos to design and build your dream house?

Here the admonition of Martin Seligman is especially relevant. Seligman, director of the University of Pennsylvania's Positive Psychology Center, and the developer of such concepts as learned helplessness, learned optimism, and authentic happiness, cautions that the only people worth taking advice from are those who have already achieved success in the area in which you aspire to be successful, and who are recognized as experts in their field.

It is not unusual for a participant in a writing workshop, whether in or out of academia, to strive to please one's peer readers by writing to the groups' collective taste, or by placing great weight on the opinion of one or two of those peers. Nothing is more deleterious to an individual's development as a writer. Opinions are a penny a dozen, but few, if any, of those amateur opinions should matter to a writer.

Only a professional writer, agent, or editor who has been in the trenches for several years and continues to keep an ear to the ground can look at your manuscript line by line and tell you where it fails and succeeds, and what your chances are in the current marketplace. Likewise, an insightful mentor who is as generous with criticism as she is with encouragement can improve those chances. But if you come to a workshop or MFA program resistant to that criticism, convinced that every page you write is sacrosanct, you are already a fool and are destined to spend your life whining about the philistines who were too stupid to appreciate your art.

To become a professional writer, one must be humble enough to want to learn from those who have succeeded where you have not yet succeeded, and you must be smart enough to understand that there is no end to one's education as a writer.

At the same time, you must be confident enough not to be fatally wounded by criticism. Do you have the strength to write story after story, book after book, collecting nothing but rejections, all the while maintaining faith in yourself to someday be good enough to join the ranks of published writers? Do you have the courage to sit alone at your desk year after year, with no resources but for your own imagination, as you teach yourself by trial and error what works for that story or novel, but only for that story or novel? Do you have the courage to teach yourself all over again with every new story and novel?

Do you possess the psychological wherewithal to not only endure but to cherish those hours upon hours of solitude necessary to be a productive writer? And do you have the boldness, when not writing, to confront the world in all its harshness and beauty and pathos and brutality?

Are you ready to live much of your life as a monk, and the rest of your time pursuing experience and knowledge with the ferocity of a zealot?

Unless you can answer "Hell, yes!" without an ounce of equivocation, do yourself a favor and throw your energies into another profession. Chances are, you will live a happier and more fulfilled existence than you would as an unsuccessful writer.

Do not allow yourself to be deluded by the energy and camaraderie of a writing program. Writing programs and other workshop venues are in many ways a false microcosm of the professional writer's world. Most workshops are overwhelmingly supportive and encouraging, permeated by a "We're all in this together" synergy.

The real world doesn't much care how you ache to be a published writer, or how many sleepless nights that ache has caused you, or how far in debt you are after paying for your degree. The real world demands results. All that matters is a good story, well told, that will appeal to a wide audience of people *willing to pay for it.*

Until you receive that validation, you are an aspiring writer but not yet *A Writer*. Know the difference. Talking about stories you plan to write, and longing to be a writer, and thinking you have some terrifically interesting stories to tell, is a common affliction. Anybody can call herself a writer. Few will have that distinction bequeathed upon them by others.

An agent or editor could not care less if your workshop peers laughed until they cried when they read your story. What they do care about are the words on the page, the writer's gift for keen perception and clear expression. They will also assess the marketability of "the whole package," which includes not only the submitted manuscript but the writer's plans for future work, the writer's platform, and the writer herself.

Do your research.

If you are working with a mentor, in or out of an academic program, know your mentor's work. Read your mentor's books. And if you don't respect your mentor's work, if it doesn't touch you or move you or fill you with envy and admiration, do yourself and the mentor a favor by getting a different mentor.

When the time finally comes to submit a manuscript into that vast, crowded, piranha-infested pool that is the publishing world, know the history of the agent or editor to whom you submit your work. What are their preferred genres? What authors do they represent or work with? What can you glean from online profiles and interviews about that person's basic temperament? If you don't get good vibes in all of these areas, keep looking.

Once you have compiled your list of dream agents and editors, but before you send out your first email query, start anticipating and preparing for the questions an agent or editor might ask when they call to say "I love it!" Know the work of some of the writers on the agent's or editor's roster. Know your own genre and be able to speak with some familiarity of past and contemporary masters of that genre. Have a sense of where the genre has been and where it is headed. Know where your work fits within that genre.

Elsewhere I have written about my own practice of not thinking about genre when composing a piece of work. I encourage you to do the same. However, the publishing world is a whole different place now than it was when I started out. Now you will be expected to tell an agent or editor, whether in your query or by telephone later, your work's principal genre. In other words, first write the piece without trying to shape it to fit the parameters of a particular genre. Then polish it until it is the best it can be. Then, and only then, ask yourself the same question an agent or editor will ask you: What kind of story is this? Can it best be marketed as science fiction? As urban fantasy? As magical realism?

As a so-called multi-genre author, I would also suggest that you avoid pinning any genre label on yourself. When reviewers refer to me as "a veteran crime writer," it is only because their reading habits are limited. My writing habits are not. I like to experiment with genres. I like to mix them together, just as I used to mix chemicals together with my first (and last) chemistry set.

I resent and resist any attempts to pigeonhole me as a writer. For purposes of marketability, however, I recognize that an individual work will sell best when directed at a particular audience. That doesn't mean a writer has to live and work in only that particular box. Follow your instincts. Follow your imagination. Follow your heart.

Know the demands of the marketplace.

What the marketplace wants is subject to change. J. K. Rowling ushered in a new interest in YA fantasy novels, but now, many years after Harry Potter first hit the shelves, there is a glut of mages and wizards. The same is true for all popular genres. Your novel must be truly unique to catch the attention of an agent or editor. Imitative fiction will warrant, at best, a yawn.

However, there is one demand that never changes: a good story. And the single most common shortcoming I encounter among aspiring novelists is in not knowing when the story starts. The time is long past, and will not likely return unless an electromagnetic pulse wipes out all electrical devices, when a novelist like Henry James could spend the first fifty pages of his novel delineating family histories and back stories.

Today's commercial novels start on the first page. Here's how Chuck Sambuchino, book editor at Writers Digest Books, put it in a blog written for the *Writers in the Storm* website: "Today's novels – especially debut novels – must grab readers from the first page, the first paragraph, even the first sentence."

Literary novels are granted a bit more leisure, but only in terms of plot. The first page must still command attention, whether by virtue of the author's voice or the pull of the characters and their situations.

To see this marketplace demand in action, read the first two pages of several *current* novels in your favorite genre, especially those of first-time novelists whose success was not the result of having an established audience and track record.

Practice your pitch.

The two-sentence pitch is often your first opportunity to "sell" your novel, especially if you are attending a conference where editors and agents take pitches, or where you might find yourself cruising the buffet table beside a publishing professional. Long before such an opportunity presents itself, however, you should have composed your pitch, not initially as a marketing tool but as a tool to focus your creative energies. You should write that pitch before you ever start composing your novel, then rewrite it again and again as the novel evolves. And the novel should evolve. If it doesn't, you are clinging too tenaciously to an outline or scene breakdown.

Writing a novel should be like raising a child: Provide a bit of guidance and a lot of love and encouragement, but let it be what it wants to be.

Here is what I ask myself when I first sit down to start a new novel: What does the protagonist want? And what is the necessary first step to achieving that goal? And what is an obstacle to that step?

Once I know the answers to those questions, I start writing. Now and then I might realize, after a chapter or two, that I have chosen the wrong point of view, that the story would work better in first person than in limited third person, or vice versa. But I wouldn't have discovered that until after writing those early pages. So don't allow your uncertainty to keep you from starting. Just start. You will learn what you need to know about that story as you go along.

That is how I work. It is not how all writers work. Some writers can't pen an opening sentence until they have a complete scene breakdown. They need to know where the story is going. I prefer to let the story evolve as it is being written. Neither method is right, neither method is wrong unless you are so married to the scene breakdown that you won't let the story breathe.

Once your novel has been fully revised and polished and you are ready to start the querying process, take another close look at your pitch: does it require its own revision so as to incorporate the changes your work has undergone?

As a polished marketing tool, your pitch is your plea for a turn at bat. So make sure the pitch hits all the necessary points and is as tight as the seams on a baseball.

Revise and polish your synopsis.

Have I mentioned that agents and editors, your lifeline to publication, are very busy people? They read at work, on the train, on weekends, on the treadmill, before going to bed. Usually they will request anywhere from ten to fifty pages of a novel manuscript, plus a synopsis. The synopsis can be anywhere from one to five pages long; best to shoot for two to three. It should make clear that you understand three-act dramatic structure, and that your novel fits some variation of that structure. Beginning, middle, and end, not necessarily in that order. Inciting incident, confrontations that produce escalating tension, climax and resolution. It has to pop. It has to sing. It has to whisper a sexy *Read me!* into the agent's or editor's ear.

The synopsis is your way of asking that person to make a commitment to you in several hours of time and energy. It is your chance to convince that person to assist you in a venture that might or might not result in the fulfillment of your dreams. This is your audition, your interview. Taking this step lightly would be like showing up for a white-collar interview in flip-flops and the T-shirt you slept in. Try that once and see how far it gets you.

Be humble yet confident.

Agents and editors have their pick of talented writers. You must give them a good reason to want to work with you. Do not, under any circumstances, whether in the written query or in a phone or face-to-face conversation, make any kind of statement about what a great writer you are or how your novel is a must-read, or any other statement that shows arrogance or cockiness. Nobody wants to work with a prima donna.

The agent or editor is taking a big risk with you. You are an unknown. You are an unproven commodity. There are tens of thousands of other talented writers lined up waiting for you to blow this opportunity so they can have a shot at it. You need the agent or editor or publisher a lot more than they need you.

So be grateful, but don't fawn or whine or beg. Don't promise, "I'll change it any which-way you want me to!" But if a suggestion is offered that the manuscript might be acceptable with certain changes, make it clear that you are not only willing to consider revisions based on their notes, but that you are eager to make your novel the best it can be. Understand that agents and editors are market-savvy in a way you are not. You should be eager to learn from them and benefit from their expertise.

Don't lie or exaggerate.

Never lay claim to accomplishments you haven't earned. This includes publications you don't have, places where you didn't study, recommendations or endorsements you haven't received.

As for simultaneous submissions, most agents understand that writers are reluctant to sit around waiting six months or more for one person's decision. They understand that you will be shopping the manuscript around to others. But if you are asked for an exclusive look, negotiate a time period, such as four weeks, then hold to it. Do not promise an exclusive look then continue to solicit other people's interest. If lightning strikes and somebody else makes an offer on the project, you will have the very unpleasant duty of letting the first agent or editor know that you have wasted their time.

Always be courteous and grateful.

If your mama failed to teach you basic etiquette – and, sadly, this failure seems more and more apparent in our populace as the years fly by – get your hands on *Etiquette for Dummies* or a similar primer and memorize it. If you are fortunate enough to be offered a bit of advice from an agent or editor, say "Thank you" even if you do not agree with the advice. Then think about that advice; really think about it. If you decide to reject it, you better have a damn good reason for doing so.

If you make a pitch, no matter what response you get, be grateful and eager to learn from the response. Send the person an email thank-you note the next day. But do not badger or harass or demean an agent or editor in any way, either by phone or email or in person; these people talk to each other. They work together. If you do something so misguided as to lose your temper or lash out in frustration, other people will hear of it. Your ego is your greatest enemy here. Tame it or suffer the consequences.

Keep your promises.

If you tell an agent or editor that you will deliver a manuscript by a certain date, make sure you turn it in a few days *before* that date. Show how professional and reliable you are. Make these other professionals want to work with you. If you miss a deadline, you have given the opposite signal. The editor or agent will think, *This writer is going to be a problem.* Author/editor and author/agent relationships are partnerships, with both people working toward the same goal. Mutual respect is an absolute must. If you let your partner down by missing deadlines, failing to return phone calls or emails, showing up late for meetings, and in general behaving like a narcissistic twit, why would anybody want to partner with you?

Understand your responsibilities as a writer.

Do not approach an editor or agent until you have the following:

- a gracious and professional attitude that encompasses all of the above guidelines;
- a polished and completed novel, and an outline for the next one;
- a platform (Facebook, Twitter, etc.; i.e. a target audience, and a way to reach them);
- a marketing plan (able to promote yourself through online and print magazines, radio, online and print interviews, email press releases, public appearances, postcards, YouTube book trailers, and so forth); and,
- a burning, inextinguishable desire to be the best writer you can be.

And in the end...

Yes, the work matters. But you matter too, especially in the beginning of a professional relationship. Your written words might be the first thing a potential teammate notices, but whether your relationship is with a mentor, an agent, or an editor, you will be scrutinized every bit as much as your manuscript will be. So be a professional. Look, think, speak, and act like a professional.

And who knows? You just might beat the odds.

Financial Planning for Adjuncts

A significant portion of an English department's adjunct faculty are writers or aspiring writers. So let's face it: You need money.

We adjuncts always need money. And it's summer again, which means we have no income unless we were able to charm our way into a temporary job at Baby Gap selling onesies to women with perpetual heartburn. Those of us fortunate to have been employed fulltime with benefits during the previous nine months have already cashed out that year's retirement contribution, have pawned our grandmother's jewelry and eBayed every beer mug and pennant acquired during our blissfully ignorant college days. Our job now is to survive the summer on a Ramen noodle diet until late August, when once again we can luxuriate in the teaching of those overstuffed classes no tenured professor is willing to teach. The most fortunate among us will receive our teaching assignments before the first day of classes, and those of us truly blessed will have textbooks available for our students before midterms.

None of which solves our ongoing financial crisis. And, unfortunately, it is a crisis predicted to worsen, as institutions of higher learning attempt to firm up their bottom lines by relying more and more on the servitude of the disenfranchised.

But exploitation is a condition we adjuncts gladly embrace. We gladly accept the lowest faculty pay on campus, even when our CVs boast more education, more experience, more publications, more literary awards, and more real-life accomplishments than those of faculty earning twice our pay and doing half as much work. We adjuncts are, at heart, a grateful and giving bunch of educators. We harbor no animus for man nor beast, whether warm-blooded Homo sapiens or ice-hearted chancellor. We only want to get along.

Hence, this primer on financial equanimity, designed to keep that goofy *What? Me worry?* smile on the face of you or an adjunct you love.

The following options to destitution are broken into the categories of *Small Effort/Short-term Gain* and *Increased Risk or Effort/Long-term Gain*. As every certified financial planner will advise (except, perhaps, for the idiot who advised you to aim for a job in higher education), a combination of both strategies is your best bet to avoiding an expatriate retirement downwind of the Panama City landfill.

SMALL EFFORT/SHORT-TERM GAIN STRATEGIES

1. Sell your blood. Plasma donation takes only about 45 minutes, plenty of time to watch six episodes of *Real Housewives* if you fast-forward through the stupid parts. You can donate twice a week, for a net profit of up to $400 extra income per month. And there's always the added possibility that: (a.) you will fall in love with your phlebotomist (annual income over around $35k/year) or (b.) your phlebotomist will be so incompetent, bored or distracted by *Real Housewives* that she will destroy an artery, which will cause your arm to wither and die, leaving you with a dead seal flipper for a limb but a very nice settlement from the blood bank.

2. Sell your sperm or eggs. Again, a very altruistic act that is also nicely profitable. However, when it comes to profit, the guys lose out on this one. A young, healthy, disease and drug-free male of more than moderate intelligence and education can pocket $200 or more every five days. But those five days between donations might make you squirm. During those intervening five days,

boys, you must remain "master of your domain." Yikes. Females, on the other hand, have no such restrictions, but must submit to a less pleasurable method of delivery. Not to mention a regimen of injections leading up to the egg harvesting procedure. According to FertiltyNation.com, the going rate for egg donation in a major metropolitan American city is $3500-$5000. That's more than most adjuncts make for teaching a 3-credit, 15-week course! And this is one area where your advanced degree really matters: Look for those agencies that have Exceptional Egg Donor Programs, then watch your bank account grow.

3. Mug an adult Amish male. Yes, this option lacks the altruism of the first two choices, but sometimes, as the saying goes, "Charity begins at home." And if you've ever stood in line at the grocery store behind an Amish farmer, waiting to pay for your weekly ration of Ramen noodles while he overloads the belt with Angus steaks and sushi-grade Ahi tuna, you know that these pacifists are among the last individuals in this country to pay with cash. That's right; that bulge in his side pocket isn't there because he's glad to see you. But beware: Even though the Amish espouse a policy of non-resistance in the face of personal violence, individual adherence to this policy varies, and the Amish are nothing if not sinewy.

Increased Risk or Effort/Long-term Gain

1. Take in a renter. For an extra $500/month, what's a little extra noise, disorder, chaos, vandalism, disrespect, petty thievery, and invasion of your privacy? Also, be sure to check with your local housing agencies: Government subsidies may be available for taking in paroled felons and illegal aliens.

2. Enroll in night classes to become: an X-ray technician (For about $60k/year, you can get used to lead panties. Optional fringe benefits include free neutering/spaying for yourself and your pets); a welder (That's right; if you had listened to your father and learned a trade, you could be inhaling toxic fumes for well over $50/hour – even higher if you take your flaming personality under water. An added bonus: easy access to safe-cracking equipment); a funeral director (Earn over $80k a year in quiet, flower-scented surroundings); or an air traffic controller (Take the FAA course, pass the test, and start hauling in over $100k/year. Too stressful, you say? Have you forgotten what you now do for a living?)

3. Be a whole lot nicer to your wealthy elderly relatives and neighbors. Pay very special attention to elderly neighbors who live alone. Not only is kindness a nice thing to do, but, contrary to certain expert sources who shall remain nameless, the activity frequently cited as the most missed among old people is sexual intimacy. You might even consider becoming a regular visitor to the local nursing home. You just might discover that, in the words of Bachman-Turner Overdrive, "Any love is good lovin'."

4. Sell a nice piece of liver. I mean really, just how much liver does one person need? You have more than enough to spare. Parting with only a third of yours could fetch you a windfall of a full year's salary as the lowest paid faculty member on campus. The downside of this is that you might have to make a trip to Bangkok for the procedure. The combined costs of roundtrip airfare, treatment for your infections, and extended hospice care might well eat up most of your profits, but at least you will have taken that trip abroad that you've always longed to take.

As you can see, we adjuncts don't need to wallow in uncertainty and near-poverty. Sure, it's easy to blame the bloated six-figure administrators who seem all too willing to pad their own budgets while wringing us dry. Sure, we can't even count on our tenured colleagues for support regarding salary and other equity issues. Sure, our colleges and universities have become this country's maquiladoras, and we adjuncts, now the majority faculty on many campuses, are the least of their employees.

But we are not helpless. We are not mere pawns. Options abound.

And I never even mentioned the use of a little friendly blackmail. You know how to handle a zoom lens, right?

If This Ain't Art, What Is It?

If we agree that the purest definition of the phrase *creative art* is "a work of the imagination, sometimes but not always supplemented by memory," we can fill that capacious basket with several disciplines: paintings, sculptures, photography, and other works of visual art; interpretive dance, theatre, films, musical compositions, and other variations of the performing arts; poetry, fiction, creative nonfiction, and drama in all their guises as the literary arts. Among those many disciplines and their sub-disciplines, the single most significant *solitary* achievement has to be the novel.

In nearly every case, the performing arts all require, at some point in the work's development, the participation of multiple individuals. Directors, producers, sound engineers, set designers, cinematographers, choreographers, actors, musicians and numerous other individuals – all required to bring the art to its fullness. Because of this necessity, the creators' original creations, though probably first manifested in solitude, are eventually and in sundry ways altered, sometimes for the better, sometimes the worse. In any case, the original vision, the literary art aspect of the performing arts, will be altered, often without the original creator's approval. By far, the most egregious dilution of the creator's work is perpetrated on the screenwriter; the screenplay is treated, at best, as a naked skeleton of the finished product, which, in the end, can require the collaboration of over a hundred individuals.

Visual artists, on the other hand, typically produce their work, start to finish, in solitude, as do poets and fiction writers, with little to no interference or collusion by other individuals. Visual art and poetry, however, are, in almost every case, short-term projects that aim to convey to their audience a single sentiment, and demand only a few minutes of the audience's attention.

Which leaves us with the remainder of the literary arts. Short fiction can call forth multiple ups and downs and switchbacks of emotion for the reader, yet in scope and thematic complexity, a good short story or novella, either easily conceived of and composed over a month's time, is no equal to the solitary achievement of a good novel. Even a bad novel is an achievement in discipline and perseverance, but a truly good novel, one that is crafted with not only an original vision and imagination but also with a distinctive style and voice, so that it touches and moves its many readers, is a project that will require the writer's sustained focus for a year or longer – a full year or more of composing then honing, shaping, developing, revising, and polishing every aspect and element of the work, page by page holding onto an ever-developing concept of the whole. The work is akin to that of a single individual building a Cadillac Escalade from tin cans, except that the tin cans have been made by somebody else. Novels, like the rest of the literary arts, are built out of nothing but imagination. And that is why the novel alone, by virtue of its scope and breadth, has no peer among the numerous other products of the creative arts.

The novelist, who might consult or depend upon advice or assistance from not a single other individual throughout the entire production process, works alone. It is the novelist who must repeatedly ask, from page one of the rough draft through all the successive drafts, if every line of dialogue is sharp and relevant. Does each conversation and interior monologue illuminate character and/or advance the plot? Does every setting create the appropriate mood and effectively portend the action of the scene?

Is every character essential and believable and clearly rendered? Does the story's structure promote reader engagement and invite reader immersion? Is every scene vividly and memorably depicted? Is the story itself free of clichés and stereotypes yet universally relatable to the reader? And does the cumulative effect of all these essentials leave the reader, who has stayed faithfully with the story for seven or eight or more hours, reluctant to close the cover and pull herself out of the fictional world she has been inhabiting?

It might be argued that an editor and publisher are essential to bringing the writer's novel to its fullness, as are the copyeditors, the cover and page designers, the marketing team and bookstores. But those individuals, if they are doing the work they should, do nothing to alter the creator's original vision. Their job is to catch small errors and weaknesses, or to *sell* the work, not to alter or dilute it through their own participation, as only the worst of editors are wont to do. The work itself, which is the story and not the wrappings of the story, i.e. the words chosen by the writer over a year or more of solitary focus, remain intact.

Yes, a lot of poorly written novels get published every year, some by the biggest of publishers and many by the authors themselves. But bad writing is not art. Art can and should entertain, but if that is all it does, it is at best a minor art. Great art illuminates. And the light it shines is never meant to fall upon the writer, who by then should be hard at work in the solitude of another novel, but only on the reader.

Lost In the Words

Many of my fondest hours have been lost between the library stacks, ensconced in words, as happily oblivious to the world and its calamities as a dipsomaniac at an open bar. For example, an afternoon in the archives at the Memorial University of Newfoundland library comes to mind, where I pored over photographs a hundred years old, tantalized by the prospect of imminent discovery.

And the dark, crowded library off the Grand Place in Brussels, where, half-starving and nearly out of money, I first discovered Sartre's little masterpiece *No Exit*, devoured most of it in a single swallow, and then, dizzied by what I'd read, staggered out onto the rainy streets.

And the sweltering one-room library above the police station in Sunset Crest, Barbados, where I found a book about Bajan idioms that opened up the lilting language to me at last, and turned babble into music.

And how many hours of my life were passed in the old Carlson Library here on campus, where you could find me on the second or third floor, following the trail of Dewey Decimal clues to the reward at journey's end? To say I felt adrift and rudderless when the library was dispersed across campus is to scarcely hint at my disorientation.

Books have always been my compass. Like Flannery O'Connor, I write to hear what I am thinking, but I also read to hear what others are thinking and to employ those thoughts as a measure of my own. I suspect this is true of most writers, we who write not because we have the answers but because we are plagued by questions. And so we turn to one another for guidance, for direction, and, sometimes, just for solace.

So what a fine day it was for me on the day the new Rena M. Carlson Library swung open its doors. I felt washed ashore at last; again on solid ground. And what a shore it is! With its current inventory of 300,000 volumes, this feast can never be depleted. More books and magazines arrive every week. I cannot tell you how happy I am made by this fact, that there will always be another good book to read, another universe to unfold at my fingertips.

Like all good libraries, this one is constantly self-renewing. It retains the best of the old while relentlessly tracking down the best of the new. And in a library's renewal is, quite possibly, the best hope we have for our own.

We might think of a library as a place to go to gather information, and it is certainly that, but it is certainly more. It is a place where we might, as Shakespeare said, beguile sorrow. Not to mention trepidation, ignorance, anxiety, and desolation. Each time I enter a well-stocked library, I get the same heady feeling as when I enter a cathedral – that I am in the presence of something huge, something too big to embrace all at once, something I might spend a lifetime trying to plumb.

It is a fine thing for a library to be spacious and well lit, as is the new Carlson Library, but it should not be too modern; it should not feel like a mall, as the Carlson Library does not. Despite the openness of the floor plan and the generous windows and the clean lines of the furnishings – its chairs and tables unostentatious but inviting reflection, stillness, a Quakerlike calm – this library manages to retain its dignity while emanating an air of tradition.

And rightfully so. A library is, after all, a repository of human knowledge, a well of human wisdom, a reservoir of human hopes and fears. A library is a place where the world makes sense, or nearly so. As Sam Hazo points out in his poem *Wordhoard,* "the sheer jumble of the world/ seems much less daunting/ in alphabetical order."

Maybe that is why we writers, whose business it is to create well-ordered worlds, are so fond of libraries, and so grateful for them. Annie Dillard composed much of *A Pilgrim at Tinker Creek* in a carrel at the Hollins College library. Francine Prose has claimed the New York Public Library as her Muse. Shakespeare wrote in *The Tempest,* "My library was dukedom enough."

A good library is kingdom enough for me as well. I walk into the new Carlson Library, for example – have you noticed that the face of the building, the main entrance, is wide-eyed and grinning? Such a cheerful invitation! – I walk inside and turn to the right and there before me wait several shelves lined with the newest acquisitions, my first stop of the day, a lure whose seduction I can never resist. Then to the Reference Room or the stacks on the third floor. Then, with twenty pounds of books in my arms, to a comfortable chair in the well-lit study area. And then…immersion. An hour or two of sweet oblivion.

There is no war in a library. No cacophony of dissent. No creditors, no telephone solicitors, no producers or agents or editors in a manic rush. There is only a still, reflective peace. Even the records of war kept here, the images and transcripts of tragedy and sorrow, the necessary reminders, even these, in a library, engender a stillness inside.

We are hushed in a library out of respect for others, yes – for those studying, reading, contemplating – but we are hushed as well by the books themselves, the fruits of the labor of giants and demi-giants and mere mortals alike. As with every good library, there is more to the new Carlson Library than books alone – far, far more. But the big, generous, unconditionally magnanimous heart of every library is its books.

Books "soothe the grieved," said the 18th-century poet George Crabbe. "Unlike the hard, the selfish, and the proud,/ They fly not sullen from the supplicant crowd;/ Nor tell to various people various things,/ But show to subjects what they show to Kings."

And if it is also true, to quote Sam Hazo again, that "the only truth that lasts is on the page," then what better place to be than in a house built of truth, this library, this vault of our lives, this heart of the university and the community that surrounds it, this caretaker of the soul of mankind, this sanctum; and a clean, well-lighted one at that, all laid out in alphabetical order?

Scripsi, Ergo Sum

Forty-five years ago, having discovered, through no lack of trying, no comparable passion, I committed myself to the tenuous life of a writer. Fifteen years later I became a father for the first time, and then made a compromise so as to support my growing family: I will also teach those who wish to become writers.

At first, I didn't like teaching. I wanted to be writing. Wanted to be holding my new son, carrying him along a country road, watching the clouds through his wide, startled eyes, "Hello, new life! Hello!"

Moreover, the role of authority did not fit me well. All those eyes on me in the classroom, all those pens poised to write, ears eager to hear what I would say. I felt naked and unarmed.

So what did I say? I said, "Listen, I will tell you how I work and what little I have learned, but that's about all I have to offer. I've never studied creative writing. I'm not sure it's even a good idea to do so."

And eventually you won me over with your eagerness and hunger, the same hunger that drove me then and drives me still. The kind that compels me to read Hemingway and García Márquez and Faulkner and others again and again. No, not read, but devour, assimilate, squeeze and flatten like an orange for every last glisten of sustenance.

"This is all you need," I told you. "An insatiable hunger, an unquenchable thirst, an endless smorgasbord of books. And the time and discipline to write, write, write."

"Learn to live dangerously," I told you. "Learn to love the view from the edge."

I counseled you as undergraduates and graduates, as teenagers and septuagenarians, as lawyers and homemakers and FBI agents and cooks and recovering heroin addicts, aspiring writers from every walk of life and disposition, every conceivable race and gender and sexual preference. Some of you have become published authors. More of you will eventually. Most of you will not. More than a few of you have stopped trying; others of you will never stop trying. But even those of you who have given up on writing still carry in your hearts the memory of that dream, that longing, that inexpressible urge to have your stories heard.

And I want to tell you now, as my time for teaching is coming to an end, what the first real writer I ever met told me: "Never quit."

And why should you quit? Because the agents and editors you query do not respond? Because your one or two published books went straight from the printer to the remaindered table?

So what?

Okay, sure; if you first took up the pen with adulation and acclaim your driving force, then yes, give up, for yours is not the soul of a writer but of a profiteer. How foolish of you to dive into one of the world's most demanding, and over-populated professions with such expectations! Success for a writer is at best a happy accident. And commercial success is no measure of your writing's worth.

But if you chose to be a writer for the same reason you enjoy getting lost in the woods, the same reason you order a meal by telling the server, "Surprise me," the same reason you always choose Dare over Truth – in other words because the unknown thrills you, quickens your pulse, enlivens and revivifies you – then how can you ever quit writing? You look at life with a heightened curiosity and an elevated sensitivity that makes every pain sharper and every pleasure more exquisite. Everything new interests you until you come to know it; then you want another unknown. Even starvation offers the opportunity for examination, and that's good, because you don't have any money for food, having spent it all on books and writing supplies.

Only sameness bores you. You are promiscuous in every desire. When making love, or running from the police, or shivering in the back seat of your car on a winter's night because it costs too much to run the engine for the heater, you are watching yourself and trying out the best words to describe your fear, your agony, your perverse delight in watching yourself suffer. You think, *What a great scene this will make!*

You push every experience to its limit and then further yet, because this is the only way to feed imagination.. Hemingway's imagery can teach you how to describe and slow down and speed up the experience, and Márquez's details can show you how to consider the experience from some unexpected angle, but only experience itself can put the pulse of life into words, can lace those words with veins and arteries coursing full of body-warm blood.

Yes, it is the unknown that shows you who you are, especially after you have captured and preserved it. *I write,* you tell yourself; *therefore I am.*

In the end, if you are indeed a writer, a writer in deed, a maker of stories, the world is not enough for you. You need more worlds, other worlds, through which to view yourself and this planet beneath your feet. You long to live not just well but fully, in every nerve and muscle, with every breath and heartbeat. The world's misery is not enough, or not sufficiently comprehensible, so you create characters and a myriad of miseries for your characters to bear, more obstacles to encounter, more agonies to explore. And through their responses you measure your own. Through them you begin to understand and know yourself. Through your characters, you find the strength to endure.

Everybody suffers. But not everybody pulls apart the threads of suffering and weaves them into a story, as writers do. Non-writers either wear their suffering daily, piling it on layer upon layer until it drags them down, or else they manage somehow to shrug off their suffering and kick it to the curb and tell themselves they are shed of it forever, too afraid to turn and find it following.

This is an important distinction between those who write and those who do not. Writers create the stories through which the rest of the world examines itself. Everyone on the planet loves stories of one kind or another, but in the United States, only .01% of us write those stories. Think of how terribly, irremediably bleak this life would be if there were no novels, no television dramas and sitcoms and serials, no films and stage plays and narrative poems and urban legends and creation stories to enliven and edify generation after generation.

The earliest known piece of true writing, carved on a stone in ancient Sumer, tells a story. Most of what we know of our past, we know from stories. What we know of our future, we can only speculate, an ability we glean through the stories we tell each other and ourselves.

We live in a time and place – now, in this country – when artistic endeavors are ignored, derided, and demeaned unless accompanied by a dollar sign and a minimum of six figures. And by artistic I refer to anything crafted with care and deliberation, with precision and a quality of distinctiveness. The marketplace, unfortunately, thrives on the mediocrity of imitation, on what is sensational and crass – products no true artist would waste her time on.

I really don't like the word "artist." It's a narcissistic, look-at-me distinction that makes me uncomfortable – as it does, I think, many writers, since our profession is heavily stacked on the side of introverts. What we are is creators. Every human being can and should be a creator, no matter one's profession. If you aren't creating something through the sweat of your hands or brain or heart, whether it is a hub cap or a glazed vase, a healthy investment portfolio or a new genome sequence, a child's smile or a lover's sigh, you are merely a consumer of others' creations, and what a hollow life that must be. We were created to create, so that through the story of our lives, our creator can better know itself.

The most important thing fiction writers create are emotions. Through meticulously chosen words and sentences and images that accumulate in power layer upon layer, we create anticipation, empathy, excitement, a shared sorrow, grief, triumph, or joy.

Because music was my first love, and because I still try to find as much harmony in my written words as possible, I like to think that my stories sometimes sing into the ears and hearts of readers, subtly reminding them that they are creators too – and of the very emotions my stories sing to them.

This symbiosis between writers and readers is a reflection of the necessary symbiosis between all people if humanity is not only to survive but to prosper. As an introvert I spend ninety-five percent of my time alone, but I reach out through my books. A book is my handshake, my hug, the kiss I lay upon your cheek when you turn the final page. If you hold the book on your lap for a few moments after you've finished the story, if you smile, if you wish there were more pages to read, you are kissing me in return.

If that is not your aim as a writer – to reach out, make contact, commune, and collaborate – you will probably be happier as a speech writer than as a novelist; happier as a rhetorician than as a playwright; and certainly happier as a polemicist than as a screenwriter.

We storytellers aim for the heart, not the head. Yes, I also like to throw a jab or two in my fiction; stories are fine places from which to hurl a harpoon at some aspect of society. But we do it because we love this world and want it, in turn, to be more loving. Writing, then, is an act of faith that a better way is possible.

Writing must also be a journey of discovery through which the writer attempts to improve herself. It is not easy for me to love my neighbor when his dog has been barking untended for the past five hours, but I find that by letting my protagonist vent his frustration through angry words, upon which he later reflects, he, and I through him, can then rediscover a nobler emotion, the kind that would ennoble all of humanity if only we could all be made to feel it.

You don't need a million readers for this, though readers are good. Readers help. Appreciative readers help most. Even if only one.

I am reluctant to speak of spirituality in an essay about storytelling, not least because I believe spirituality to be a private matter between each individual and his or her God. But if I am to speak comprehensively about the writer's obligation and motivation, spirituality must be included. If writing is an act of love, an act of faith, and an attempt at communion with hearts unseen, how can it not also be a spiritual endeavor?

Few would deny that the best poetry, no matter how secular, is also highly spiritual. Why not stories too? Why not plays? Why not, even, and sometimes, movies? If you weep while reading or watching, if you laugh, if you clutch your chest and gasp, it is because the writer has touched you. Why is that connection any less spiritual than the one you feel when you hold your child or grandchild or lover or friend?

As writers, we sit at our desks each day and gather around us (though they are always there, bidden or not) every slight and fear from childhood through yesterday, every memory broken, lost, or fresh as fire, every pain suffered and pleasure savored. And from this wet clay we mold our Adams and Eves, our Cains and Abels. We set them down in their gardens in medias res, then turn them out with our flaming sword, and send them east to the perilous land of Nod.

We writers are outcasts too, wanderers endlessly wondering. We stop wandering only long enough to write down what has happened thus far. But we never stop wondering. We never quit.

Nor should you, my students of days past. Never stop wondering, never stop learning. And if you must use comma splices when you write, splice deliberately. If you must use sentence fragments, fragment deliberately.

Love deliberately.

Breathe deliberately.

If you do that, it matters little if every agent and editor on the planet forsakes you. Write to feed yourself on the unknown. Write to drink the hope that another planet will soon be discovered inhabited only by agents and editors all starving for a writer, with its twin planet a mere ladder rope away and inhabited only by readers all starving for a good story.

Ultimately, however, do not write for validation. Write to preserve the memory of your life and imagination for your children and grandchildren. Write to sound your barbaric yawp. Write to sing the song of yourself. Write to live. Write to be.

On Titles and Those Who Make Them

Writers and the people who market books see their product and audience in different ways. Writers see that vast invisible sea of potential readers as living, breathing people with desires and emotions. Marketers see them as wallets to be pried open. Writers also manipulate, but with the aim of touching and moving the reader, of making a connection through the story's characters. To the marketer, the purpose of words and images is to grab the reader's attention and hold onto it all the way to the cash register. What happens after that is of no concern to the marketer. To a writer – to most writers, I hope – this is the equivalent of dishonest storytelling.

Dishonest storytelling happens when the writer deliberately misleads the reader into believing something that isn't true. The honest storyteller does give the reader an opportunity to mislead herself, but he doesn't take her by the hand and lead her in the wrong direction. There is a fine line here, to be sure, just as there can be a fine line between bad and good writing, and good and great writing. Writers who aim for honesty are offended by not only dishonest storytelling but also by dishonest messaging in the marketing of their story.

What matters to me professionally is the use of words, that they are used deliberately, effectively, and honestly. Take a name, for example. I have always thought it unfortunate that in our culture we are not afforded the opportunity to choose our own name, one that best signals who we think we are and who we wish to become. Names, as studies have shown, can affect the way people see us, at least initially. Later they might look at us and say, "You don't look like a Betty. Would you mind if I call you Beth?"

The same holds true for a book's title. What we name a book is the first thing a potential reader knows about the story inside. Therefore it is logical to argue that, since books are not born with their titles already assigned, as people usually are, we must choose a title that reflects some important quality of the story inside. This writer believes that the title (and the cover art) should suggest something about the guts of the story. Marketers, on the other hand, aim to employ the cover as a kind of bell to induce a Pavlovian response in the potential book buyer, so that the buyer, already salivating, thinks *romance!* or *mystery!* or *fantasy!* or whatever the genre might be.

It is this salivation, followed by the reaching for one's cash or credit card, that concerns the marketing department. Too often, however, a title and cover image chosen by a marketing department will leave a bad taste in the reader's mouth, just as the greasy, skinny burger with wilted lettuce and a square of unmeltable cheese facsimile on a stale bun will do when compared to the vibrantly colored poster featuring a tower of succulent beef and bun and condiments plastered to the fast food restaurant's window.

A title and the accompanying cover art should entice the reader, but my experience tells me that readers also want to recognize, whether on page 20 or page 300 or anywhere in between, exactly how the title foreshadows the story. The best titles are ones that generate a balance of wonder and understanding in the reader, and which eventually will come to feel so organic to the story that no other title could have fit as well. Consider *For Whom the Bell Tolls*, for example. *Of Mice and Men*. *The Grapes of Wrath*. *A Canticle for Leibowitz*. Read each of those novels and suggest a better title. I bet you can't. Each title is sewn seamlessly to the heart and soul of the story.

It is also, therefore, logical to argue that no one knows the heart and soul of the story better than the writer. Only he or she, at the title-assigning stage of the game, has the understanding necessary to render down four hundred pages of grief and struggle and transformative joy into a few encapsulating words. To suggest that someone else, having never read the novel or having read only a brief synopsis of it, can deliberately, effectively, and honestly choose the right name for that story, is nonsense.

Writing and marketing share an uneasy alliance. These days, marketers want to start marketing their vision of a novel well before the manuscript is finished instead of marketing the author's vision of the novel after he or she has lived and breathed and dreamed that story for a difficult year or more. This is a relatively recent phenomenon in the literary world, one engendered by the increasing shallowness of a society that often values the marketing of a product more than the product itself. Were Michelangelo to finish his sculpture of David today, he would likely be told, "Looks great! But let's give him bigger muscles and a bigger package and maybe put a naked woman lying at his feet. We'll call it *His and Herotica*."

Publishers, of course, have to make money on a book. So do authors. But both should aim to profit from that numinous connection between story and reader, not from a misrepresentation of the story inflicted by a dishonest or misleading title and cover image. Any title that leaves the reader shaking or scratching her head at the end of a novel is a bad title.

Sometimes the author's name above the title can save a book from being misunderstood at first glance, but in that case only readers familiar with the author's name or interested in the promised subject matter will lift the book off the shelf.

Sometimes a novel with an atrociously bad title – *The Effects of Gamma Rays on Man-in-the-Moon Marigolds*, *Appointment in Samarra*, – will overcome the burden of its title and become a rousing success. But in these low-attention span times, this happens rarely. Few of us have hours of spare time for wending our way down a bookstore's aisles while reading back cover or flap copy for a hint of the story's nature.

A beguiling title or author's name must first make us pause. Had I not known that Melissa Banks is a fine writer of funny, tender, and observant prose, I would never have read *The Girls' Guide to Hunting and Fishing*. Without that knowledge, this is niche marketing that misses its niche.

How do you know when you've chosen a good title? A title "should have a mystery to it," said Joyce Carol Oates. "It can't explain everything." Walker Percy voiced a similar criteria: "A good title should be like a good metaphor: It should intrigue without being too baffling or too obvious."

For me, a good title is one that is memorable, that truly reflects the thematic essence of the book, and that possesses what Hemingway called "magic" – a poetic and seductive enticement to the reader to open the book and read the first page. And by "poetic" I mean exactly what Oates and Percy said: metaphor and mystery.

Marketing departments seem to believe that most readers make their buying decisions based on genre. I hope that isn't true, and I suspect it is not. A truly well-written and compelling novel should be marketed as such to all readers who love a good story, not just to those who read a certain genre. Should *The Old Man and the Sea* be marketed today as a fishing story? *Killing Mister Watson* as a crime novel? *The Handmaid's Tale* as science fiction?

I want to be able to linger over a title, to savor the sound of it and to wonder about the nature of the tease it presents to me. This isn't a new argument, but it is worth making again, as the division in philosophy as to the title's job often has the writer and publisher working at cross purposes. If all a title does is to signal the genre to potential readers, it's a bad title.

A Writer's Education

I never felt at a great loss without a living and breathing mentor, a guide, a comforter, as so many young writers seem to feel today. I sometimes wished for an expert who could field a question or two, who might respond to a scene or paragraph I felt uneasy with, but by the time I finished college, I had read, on my own, all of the previous generation of American writers plus most of the European and South American and a few of the Asian masters.

Other aspiring writers my age had read Vonnegut and Ray Carver and thought they knew everything there was to know about writing. I read all of Vonnegut in high school, long before I'd had a single thought of becoming a writer, and even adopted a world-weary "So it goes" as my motto, at least until my sophomore year in college, when I was still an accounting major.

Having also read all the modernist and mystical poets and playwrights on my own by then, I switched majors for my last two years in college when I discovered that I had already taken, as electives, enough literature classes to satisfy the requirements for a degree in English, and enough psychology classes to satisfy as a minor, and enough credits in business and economics for an associate's degree in business administration.

I too read Carver and the other minimalists of my generation, but, having feasted on the sumptuous prose of previous generations, I found minimalist writing to be artless and easy, as satisfying after a five-star five-course meal as a fortune cookie. So I kept studying the writers I admired, the impressionists and meta-fictionists, the transcendentalists and existentialists, the surrealists and absurdists and modernists, the writers whose prose moved like a thousand rabbits in a maze as well as those whose prose sounded like the song of a pod of blue whales mating, and especially those whose prose moved like an iceberg with most of its mass and power submerged. These were the only writers who had anything to teach me, though I did learn from the minimalists all that I wanted my prose to avoid.

My first job out of college was as the sports editor and photographer for a weekly newspaper, but I spent so much time in the darkroom playing with the pre-digital era equipment, or writing a weekly column aimed at shaking up the provincial readership, or day-dreaming about writing a novel, that, near the end of my first year, when the publisher confided that he expected me to take over editorship of the paper within a few months, I turned in my resignation, drove to Florida, and took a job sweeping floors in a hospital supply factory. Thus began my real writing education, which had nothing to do with studying prose (a lifelong vocation), but with studying human nature (another course of study that never ends).

After that job I worked in a factory that manufactured the thick rubber liners for truck tires, then as a house painter, a tennis instructor, a swimming pool installer, an emergency services caseworker, a tree trimmer, a summer replacement in the accounting department at a U.S. Steel sintering plant, a bartender, a game operator in an amusement park, a substitute teacher, a singer and keyboardist in three different bands, and as a broker in a San Diego company that traded in barter points that could be redeemed for restaurant meals, clothing, gasoline, and any other commodity you can think of, including, in my case, a diamond engagement ring.

Before the ring, I backpacked through Europe for a few months, lived in California three different times, soloed in a Piper Tomahawk and accidentally put it into a near-fatal spin, slept in the bushes on the Isle of Wight, almost signed up for the Navy at the height of the war in Vietnam (until my mother pleaded with me not to), got turned down for an entry-level job with the FBI, almost joined the Peace Corps (but, being high at the time of my interview, didn't do that either), almost starved to death in Belgium, ran from muggers in Tijuana, hitchhiked or walked but mostly drove over much of North America, fell in love and out of love at least twenty times, ran from the police at least a dozen times, put a couple of cars into a couple of ditches, got lost in the deep woods more times than I can remember, almost drowned in class-IV rapids, almost broke my neck on a ski slope, contemplated suicide many times and made one half-hearted attempt at it, did a handful of really stupid things that still make me wince, and had a number of wholly concrete but totally inexplicable encounters with the supernatural.

During those years I wrote no fewer than four novels, a hundred short stories, a hundred songs, and at least a thousand pages of bad poetry. I got a master's degree then started and dropped out of two PhD programs that had offered me full tuition scholarships.

The summer I turned thirty, I sold four short stories to obscure literary magazines. Three years later I was awarded my first literature fellowship award from the National Endowment for the Arts. The next year, with forty dollars to my name, and ready, or so I told myself, to throw in the towel as a writer, Joyce Carol Oates awarded me the Drue Heinz Literature Prize for a collection of unpublished short fiction. Not until then did I stop calling myself an aspiring writer. But even then, and even now, my education as a writer continues.

Books: What Are They Good For?

When I was fourteen I lined up my collection of Hardy Boy mysteries and Tom Swift books, the complete sets, and unloaded my Daisy air rifle into them. A typical BB would penetrate a cardboard cover to page twenty or so. But I kept firing until a ragged hole had been blasted clean through every book. All of my Superman comics and my sister's collection of Nancy Drew books succumbed to the same fate. Then, to cap my afternoon of miscreancy, I piled the ruined books in the backyard trash barrel and had a mighty blaze going for a while – until both parents returned from work and I was tongue-lashed to within an inch of my life about the evils of waste and senseless destruction.

Had I kept those books intact and in good condition all these years, they would be very valuable now – hundreds, even thousands of times more valuable than the ninety-five cents originally paid for each hardcover volume. I might be so affluent by now that I would never have been compelled to write this essay, nor anything else. I might be so rich that I would have no ambition at all.

And this, perhaps, is the most obvious value of books, though hardly the most important one. Books become collectable. They increase in value. They make some of us rich. They make some of us sick with regret.

———— ∞ ————

Books accrue value in other ways too. Books teach us things; nobody can argue with that. Sometimes they teach us the wrong things.

I saw my first naked woman in an art book I had pulled, innocently the first time, from a shelf in the elementary school library. She was a concubine being offered up for sale at an Egyptian slave market. A tall woman, raven haired, voluptuous to an eye-popping degree, and covered from head to bejeweled toe in nothing but her own milky skin. Because I knew no better at the time, I saw nothing strange in the fact that she was totally devoid of body hair. So was I. Three or four years later, when I discovered that even milky-skinned girls blossom just as hirsutely as boys in certain mysterious parts of the body, it came as quite a shock to me. I'm not sure that I've ever gotten over it.

I mention this trauma as a case in point: We writers must be careful about what we put into books. Word and picture alike have the power to inform and misinform. To elucidate or obfuscate. To teach us big words like elucidate and obfuscate. Or, better yet, to teach us, in little nuggets that accumulate over time to a mountain of information and, with luck, wisdom, how to live.

Books can provide us with facts and statistics but they also give us examples that are not so easily quantifiable. Metaphors about the healing and destructive potential of love, for example. Allegories about the pitfalls of greed and excessive pride. Lessons about the rewards, sometimes discernible only to ourselves, of integrity. There is no predicting when or which book will grace us with such nuggets, but it is my belief that if we read enough, the right book will come along.

Take the Emersonian oversoul, for example. I knew all about this notion in theory long before I left adolescence, but that's all it was to me, a lovely little abstraction, until I read, of all things, Henry Miller's *Tropic of Capricorn*. It was a Saturday in June, I was nineteen, home from my first summer away at college, relaxing from my summer job on the labor gang at the steel mill.

In search of some greenery and solitude, and maybe even something less reducible to word, something like the return of innocence, I found myself sprawled in the grass of the Little League outfield, where I read a passage from *Capricorn* that suddenly, unexpectedly, made the air before my eyes begin to shimmer, made the whole world seem to open its arms to me, take me in, enfold me in an everyplace that existed outside of time and indifferent to it. For once in my life I was content, and for no apparent reason; no sadness, no worry, no questions; no answers either but no need for them.

The honking of a car horn started a gradual evaporation of my serenity, a kind of drifting down from the sublime to solid earth. Still, it was a remarkable few minutes. The afterglow, like sunlight through a curtained window, has stayed with me all these years.

I have tried on numerous occasions to recapture that euphoric feeling by reading the same passage – indeed, the entire book – but without success. Often a book's power will depend upon the vagaries of the moment. On the sunshine and the scent of grass. On the sliding board glinting hot in the sun and on the squeaking chains of a child's swing.

The power of a book to teach us, to move us, to change our lives with an inexpressible insight, to give us new eyes and a new heart and a new will to live, is seldom conspicuous in the ink and paper. The power of a book can be as sudden and upsetting as the prick of something sharp, or as soothing as the stroke of sunlight on bare skin.

In collusion with a playground, or at other moments in collusion with a leather wingchair in a windowless room, in collusion with the external and internal vicissitudes of the reader, some books have the potential to nudge us, one reader at a time, toward a better state of affairs. A book, if we as writers are careful about what we put into it, and we as readers are magnanimous about what we bring to it, has the potential, at least for a moment or two, to turn aside anger and misery and self-pity, and in so doing to suggest to us a finer way to be.

This is the magic of story. The power of narrative. And it is not a power that, as many writers fear, will be diluted by technology. Far more stories and poems and personal essays now exist in cyberspace than ever could or ever will exist in print; more narratives even than scientific tracts or religious and philosophical treatises.

The impulse to tell a story is humanity's heartbeat. Is there anybody who doesn't tell somebody else a story, long or brief, true or made-up, at least once every couple of days? We tell stories about things that excited or frightened or confused us. We tell stories about other people. We tell stories about what happened at school, what happened at work, what happened in last night's dream.

We tell stories so as to feel connected to the world at large. So as to peel back a layer of the onion; to share the onion; to be, for a moment, not so all alone.

Narrative is primal. Metaphor is our ancient and elemental language. As long as humanity survives, there will be stories. That, in the end, might be the one trait that elevates us above all other species on this planet. We are the only animal that tells each other stories.

--------⌒∞⌒--------

A distinction must be made, though, between the impulse to write and the technological changes in how that impulse is made tangible. Technology simply presents us with a few more ways to distribute and preserve our words. Originally we had only the oral option, soon to be augmented with vegetable dye daubed on a cave wall. Then came Gutenberg, then Metro-Goldwyn-Mayer and Playhouse 90. Then, audio books. And now we have books on CDs and jump drives, books on a screen, books sent from one reader to another like a kiss blown across a busy highway.

There was a time when I worried that the lightning advance of technology would render paper books obsolete. But writing and reading about this subject has cleared my head, and I fear no longer.

A printed book, from the moment it is carried from a bookstore, begins to assume a singular identity. My Heinemann New Windmill 5th edition hardcover of Camus' *The Outsider*, purchased thirty-five years ago in a dusty bookstore off the Grand Place in Brussels, will not look like yours or anybody else's copy of the same edition. The dog-earing, the marginalia, the coffee or sweat or blood stains, the bookmarks made from note cards and paperclips.... A book soon becomes as individual as its owner. In this way a printed book grows; it evolves into a hybrid of the people in its life, its author and its reader. It is the offspring of intellectual and emotional intercourse.

Unfortunately, the same cannot be said of a book on CD or DVD or on nothing at all, the e-book. These too will assume wear-and-tear but theirs is a superficial aging, whereas the maturation of a paper book is internalized by the book. CDs and DVDs and hard drives are made to be immune to the magic of human touch. They do not respond to handling as a book will; there is no reciprocal warmth as exudes from a book. They are never quite as alive, never quite as vital as a printed book.

And among all the options, the e-book is the least substantial. It is a book that doesn't exist. It is beamed from the online vendor to a reader's device and presents the illusion of existing inside that device. The e-book can be read but it is a vaporous, ephemeral thing.

Even more so, the audio book. When converted into audible sound, the voice of the story might be mechanical or that of a stranger or even that of the author, but books were meant to be read in the voice of the reader and in the voices of the characters the reader imagines. When anyone but the reader narrates the book aloud, the listener is getting somebody else's rendering, somebody else's interpretation of dialogue, somebody else's translation of words into feeling. Only awkwardly can a listener pause to reconsider a sentence or phrase from an audio book. Only clumsily can the listener juxtapose her own translation atop the narrator's.

There is a certain solidity to a physical book that no computer screen or interface can ever impart. During a grid-down incident, physical books will still be there on your shelf, waiting to get you through the night. After the apocalypse, physical books will still exist. You can still tuck a book under your arm, set it upon your lap, lay it open atop your chest as you drift off to sleep. The sheer physicality of a book comforts as steadfastly as the hand of an old friend. Books erase the trepidations of solitude. They shorten lonely nights. They people empty days.

There is a corporeal sureness to a physical book, a sense of fraternity that emanates from its pages. Just possessing the book fulfills an elemental need. It is why we turn them over in our hands, carry them about with us, leave them lying here and there so that the eye might chance upon them from time to time. Books fill the hole of separation that darkens every human psyche.

I believe too that when we hold a book in our hands we can feel something of its author in it. Maybe this is because of the author's photograph on the dust jacket. Or maybe it is because the organic composition of the paper has absorbed the spirit of the author's thoughts or voice or intentions. Because a physical book is organic. The pages of a physical book live in there interaction between writer and reader. Each time you open a book, it breathes. Its heart beats with every page turned. Its whisper speaks to you every time your fingers slide across a page, leaving a tiny bit of you with every tender rub and scrape of your skin. And in the end the book leans back and looks at you after you have turned the final page, and, if you are lucky, you say goodbye to each other with a smile.

A book is an amulet in a way no computer screen or sound wave can ever be. I know of readers who will carry a book around for days after having read it, because the experience of having read it, of connecting with the characters and their author, is so moving that one is reluctant to break that connection. It is an experience akin to bumping into a friendly guide with a flashlight when you have been wandering lost through the catacombs. Akin to religious epiphany or the sublime intimacy achieved only in the best and rarest of sex.

It feels something like a small death when a particularly good book comes to an end. This was how I felt on that afternoon so many years ago when the air finally cleared of the scent of lubricating oil and hot BBs and I stood looking at the carnage I had wreaked. A lifetime of good reading reduced to confetti. I knew myself then to be some kind of perverted little assassin to take my rage out on the things I loved most in life. That is why I then piled all the books in the trash barrel and set them ablaze. Because there is a dignity in fire, and I needed to cleanse myself and my victims of the ignominious way I had behaved.

And now I find it very difficult to deface, disfigure, or demean a book, any book, even a cheap mass market paperback. I would rather give a book away than ever destroy one again. Because books are like bullion to me, wealth waiting to be cashed in, though their currency is spiritual rather than financial. The closets and my attic and my office are stuffed with them. In fact every book is another room in my house, rooms full of people or wildlife or wind-seared solitude, rooms where Krakatoa erupts and bulls stampede through Pamplona, rooms where on a winter's day, just by opening a door, I can lift a cloud of monarch swallowtails off a pine bough, or sweat with Schweitzer in a malarial steam.

Printed books never have to be turned on or plugged in or have their batteries replaced. They don't harbor viruses or flash error messages or become inaccessible because you lack sufficient memory. And when you come across something in a book that you don't understand, you don't have to spend three days waiting for Tech Support to answer the telephone in an accent you can barely decipher, you refer to another book, a dictionary, an encyclopedia, you graze from one to another as happy as a cow in sweetgrass. You gorge yourself. You feast.

Physical books take up space, yes. But isn't that the point?

All in all, I no longer worry about the fate of printed books. Books will endure. Twenty years from now, or ten, five, or even next year there might be fewer of us who hold printed books precious, and fewer books published worthy of being held precious. But there will always be good books around for those of us who need them. We will write and publish them for one another if need be, a few good books for us to carry around like amulets, or to line our walls like bullion, to expand our homes, or even, in desperate moments, to consign to the flames in primitive rituals of purgation and catharsis. And for those hours when the bookstore and library are closed, when nothing between covers calls out from the bookshelves, there will be a million other books too, just a mouse click away.

Printed or not, books open windows on our souls; they bring in new air. And this – this is what books are good for. They remind us to breathe, and to breathe more deeply. They help us to stay alive.

Indefensible

On some mornings the engine is cold and hard to get started. On some mornings I stand at my desk and ask myself why I should even bother to sit down, why should I spend another five or six hours pounding the keys. Yet I sit. I always sit.

Still, I frequently wonder what it is that drives me to spend several hours every day writing, as I have done for nearly every day of the past fifty years. Why do I feel that a day without writing is a wasted day?

I was not yet twenty-one when two different men – both with the credentials to suggest they knew what they were talking about what – pointed out to me that I had a talent for writing and storytelling. I, theretofore clueless as to the path my life should take, immediately seized upon their observation and resolved to make my life as a writer.

It made sense: I had always been a reader and had been making up stories since but a newt to entertain myself and the neighborhood kids. Writers, without my ever having recognized it, were my heroes. So, at least in the beginning of my career, I was motivated by a desire to join that lofty pantheon. And though my opinion of writers as a group has taken some dents, my own ambition after twenty-six books, critical acclaim, and a basket full of literary awards has flagged from time to time but has never come to a complete halt. How to account for such insatiable masochism?

I was never driven to writing, or to anything else, by a lust for fame. In fact, one of the strongest appeals of the writing profession is that it is a solitary art. I can remain as anonymous as I wish. I did hope, for the first twenty or so years, that writing would be more financially remunerative than it has been, but great wealth was never a goal either. All I hoped for was a comfortable life for myself and family. Yet when that goal was achieved only erratically, I continued to be faithful to the discipline. And I do recognize the folly in that, just as a man who is repeatedly cuckolded by his lover yet refuses to cut her loose must recognize his own folly.

So I must assume, though I am only guessing here, that my motivation lies at the root of who I am. I am still that little boy who loved to make up stories and loved to read and watch them. Nobody has ever offered to pay me to read books or watch TV and movies, jobs eminently easier than knocking off a hundred thousand words every year, or else I would be so employed. But still, a question arises: Why do I love storytelling so much?

The answer to that question hides out at the cellular level, I think. To begin a tantalizing story, as either a writer or reader, is to venture into the unknown. Where will I end up? What will I discover there? And what will I learn over the course of the journey?

Ah, yes. The lure of the unknown. The seduction of what is unproven, not yet suspected or gleaned, not yet experienced. I love the challenge of it, the titillation of surprise. Ask me to choose between a fine dinner at a restaurant where the chef knows precisely how I prefer my steak or a dinner at an unknown restaurant where the food will either have me swooning with delight or vomiting into a bucket, and I will choose the latter. I have made that choice numerous times, and will so again. My tolerance for repetition is low and my failure rate is high, but I don't mind failure. Failure is often the best teacher. Failure can be its own revelation.

The opposite of risk averse, I am and always have been giddily foolhardy. It's the unknown and unpredictable that beckon to me, the Siren's call, the path untraveled, the sketchy and improbable, the fanciful and absurd. Over the course of my lifetime I have turned down three offers of tenure, one as a senior editor at a weekly newspaper, another as a factory foreman, and a few others as a salaried cog in the greasy wheel of commerce. And for what? A tenuous, frustrating, capricious life as an underpaid storyteller.

But is even that enough motivation, the pleasure derived from thumbing one's nose at convention and practicality, of marching to the fibrillating beat of one's own drum? Enough for a few years of effort, sure, but a lifetime? No. I have quit the profession of writing several times. Cried *no mas! no mas!* to the pummeling I was taking. Yet, within a day or so, I always picked up the pen again. There must be another reason, some motivation scarcely visible and nearly inexpressible, for why I cannot quit.

Ask any scientist in the world, whether strict materialist or mind-soaring quantum theorist, how brain chemicals and electrical charges create a poem, or a song, or fictitious characters that will move others to tears or laughter or an examination of one's own soul, and that scientist, after maybe fumbling and groping philosophically for a beat or two, will concede this: Nobody knows. Nobody has any idea how the creative mind works.

When an idea pops into my head from out of nowhere, when the image of a character fully formed appears in my mind's eye, when I hear or read a casual phrase that suddenly sparks a whole new world in me – where does all that come from? I have populated hundreds of worlds by now, thousands of characters in novels and stories and poems and plays and screenplays. With a few million words – which are nothing more than arbitrary symbols given meaning though a consensus of our culture – I have put those characters through hell then brought them back into the light. They have loved and laughed and despaired and wondered because of me. They have lived and died in places I have visited and known as well as in places I have never seen or have made up out of thin air. And they have become so real in their fabricated worlds that individuals in *this* fabricated world were moved to tears and laughter and love by them, have cheered them on, worried for them, applauded for them, and have taken them into their homes and hearts.

What a miracle that is!

There is no logic to it. No practicality. No justification. And I like that about writing. It's indefensible and inexplicable. And for that reason, I find far more exhilaration and fulfillment in the unlikely endeavor than I have found in any other.

Reading, Writing, & Teaching Fiction That Matters

Why reading is good for the bottom line

Not long ago I read that a group of business leaders had concluded that the most valuable personal quality among employees is empathy. Their implication was that empathy is in short supply in the world of business, and that their businesses suffer from this dearth. In short, they concluded, without actually expressing this conclusion, that long-term productivity and profit are inextricably linked to empathy.

Business success and a sense of shared humanity entwined? Capitalism and morality in a symbiotic relationship? A GNP that can rise or fall according to the nation's empathy barometer? What a startling and revolutionary notion!

Well, it's not revolutionary to those of us who have long recognized the not easily quantifiable rewards of a liberal arts education – a system of education once commonly viewed as the ideal until kicked off its pedestal in 1987 by Gordon Gecko's short-sighted pronouncement that "Greed is good." Greed, of course, is a component of ego, and ego is at odds with empathy.

The current business leaders who admit to recognizing the hole in the soul of corporate America are to be commended for exposing the truth. Like the innocent child in *The Emperor's New Clothes* who cried out, "But he isn't wearing anything at all!" they have forced others to see a starkly unpleasant image.

Unfortunately, they were at a loss as to how to identify empathy in a new recruit, or how to teach empathy so as to make it part of every new graduate's skill set. Surprisingly, not one of them mentioned the reading of fiction as a possible fix.

In a recent Internet health blog, journalist Lisa Collier Cool summarized the findings of several research studies as to the benefits of reading. The research, reported in *The New York Times* and *USA Today*, and originally published in *Plos One*, *Neurology*, *Creative Research Journal*, and the journal Proceedings of the National Academy of Science, was conducted at The New School for Social Research, the Institute of Education of London, Brigham Young University, Case Western Reserve University School of Medicine, The University of Sussex, and The University of Toronto. The conclusions reached by these studies were, in a word, overwhelming:

- children who read perform better in tests of vocabulary, spelling, and math skills;
- reading can enhance growth and healing in children;
- reading can enhance creativity and open-mindedness;
- reading can slow mental decline and memory loss;
- reading fiction can increase empathy and social perception of the mental states of others; and,
- increased empathy will, in turn, increase one's longevity.

In other words, if you want healthy, creative, intelligent, open-minded, and empathetic employees, hire bookworms.

But, you ask, how do we identify these people?

Empathy is not at all difficult to identify, not even in a twenty-minute interview session. A question of two will easily reveal the absence or presence of empathy in the interviewee (provided the interviewer is empathetic enough to discern it).

You might ask, for example, "If Bartleby the Scrivener were alive today, how would he view our society?" Or, "Do you know anyone who behaves like Rabbit Angstrom, and, if so, how do you feel about that person?" Or even, "Name two novels that were important to your growth as an individual, and do your best to explain why they were important to you."

There is no doubt that any of these questions will give most business graduates pause. They will give pause to most individuals, whether right or left-brain dominant. In every case, though, the response will be edifying.

Unfortunately, in today's America, most bookworms are also introverts. And introverts comprise only a quarter or so of the population. Plus, introverts would rather poke themselves in the eye than to engage in the kind of social interaction necessary for success in the corporate world.

The question for that world then becomes not *how do we keep all our employees from poking themselves in the eye all day long?* but *how do we fill our ranks with personable individuals who also read a lot?*

Earlier in our country's history, Great Books programs flourished in our universities and colleges. Reading lists were a part of every curriculum, a prerequisite for every graduate. Those institutions' administrators thought of themselves more as educators than as bean counters, and they understood that whatever other professional skills were developed in their students, none was as important, none as influential on every aspect of human endeavor, as the sensitization of the human psyche. They understood what so much of our current information-spewing, profit-grabbing, status-seeking society has chosen to forget: that the heart of education is the education of the heart.

Unfortunately, this amnesia is no longer limited to the business world. Even as the business world is slowly awakening to its myopia, the business of education is succumbing to its own form of blindness.

Slip-slidin'away: Why our students can't write

In my nearly thirty or so years of teaching everything from remedial freshman comp to advanced creative writing, I have been approached by several students who attempted to bribe me for a grade they didn't deserve. Others who were not my students but knew that I am a writer wanted to hire me to write a paper for them. I've been offered everything from dinner to money to sex. When the bribes failed, the students played on my compassion or tried to shame me into complying. *You have no idea what my parents will do to me if I fail this course! I'll lose my athletic scholarship! I'll lose my financial aid and it will be your fault when I do!*

The lack of basic writing competence in the average student in higher education never fails to stagger and sadden me. A recent article in the *Chronicle of Higher Education*, authored by an employee of an online company that provides completed student papers from freshman to graduate level, all written to order for a fee, should stagger and sadden every individual who reads it. Cheating is rampant. And much too easy to accomplish.

The truth is clear: Our students come to college with substandard writing and communication skills. Too frequently they graduate from college with little improvement in those skills. This can only happen when the skills themselves are not valued – when only the grades are valued.

Fortunately, a remedy for this epidemic exists. And the sooner in one's life the remedy is applied, the more complete the remedy will be.

Do you ever wonder why America's literacy rate lags behind that of Cuba, Latvia, Lithuania, Slovenia, Tonga, Azerbaijan, and over a dozen other countries? Ever wonder why South Korea's high school graduation rate is a full twenty percent higher than the United States'? Ever wonder why this country's average IQ ranks 29th in the entire world?

I am convinced that the answer to helping students become better writers and readers is much simpler than non-writers, and especially school administrators, are willing to admit.

Writing is a skill that cannot be taught by lecture, nor assessed and graded by computer. Grammatical and spelling errors can be caught by computer programs, but those elements play only a small part in good writing. And some of the best writing deliberately breaks the rule of grammar.

My perspective as not only a teacher of writing but also as a successful professional writer is that there are no right or wrong ways to write, there is only effective or less than effective writing. Successful teaching of writing depends on, at the least, small group instruction, or, at best, one-on-one interaction between the student writer and the instructor. Only when I sit with a student and show her why this sentence works or what makes that phrase murky or why this paragraph is unfocused – only then does the light bulb flare on for her. Increasingly, however, administrators attempt to cut costs with solutions that erode effective teaching and shortchange the students themselves.

When I first began teaching writing at the university level in the late 80s, each class had an average of 18-20 students – still too many for an ideal writing class, but manageable. I was able to give each manuscript a few minutes of personal attention each week, enough that I could pinpoint for the writer some particular strengths and weaknesses. My most recent undergraduate writing class had an official maximum of thirty students, each one turning in a new draft every week, and a completely new piece of work every three weeks. By the second assignment, I was so buried in manuscripts that I would not see daylight again until the semester's end. Even with extended office hours I was unable to give each of my 120 students and the three drafts of each of their five assigned papers (that's approximately 5000 pages of work to read, line edit, and critique) more than a few minutes of personal attention each semester. Some assignments were not seen by me more than once during the three-draft process, and a few not until the final draft was turned in – which meant that the student was guided only by those few bits of instruction conveyable by lecture and by the editorial insights of her peers, many of whom provided less than insightful advice.

Considering the lack of preparation and the abysmal writing skills my freshmen, upper classmen, and even my MFA students bring to our first class meetings, I can only assume that elementary and secondary school English teachers are facing the same dilemma.

Yet there is another reason why our students cannot write proficiently and are unlikely to learn how to write proficiently unless current methods of teaching writing are amended. The problem is not due to computers or TV or popular culture. Emailing and texting and tweeting are all forms of communication, each with its particular language demands, and the differences between these forms of communication can easily be learned by students, just as an observant and disciplined writer can easily learn the different demands of poetry, screenwriting, and writing for the stage.

Our students can't write proficiently because, from pre-school through college, they are no longer expected to read the finest examples of writing available for their grade level. Frustrated middle and high school teachers, forced to teach an overcrowded class of students from the entire spectrum of reading levels, have no choice but to teach to the lowest level, which means hauling out the Easy Readers and graphic novels instead of exposing those students to the galvanizing power and beauty of finely-crafted stories and poetry and plays. I have witnessed the consequences of this kind of politically correct insanity in every college writing class I have ever taught.

Fully fifty percent of my MFA students lack the basic grammar competency that was required to pass ninth grade English in my rural high school back in 1965. And these are students who fully expect to become writing teachers themselves, especially if their dream of becoming a best-selling writer doesn't pan out.

At least as many of these MFA students not only admit to having never read a book by Hemingway, Steinbeck, Faulkner, Flannery O'Connor, Joan Didion, Norman Mailer, Russell Banks, Andre Dubus, Margaret Atwood, or García Márquez, but also admit that they have never even heard of Dos Passos, Umberto Eco, Richard Yates, Harper Lee, William Gass, Stanley Elkin, Knut Hamsun, Heinrich Boll, Jim Harrison, Phillip K. Dick, Albert Camus, Kate Chopin, Joseph Conrad, D. H. Lawrence, Katherine Mansfield, and dozens of other essential literary masters. These aspiring writers might have seen the movie "The Color Purple" but have never read the novel. They recognize both the name of the author and the book's title character but have never actually read *The Adventures of Huckleberry Finn*. They know the phrase "catch-22" but have no idea that there is a brilliantly acerbic novel of the same name. Nor do they know what *acerbic* means.

Good things happen when students are regularly exposed to excellent writing throughout the course of their education. First, they acquire essential grammatical skills by repeatedly reading examples of correctly punctuated and precisely expressed syntax. Secondly, they learn – by the same kind of osmosis as they learn to speak and sing – how to manipulate voice and tone and rhythm and pacing of their writing for the desired effect. Thirdly, these students broaden their exposure to humanity itself, and in so doing acquire a more extensive catalog of options as to what constitutes humane conflict resolution and what does not. In other words, when they become immersed in the lives of others through literature, they acquire a greater depth of understanding, even compassion, for these characters, and, by extension, for all of humanity. They develop *empathy*.

Fiction and drama, among all genres of writing, best accomplish these results. Not many individuals have the means or opportunity to regularly enjoy dramatic performances, however, but nearly everyone has access to a never-ending supply of good fiction, whether from their schools and libraries, online, or at the local bookstore.

Unfortunately, these benefits from reading excellent fiction require a return to a demand for excellence from elementary, secondary, and university students – a demand that has become next to impossible for teachers to make. Today, school administrators at all levels are abdicating their role as educators concerned with providing quality education and instead are retreating to the role of miserly bean counters who rely on the easy fixes of cramming too many students into one classroom, and of increasing instructors' course loads, thereby stripping the writing instructor of the opportunity for the individual interaction with a student that would affect a meaningful improvement in the students' writing skills.

At the same time, public universities in many states, my own home state included, are cutting programs and whole departments that do not lead directly to a specific job currently in demand. In a misguided attempt to cut costs and attract more students, public universities that once took pride in producing thoughtful, well-informed, empathetic individuals sensitive to the entire range of the human condition are hurrying to convert themselves into vo-tech schools that turn out worker bees with a very narrow set of skills.

Whether this solution is advocated by a governor, a Congressperson, a university president, provost, chancellor, dean, district superintendent, principal, or school board, it is a mindlessly lazy, irresponsible, and short-sighted decision that can only hasten the downhill slide of literacy and overall educational quality in this country.

And just what do our children's declining reading and writing skills have to do with empathy in the business world? And what place do either of these considerations have in an essay about reading, writing, and teaching fiction?

Like fever, nausea, lassitude, and other symptoms of the swine flu, they are all related, and all are indicative of a dangerous pandemic illness.

Read a good story and call me in the morning

Henry Skolimowski, author of *The Participatory Mind*, argues that a more peaceful and harmonic society can emerge only when society begins to value those virtues more than it values individual and often exclusionary rewards. Building a peaceful, harmonic society is a lovely idea, and maybe even possible a few hundred years down the road if our mental and spiritual faculties can ever develop sufficiently to lift us out of our swamp of me-ism. For now, in a world where capitalism is still our best and fairest option for the pursuit of happiness, a quicker path would be to embrace the moral capitalism advocated by Michael Novak in his address to President Bush's 2002 Economic Forum.

As Novak pointed out in that address, compassion and empathy toward shareholders, and toward the American public in general, is a sound business practice. People are unlikely to invest in a company if that company is known for unethical practices.

However, even an argument as rational and commonsensical as that one is unlikely to evoke a sense of morality in individuals who lack empathy. Morality is a consequence of compassion, and compassion arises from being able to see one's self in another person's shoes, which is the essence of empathy. It would be naive to expect individuals schooled only in the truths of percentages and formulas to decide suddenly that profits matter less than the manner in which they accrue.

Unless....

Unless the individuals making those decisions have undergone a subtle alchemy of perspective, one they were not even aware of, because it has been taking place ever since they first held a book in their hands.

Of all the ways to improve writing skills, and to do so with an absence of onerous grammar exercises and boring prescriptive rules, and to do so in a way that is actually enjoyable and entertaining, and in a way that actually alters the structure of the brain by creating more neurons and synapses that will make the individual more informed, more intelligent, more articulate, a clearer thinker and better communicator, none is more effective than a lifetime of reading good fiction.

Of all the ways we humans can be sensitized to the plights of others, can be made less cynical and more compassionate, less selfish and more altruistic, less divisive and more inclusive, less intolerant and more embracing of our differences, the least painful way is through stories.

------ ⌒⌒ ------

Stories and storytellers have always existed. They are as old as language itself. Human beings crave stories. Back in 1998, in an article I wrote for *Fiction Writer* magazine, I espoused my belief that the human need for a "well-told story is a genetic need. It's written on our DNA. We need models of behavior that are a remedy to chaos. The human psyche, if it is to persevere day after day through the bog of violence and greed and deception that is American life, requires reassurance."

And not only reassurance, but affirmation. Options. A window into a world larger than our own, while also being a window into the depths of ourselves, into the realization, as I wrote last year in an essay for *The Chronicle of Higher Education*, that each of us is "not one lone cell stranded in the desolation of the world, but one of eight billion cells conjoined by the world, all hearts echoing the others in the song of one enormous heart."

If we have any hope of fostering a society, and a world, that values peace over conquest, cooperation over dominance, people over technology, acceptance over division, and free and open communication over politically correct censorship, we have to develop educational strategies that emphasize these values and their very real rewards. But how do we reverse an educational system that is already a long way down the wrong path?

In an economy-driven society, education will change only when employers start seeking out and hiring individuals who have been taught to possess a wider range of knowledge and skills. If today's business world lacks empathy, and many business leaders now recognize that it does, employers need only know where to find more empathetic employees. Which brings us right back to where we started: back to fiction that matters.

———

When you toss out a phrase such as "fiction that matters," you had better be able to explain what you mean by that phrase. This is especially true in our country's current culture of "you either agree with me or you are my enemy and need to be silenced" – or especially irrelevant, depending on your inclination.

You might argue, for example, that a poorly written but best-selling erotic romance matters because of the titillation and enjoyment it gives to millions of readers. And you would be correct. Reading done for pleasure does matter. But for the purposes of this argument, it matters on the same level that a play-off game between the Ravens and the Steelers matters. Not only do both events provide a few hours of pleasure to their respective audiences, but they also provide economic enrichment to everyone involved in producing those events.

On the other hand, perhaps you believe that art is mankind's way of reaching for something noble in ourselves, a way of stretching our imaginations toward a consciousness of self that might one day justify and give meaning to our existence.

So let's start there, with an assumption that fiction can matter on a plane of significance higher than mere entertainment and diversion from life's banality, and that the creative impulse behind it is not as attenuated as a snapshot of our society might suggest. The term "serious fiction" has also been used to describe such writing, but the word "serious" gives the definition a weighty, even leaden feel to it, as if to warn that this fiction won't be fun to read but it will be good for you, a kind of cod liver oil squeezed from the juice of bitter words.

The term "literary fiction" is no more optimistic; in our bottom-line publishing industry, it can be the kiss of death. I learned never to use the term when pitching a manuscript to a former agent, because the response was inevitable: "My eyes just rolled to the back of my head."

And how many nonacademic readers are likely to get excited about a fiction called "literary"? When even agents and editors scurry to get out of range of the term, and instead latch onto buzzwords like "upmarket" that don't set their eyes to rolling quite so violently, perhaps the time has come to lay "literary" to rest. Perhaps the best reason to do so, however, is because of the snobbery too often inherent to the term. There has become no more exclusionary term in publishing than "literary," and, like all forms of exclusion, this one is unfair and short-sighted, for reasons to be considered a bit further along in this essay.

In the meantime, we might even use here the term "fiction that lasts," as Hemingway did in his famous *Paris Review* interview. But that term, when I first read it as a young man, gave rise to the question, "But Ernie, what makes fiction last?" And the answer is, "It lasts because it matters." So now, of course, having chased our tail back to where we started, we have to inquire, "But what makes fiction matter?"

The truth is that fiction can matter but fail to last because, in this very crowded field of print and digital publications, and in this increasingly semi-literate society we live in, serious, distinctive, original, and meaningful fiction has a more difficult time finding an audience than does more titillating and predictable work. The trick, for those of us who care, is to find a balance between serious and popular fiction, a reconciliation of the marriage that Norman Mailer pronounced dead some four decades ago.

And so, still at the beginning: "What makes fiction matter?" It matters because, perhaps, it will be read down through the generations, but more importantly it matters because, through its construction and intent, such fiction provides more than a momentary titillation; it makes possible a deep connection between writer and readers. Additionally, it is the vehicle for a singular view and take on the world, a view that is singularly and compellingly expressed, and which concerns itself more with the exploration of significant questions than with the posture of easy cynicism and the positing of easy answers.

Fiction that matters is not about the physical events that happen in a story – the inciting incident, the quest for treasure or success or love, the plot reversal, the climactic confrontation with opposing forces, and the resolution. We call these events the plot, and plot is important because it keeps the reader reading, and, if handled properly, provides a kind of emotional satisfaction that feels true and genuine to the reader, and consequently incites the reader to want more of the same. I would argue that plot is essential if one wishes to craft a compelling and memorable story.

But plot, the external events of a story, is not what makes fiction matter. Plot is a tool. It is the locomotive that pulls the cars. It is the crane that lifts the building stones into place. It is the shovel that uncovers the buried treasure.

Plot is the device that subjects the main characters to conflict, and in so doing forces those characters to examine their own hearts, and in so doing opens up *our* hearts and souls to those characters struggling for meaning and understanding.

And that, coupled with a distinctive and seductive voice, another of the author's tools, is what makes fiction matter. Fiction that matters is not about what happens in the plot, it is about what happens in the characters as a result of the plot. And, consequently, what happens in the reader.

I am not going to demean any writer's work here by comparing specific examples of writing that matters with writing that matters not so much. It is my belief that all writers strive to write to the best of their ability. Even those who deliberately write by formula, with little concern for the beauty of language or how it conveys the protagonist's transformational journey, write out of a love for story and the desire to craft the best story they can. These books are not written to matter. They are written to provide a few hours of distraction from the harshness or tedium of life, and then to be left behind on the beach or the bus seat. They are as memorable as a potato chip. And, ultimately, just as nutritional.

Fiction that matters is more sumptuous fare. It is the only kind of fiction that can satisfy the hunger of existence. Yes, it too provides a temporary satisfaction, but also a cumulative one. I am old enough now to have my mailbox stuffed with flyers and pamphlets from AARP, and if asked to compile a list of the books that have sustained me through those twenty thousand days and nights, the list would be a long one. No single volume was capable of providing all the nourishment required to keep the heart beating from birth till now, but each one left its taste upon my tongue. Each added its rhythms to the sometimes clenching, sometimes gasping, occasionally laughing beat of my heart.

Fiction that matters changes us, one story at a time, one novel at a time. Each piece executes an incremental increase in our understanding of and appreciation for what it means to be a human being.

That is why we read fiction that matters and why we write it, and why we must teach it to those younger hearts that have not yet found their rhythm. We must awaken those young hearts, again and again and again, to the startling beauty of words and sentences carefully wrought, and to those invisible yet unbreakable threads that tie us all to the characters created by those words. We must help our children and our students to experience the very real emotion produced by imagined lives, the desires and needs and fears and impulses that bind all characters with all readers regardless of ethnicity or gender. We must let literature do its work on them year after year, shaping and stretching their DNA, providing it with the elasticity to endure life's blows without hardening, and to withstand the storms of life without being uprooted, and to survive the tides of time without eroding or being pounded into the sand.

The goal of literature, of fiction that matters, is nothing short of the Philosopher's Stone. The ultimate goal of fiction that matters is a transformation of the soul of mankind, a transformation that must take place a single soul at a time. The chemistry for this transformation is not the least bit arcane. Transformation requires only a steady application of tears and smiles, the indigo midnight ache of loss, the tangerine sunrise ache of love.

Hey, teacher, leave that kid alone!

Where high school and college literature classes go wrong – and sometimes fiction writing classes do too – is in trying to reduce a story to its meaning. The meaning of a story *is* the story, the experience of the story and the emotion generated from that experience. If every scene and every sentence and every word of a story is essential to the rendering of that experience and to the evocation of those feelings, then how would it be possible to reduce a story to a line or two of abstract summarization supposed to convey the entirety of the story experience? It isn't. But teachers resort to asking, "What is the theme of this story?" because it is so much more difficult and time consuming to ask twenty-five students, "How did you experience this story?"

And many students are uncomfortable with this kind of question. They prefer to answer, "The theme of this story is the indifferent brutality of nature," rather than to spend five minutes analyzing their discomfort at various moments in the story, their rising fear and finally their sense of dread or joy with the resolution. They would rather not talk about how they see themselves as the main character, how they see his poor choices as a reflection of their own incompetence. They would rather not talk about the way this story makes them fearful of the world outside their little rooms, because what happened to the hero in this story could happen to them if they are not very careful. And they would rather not talk about the secret sense of glee they feel when the hero dies in a slow agony. Or the hope they are given when, against all odds, the surviving lover takes comfort in her memories of love shared. They would rather write in their essay books, "The theme of this story is the indifferent brutality of nature" and receive five points for their answer and an A for the course. And the teacher would rather grade that answer than to struggle with twenty-five booklets filled with painful self-analysis that defies assessment by grade or by any standard but the standard of the heart.

How, then, do we teach stories? Certainly not by lecture. If it is a writing course, we ask, "What words in this description of weather establish the mood of the scene and signal the protagonist's emotions?" We ask, "How does the main character's dialogue in this scene convey the barrenness of her heart?" We consider what the writer has done and how she has done it. If we are teaching a literature class, we ask, "What do you think of the choice the character made in this scene?" or "Why was this ending inevitable for her?"

In writing classes we should examine technique. In literature classes, choices and their consequences.

We mislead students when we ask, "What is the theme of this story?" Ask any writer to tell you the theme of his story and, after he struggles for an answer, he will tell you, or want to, "Stories don't have themes, they have lives. So tell me the theme of your life, and I will tell you the theme of my story."

What makes the teaching of stories so problematic for non-writers is the discomfort many students and teachers alike feel when publicly exposing their inner selves. But this is precisely what a story does. It lays lives bare for our examination. It denudes at least one character in every story, strips away not only the costumes and masks but also the skin and bone and musculature and tissue, leaving visible what no anatomist, no matter how skillful, can expose. The soul of that man, that woman, that character. And why does a story do this? So that we can experience what that denuded character experienced, and then consider our own souls denuded in the mirrors of our minds.

The power of literature is not invoked by asking students to memorize titles and dates of composition, or to match characters with titles, or to summarize in so many words the author's theme. The power of literature lies in asking readers to look carefully at the characters' decisions and to see in those actions their own lives and their own decisions. Literature is one of the most potent tools for personal alchemy our kind possesses.

Finally, I would also argue that fiction that matters is fiction that examines the consequences of mankind's narcissistic and destructive behavior, on both the micro and the macro levels. Fiction that matters to this materialistic, consumer-driven society we find ourselves in should provide evidence of the shortsightedness of revering progress over nature, ambition over cooperation, self-aggrandizement over equality. The power of literature lies not in its authentic portrayal of life as it is, but in its subtle yet insistent suggestion that we can and should strive to be better at who and what we are.

A society whose members feel no concern for the welfare of others, or who feel outright contempt for those who fail to conform to an arbitrary norm, has ceased to be a society. The connective tissue has dissolved. That society might give every appearance of still being whole, a complete body, but inside its bag of skin the bones no longer work together. The right hand is busy raking in all the gold it can reach while the left hand is counting out coupons at the grocery store. The right foot is kicking in a stranger's door while the left foot is struggling to keep the door closed. The right eye is scanning the employment ads while the left eye is peering through the neighbor's curtains.

Now try to imagine a society in which, at every instance of human interaction, empathy is the most immediate response among all parties involved. Impossible, you say?

According to two separate studies published in *Science* and *PLOS One*, readers of fiction, and especially of fiction that matters, enjoy an enhanced level of empathy and insight into the mental states of others. Researchers David Kidd and Emanuele Castanoe state in "Reading Literary Fiction Improves Theory of Mind" that reading fiction leads to "better performance on tests of affective ToM," i.e. the ability to understand others' mental states, "and cognitive ToM compared with reading nonfiction, popular fiction, or nothing at all."

Researchers Matthijs Bal and Martijn Veltkamp, in their article "How Does Fiction Reading Influence Empathy?" concluded that "imaginative processes, evoked by fictional narrative experience, make people more empathic," and that "the effects of fiction on empathy...manifest themselves over time."

The more you read, the more empathy you feel and display toward others. The more you read, the better you become at writing and communicating. The more you read, the better you become at math, the quicker you will heal, the less memory loss you will suffer, and the longer you will live. Reading fiction that matters, it seems, will make you a better person. So when Mark Twain observed that the person who can read but doesn't is no better off than the person who can't read, he understated the problem. The truth is this: the person who can read but doesn't has no one to blame but himself for failing to become a better person.

What's it all about, Alfie?

Fiction matters when, through the quality of its voice, the insightful portrayal of its characters and settings, the sensitive and wholly credible resolution of its conflicts, and the transformation, whether nuanced or conspicuous, of one or more characters, the story engenders in its reader a subtle deepening of one's empathy with the human condition.

Any individual who has made the acquisition of wealth or fame or power the driving force of his life, only to watch his child, parent, spouse, or friend succumb to an illness or accident nobody's wealth or power or fame could assuage, has surely come to recognize the ultimate impotence of those acquisitions. All but the most resolute of narcissists and sociopaths among us will sooner or later come to that recognition. Life will see to that.

What is life all about? is a question we will all ask at some point in our lives, and should ask every day.

Fiction that matters asks that question for us. And in the asking, it also provides the only answer available. Fiction that matters reminds us to care.

The Hell Called 'The Mall'

For many authors, including me, making a personal appearance is an energy-draining affair. I have participated in such appearances at least a hundred times over the years. Readings, group book signings, individual book signings, library appearances, Q&As, lectures, panel discussions – every type imaginable. In addition to the emotional and psychical toll these appearances take on writers, there is often a significant financial toll as well. Publishers seldom assist writers in the cost of attending such events in order to promote a new book, the promotion of which helps the publisher as much as, if not more than, it helps the writer. Other venues, too, including libraries, small universities, and community events, offer no monetary compensation, not even travel expenses; often they assume they are providing a benefit to the author, who should be happy to give away his time and expertise.

What many of these event planners do not realize is that a one-hour appearance by a writer will derail that writer's entire day. Preparation, apprehension, rescheduling of family events, rescheduling of writing habits and the necessary self-discipline of maintaining those habits – it is all disruptive and often upsetting. And that is why I now limit myself, as I have done with few exceptions for the past thirty years, to only three types of personal appearances.

The first are publisher-funded appearances, and especially to those that put me in front of a large audience of booksellers. These are very beneficial appearances because I am pitching a book not to an individual book buyer but to a few hundred individuals, each of whom will promote my book to thousands of potential book buyers.

The second type of personal appearance I am willing to consider is an individual book signing or reading or a presentation and Q&A to a sizable audience that has come to the event for the express purpose of listening to the author talk about his/her work, and/or to purchase an autographed copy.

Here the term "sizable audience" is flexible. If I have to drive three miles to the local library for an appearance, ten book lovers is enough. If I have to drive a hundred miles to speak to an audience of thirty, I will need expense money plus a promise that most of those thirty attendees will purchase a book. If I have to fly somewhere, and the event is not underwritten by my publisher, compensation for travel and overnight accommodations must be part of the deal plus $750-$2000 as remuneration for the loss of up to three days of work and time with my family.

It has always puzzled me why venues so often expect an author to work for free. Even the most mediocre of corporate speakers will receive thousands of dollars to present a day's workshop, but authors are often expected to speak to multiple classes full of writing aspirants for nothing but a meal of rubbery chicken and lumpy mashed potatoes.

The worst type of author appearance by far, however, is the kind held in a mall. These appearances range from the least offensive to the most: from the mall bookstore appearance to a full-blown writers' conference held in the mall's main hallway.

The first kind can be commercially successful for both the bookstore and the author but typically benefits only the bookstore. Success for the author depends on how well the event has been advertised by the bookstore, and how many patrons actually show up to hear the author read and answer questions. I have read for an audience of two and an audience of fifty in mall bookstores; most audiences fail to achieve double digits.

The writers' conference type of mall appearance is nothing short of brutal and defeating for most authors. Out of the dozen or so writers asked to speak at such an event, only the keynote speaker will have long lines of individuals waiting to purchase his or her book while the other authors in attendance are ignored.

I refuse to ever do another mall appearance. There is nothing more demeaning to an author than to sit in front of a stack of books while answering again and again the question, "What's your book about?" to people who have come to the mall only to buy a new pair of Skechers or a cheesesteak from Charleys. Those writers, and I was one of them a few times, will end up selling only one or two books and exchanging a few more for books by the other writers who also spent the day selling next to none.

The third type of mall appearance, and the only one I will participate in, is the guerrilla appearance. Unannounced, and often wearing sunglasses and a ball cap, I will enter the mall bookstore without notice and peruse the shelves for copies of my books. I always find some. I will then carry one or more of those books to the information center or checkout counter and ask, "Would you like me to sign my books while I'm here?"

The element of surprise is very effective in these situations. More than once the store manager or an assistant has pulled every copy of my books off the shelves and out of the back room, then stood by smiling as I signed them. What makes this guerilla strategy productive is that autographed books cannot be returned to the publisher. Once signed, they are as good as sold.

There are always those few authors who will trip over themselves for any chance to talk about their work. No venue is ever turned down, no audience too small. In an age when digital promotion reaches far more potential readers than in-place promotion, I find this behavior difficult to understand other than to suspect it is fueled more by ego than by dedication to the craft.

Those of us who view self-promotion with disdain as a sometimes necessary evil will come home from such events drained of energy and wanting only to crawl into bed for a few days with the covers pulled over our heads. And the only thing that will bring us out of that funk is to crawl to the desk, take our chair once again, and write until the stink of self-promotion begins to fade.

By Jove, I Think I've Got It!

Ah, the epiphany. The moment of grace. The *kenshō* experience, the awakening, the lightning bolt, that *aha! eureka! holy crap!* sudden flash of insight and understanding.

For this reader, good fiction is all about that moment. All about the completion of the arc, the protagonist's journey from turmoil to self-awareness. In mainstream and literary fiction, the epiphany is essential if a designated character is to grow and change. Here the epiphany is often that moment when innocence is lost, when a character recognizes the cruelty or fragility of life, the certainty of death, the illusion of permanence, and so forth. In Hemingway's "My Old Man," a boy who has idolized his father hears other men talking disparagingly about the man, and he realizes that his perception of his perfect father has been wrong. The exact opposite happens in Tobias Wolfe's wonderful short story "Powder," when a boy realizes that his father is not the narcissistic incompetent his ex-wife has made him out to be.

One of my favorite epiphanies is the one that must have been experienced by novelist Graham Greene (and which serves as the introduction to my forthcoming novel *The Deepest Black*), who wrote in an essay, "Human nature is not black and white but black and grey."

In some plot-driven fiction, and especially in series fiction, no such moment is required, since the emphasis of the story is not on character growth but on the completion of the plot, whether it is the consummation of a romance, the salvation of humanity from an asteroid, an alien attack, or an epidemic. But even then the epiphany can come into play: the haggard neuroscientist, ready to throw in the towel and let all of humanity succumb to brain-eating parasites, suddenly realizes that the parasites can be rendered impotent by activating the pineal gland to release a squirt of psilocybin.

In murder mysteries, the final outcome, the identification of the murderer, often comes thanks to a variation of the epiphany, the investigator's sudden remembrance of an overlooked clue, the casual but incriminating remark. This is the hunch, the vibe, the little voice in the head, the shiver up the spine. It is a way of knowing something without knowing how you know it. You just do. Crime solved.

Epiphanies in genre fiction, however, do seem to have greater influence on the story's plot than on the main character's self-awareness. For my Ryan DeMarco mystery series, I wanted both – a continuing arc of growth through all five books for DeMarco, plus a satisfying but unpredictable resolution for each of the five separate mysteries. The trick was in making all the epiphanies seem like natural and believable occurrences in two people striving to hold onto love throughout their drama- and stress-filled lives.

We all have had these sudden, inexplicable insights. They are an essential part of growing up, of learning, maturing, and coming to a clearer understanding of ourselves and the world. In life, most of our epiphanies are small, but that doesn't mean that they are unimportant. They influence our decisions, and those decisions change our lives, sometimes for better, and sometimes, when the epiphanies are false, for worse. But even from the false epiphanies, something can be learned.

Originally the word *epiphany* referred to an insight sent from the divine; initiation rites in the ancient mystery religions were intended to produce spiritual epiphanies. In his *Poetics*, Aristotle termed that moment in a play when a character achieves a sudden understanding or crucial insight as *anagorosis*, and called the change of course brought about by that insight *peripetia*.

My favorite description of the epiphany comes from William Burrough's psychedelic *Naked Lunch*, in which the author describes the epiphany as "a frozen moment when everyone sees what is at the end of the fork."

Most of society will claim that these moments are whispers from the subconscious mind, attempts to bring the more limited conscious mind into the loop. Some will recognize them only as symptoms of mental illness, or, at best, as flights of the imagination. Others hold that these moments have a supernatural or otherwise outside source, and that they are a gift of encouragement, a reward to the receiver.

These latter insights are all generally positive ones, and a necessary first step to enlightenment. I have had a few of those too – sudden and unexpected realizations of the connection of all things, that the body as a solid object does not really exist, that nothing material exists, and that each of us is an integral part of that exquisite nothingness.

In fiction, a narrative overpopulated with epiphanies with no discernible cause-effect relationship to the protagonist's actions – otherwise known as coincidences – soon loses its credibility. To be credible, an epiphany must be earned. They shouldn't just pop up like moles in a game of Whack-a-Mole, but must be precipitated by a lot of leg work and head scratching, a lot of trying to piece together the puzzle at hand.

In this light, the epiphany can be seen as a kind of deductive logic – the last but least predictable step in a syllogism: "I know it sounds crazy, but look at this. Ninety-nine percent of the brain is mush. All except for the pineal gland; it's untouched in all six samples. It's almost as if the microbes are afraid of it. We already know that serotonin has no effect on them. So it has to be the DMT or psilocybin! What else can it be? Distribute magic mushrooms to everybody!"

In some fiction, it isn't the character who experiences the epiphany, but the reader. In these stories, the main character remains precisely the same person he or she was on page 1, but the reader, at the end of the story, nods and smiles to herself, understanding not only the story but herself or the world a tiny bit better.

To whomever the epiphany occurs, and however it occurs, the epiphany has been and will remain a hallmark of storytelling. The well-made story, as it used to be called, consists of a beginning, middle, and end, with each component contributing its essential elements, all building to the final resolution and, more often than not, culminating in a moment of greater self-awareness for the protagonist and/or the reader.

The non-conclusive story, disparagingly called the *New Yorker* type of story back in the heyday of minimalism, the kind of story in which nothing much happens and none of the characters evolve, still finds itself on the bookshelves now and then, but less and less frequently. And rightfully so.

Have you had your epiphany today?

The Silence that Speaks

I am not fond of being referred to as a crime writer or a mystery writer. Those words put the emphasis on a novel's plot, and I don't write plot-dominant stories. I write stories about the relationships between people, some of whom might be engaged in actions that include murder or another crime.

Crimes and their repercussions are a great way to put a character under maximum pressure. Under pressure, our true natures are revealed. And only through an examination of our true natures can we (and our fictional characters) grow and evolve. An unexamined life is not worth living or worth reading.

My goal with the Ryan DeMarco mystery series, for example, was to follow DeMarco on his own spiritual journey through a course of demanding events – whether murder investigations, romantic and other relationships, betrayals, losses, even brushes with death – that force him to assess not only his true nature but the true nature of reality. He is at an age when human beings do that kind of thing. Carl Jung called it the stage of Spirit, the fourth and final stage of life. It is when we realize that our lifetimes of accomplishments and our possessions are not all we are. We are more than that. In this stage we become the observers of our lives and learn to view life from a different perspective. These are the years of wisdom – if, indeed, we are equipped to receive it.

DeMarco is an inherently compassionate person, but for a long time his thoughts were filled with the noise of anger and guilt, which interferes with spiritual development. One of the most important things a person can do for him or herself is to mute that noise by cultivating the silence that speaks. In the novel series, with the help of Thomas Huston, Jayme, and his love of nature, DeMarco learns to listen to that silence. This is also an essential facility for any writer who hopes to produce more than merely escapist stories.

So what is the silence that speaks? None of the world's scientific geniuses has ever been able to explain how brain chemicals and electrical impulses produce ideas. That's because they don't. We know that the physical brain is somehow associated with consciousness – the mind and its infinite creativity – probably as a receiver of some kind, a filter and storage compartment. But we also know, from tens of thousands of documented and corroborated personal experiences, that an individual's consciousness can continue to function (often even more keenly) when the brain is clinically dead. So it is clear that the physical brain does not *create* ideas or any other facet of what we call consciousness. They originate from the silence that speaks, that vast reservoir of consciousness and creativity that permeates everything.

Einstein claimed that imagination is the highest human faculty. Max Planck, the father of quantum physics, was among the first contemporary scientists to understand that mind, i.e. consciousness, precedes and in fact creates the illusion of matter. J.K. Rowling, during a train ride, experienced a spontaneous flood of imagination that gave birth to the entire Harry Potter opus, the highest-selling fiction series in history. Spiritual masters from the beginning of time have been inspired and guided by knowledge that seemed to come to them out of the silence – out of what Buddhists call the no-thought, which is a mental state free of idle or discursive thoughts, often achieved through meditation, chanting, or breathing exercises. When the mind is sufficiently quiet, wisdom seeps in.

My best ideas have always come to me unbidden during some non-thinking activity, such as meditation, dreaming, washing the dishes, mowing the yard, walking in the woods, taking a shower, or riding my motorcycle. At such times, brain activity is low, especially in the neo-cortex, the reasoning, analyzing part of the brain – unless I am actively working on some concern or problem. Several studies show that low activity in that region of the brain is associated with heightened states of consciousness. That low activity mental state, called *wu-wei* by Taoists, allows us to "hear" inspiring whispers that might or might not have a relationship to personal experiences. This is the magic of creative thought. It often possesses some deeper, indescribable quality that will not yield to analysis or logic.

In my experience, more people fear silence than love it. What makes silence frightening is its aural semblance to emptiness, to impotence, to nothingness, to death. But silence is none of those things, and when you have come to love it and prefer it over its opposite you will see that silence is fullness, silence is everything at once, silence is the great connected ever-abiding all. But if you do not love silence, those words will mean nothing to you, they will be nonsense, just as all words are nonsense, are nothing, when you have learned to listen to silence with your heart and not your ego.

In *The Book of Embraces*, Uruguayan writer Eduardo Galeano introduced a word for that quality, coined by fisherman along the Colombian coast: *sentipensante*, the language that speaks the truth not through thinking, not through analysis and reason, but through feeling.

Love, I think, is *sentipensante*. As is joy. That exultant sense of gratitude and hope bequeathed by a sunrise or a star-filled night. That profound bond between a parent and child that cannot be articulated nor even understood unless one has experienced it.

This is the quality I sense every time the silence speaks. Not just the beauty of cadence and rhythm and image, which I attempt to build into my prose, but the beauty of an inexpressible truth. When Hemingway stated that the job of the writer is to write "one true sentence," this, I think, was what he meant. From that truth, everything else will follow.

This is not to say that the silence that speaks must simply happen of its own accord, as a sudden inspiration out of nowhere. It can, in fact, be courted, even cultivated. The first step is to look for ways to bring more silence into your life. Only when you have made peace with silence will it speak to you. You will never hear the silence if your lips are moving or your ears are filled with sounds of your own or somebody else's making, or if your hands are busy and your eyes are trained on what your hands are doing. You must court the silence with your own stillness. You must allow the silence to sense your respect. This is how you tell the silence *yes, I am ready, I have come to be still and listen.*

The woods are a good place for listening and so are the mountains and the seashore and a shady spot beside a meandering stream. But who can go on vacation every single day? Any private space will work so long as you have found the proper stillness *inside.* It is easier to achieve and hold that stillness in places not riddled with the clamorings of man. But even then, such stillness does not come quickly or easily, especially after a lifetime of filling the silence with your noise. But if you are patient and humble it will come, the stillness will come, and after that the silence will speak to you.

If you are very lucky it will speak to you in words but more often in images and feelings that appear and then go, appear and then go, as if it is testing you to see if you are paying attention. This is when you must hold the stillness and humility as firmly as you can but without applying any pressure or expectation. The stillness wants and desires nothing. The stillness accepts. It remains open and grateful always, even when the silence holds its tongue. This is the only way the silence can come to trust you and know that you are ready. Then it will speak to you in whatever language it chooses. It might be a scent that wafts over your face or a butterfly that sits on the back of your hand. It might be a vision or a soothing sound or a soft voice whispering a few words inside your head. It might be the caress of perfumed fingers across your cheek.

I have heard the silence in all these languages and more. At times the silence has spoken to me of love or has told me that I am never alone. It has made me weep with bliss or has made me laugh out loud with surprise and joy. Its communications are always brief but the rhythms can linger inside you for years and years as quiet ripples of an understanding you can never put into words, an unhurried wisdom, refreshing and sustaining, and after hearing it a few times, you will know that no matter how loud or varied the noises you make, you will never find any to equal the peace of the silence that speaks when you have learned to sit still and be grateful and listen.

ONE WRITER'S TIPS

There is a misconception among many of today's aspiring writers that they must obtain a degree in order to become a writer. I spent a total of more than seven years sitting in college classrooms, and I cannot think of a single thing learned in those classes that could not have been better learned through firsthand experience and self-study. The teaching degrees I received did not make me a better teacher, and not a word heard in a classroom made me a better writer. On the contrary, the degrees and prescriptive instruction were aimed at making me a better conformist. They failed to do so. That is why the only degree I value is the Doctor of Letters degree, which was not awarded for sitting in a classroom and regurgitating what I was fed, but for a body of creative work whose every word was written outside the influence of academia.

My most important educational experiences, and the ones that formed me into a writer and continue to inform my writing, began with growing up in a hardscrabble blue collar world, then at nineteen dropping out of college for a year to paint houses 2500 miles from my home, then taking a solo backpacking trip through Europe when I was twenty-six, followed by being the father of two amazing sons, and then wrapping things up with another fifty years of purpose-driven reading, writing, traveling, and living.

Life itself is the only education any committed writer ever needs.

You do not have to be in an altered state of consciousness to do most things in life, but you do to write a book of fiction or any sustained work of the memory or imagination. You must be able, two or three hours a day for most of a year, to focus your thoughts with the intensity of a magnifying glass held over dry leaves on a sunny day. Every time you waver, the heat is lost and you must start again.

Certain things help. The absence of distracting noises (which for some means total silence and for others allows the presence of sounds that have come to be reassuring – the baby's sibilant sleeping breath, the children's happy clamor outside. Some writers even prefer to work in public, in cafes and libraries!) A well-lit writing surface, whether computer monitor or legal tablet. A comfortable chair that does not encourage you to slouch or stretch out supine. An innate sense of rhythm and harmonics that allows you to be drawn into the music of language. An insatiable desire to observe your characters. A love for working alone.

A few last items: Self-motivation. Discipline. Spite. Coffee. And finally, the one requisite that renders all previous requirements secondary: A writer needs a desperate, unreasonable, possibly neurotic and indefensible hunger for wading about in the murky depths of his or her own imagination, flickering penlight in hand.

A state of intellectual restlessness that results in periodic episodes of creative self-renewal is a good thing for every individual, and essential for a writer. Prolonged complacency with any situation means that the individual, like water running downhill, will eventually settle in a low point and go stagnant. Complacency is a kind of depression. Far better to fail when taking a risk on something new than to acquiesce to gravity. For the writer, that something new can be a change of genre, voice, style, structure…. It can be anything at all that brings challenge back to the equation. If a writer isn't challenged by her project, she isn't growing as a writer. She isn't really living as a writer must. As Virginia Woolf wrote, "A self that goes on changing is a self that goes on living."

Creative writing, like all artistic endeavors, is far more likely to fail than it is to succeed. And even if a first book is a critical and commercial success, the odds against the writer become only a little less staggering. A writer has to prove herself with every single book. A school teacher, a dentist, a lawyer, a factory worker has no such gauntlet to run. You get your training, you land your job, you make a down payment on a house, you deposit your check, you live your life. Success as a creative writer requires an unrelenting obsession for excellence; every book must be as good or better than the previous one. Even the most loyal of readers will slip away if you disappoint them one too many times.

The first sentence of every story is the most important one. From that sentence, all else impends. It is not only the information conveyed in the first sentence that matters, but also the coloring, the shading, the background music, the wind through the trees. Mood. Ambiance. Atmosphere. Rhythm.

The first sentence establishes the story's frequency. And by the time that sentence is committed to paper – after the sentence has been rolled around in the mouth like a piece of ocean glass in a tumbler, smoothing out the sharp edges, grinding away the awkwardness until the end result is a shining pendant of a sentence – by then the mood and rhythm of the story are established. The heart now beats to the story's frequency. The fingers type to that frequency, behaving as a particle or wave, staccato or legato, solid or liquid, however the story dictates.

I chuckle every time I read an admonition by a writer that one must keep the writing room free of all distractions, such as cell phones, laptops, TVs, and so forth. I have written more than thirty books, twelve plays, numerous screenplays, and hundreds of short pieces in rooms where all of those distractions and more were close at hand. The secret to productivity isn't hiding from technology; it's a lot simpler than that. It's called discipline. You could move your writing space to an empty cave on a remote mountaintop yet still produce not a single word if you fail to possess and practice self-discipline.

The more time you spend in a classroom, the less likely it is that you will emerge from the classroom with an original thought in your head. Academia does not encourage and reward original thinking as much as it encourages recycled thinking. Your professor will reward you for repeating what you were told in class, just as that professor was rewarded for repeating what was taught when he or she was a student, and on and on back through all the generations of recycled thought. The best thinkers, and therefore also the best writers, are those who have forsworn the dictates of others to face the world uncorrupted. If any single reason can be blamed for the past few generations of bland, uninspired, repetitive and imitative literature, and for our generations of meek, easily offended young people, those afraid of being alone, afraid of the dark, afraid of solitude and afraid of nature, it is an educational system that rewards those most thoroughly brainwashed while ignoring and devaluing those with the courage to spurn indoctrination.

It isn't the act of learning about the basics of creative writing that stifles creativity, but the act of clinging to those conventions, and the act of believing in them as solemn and indisputable gospel. A rigid adherence to conventional tropes, story structures, themes, or any other element of creative writing is the sign of an unimaginative and timid writer. The best writers, and in my opinion the only ones worth reading, are fearless, even reckless, and will abide no constraints on what or how they write. This is not to suggest that undisciplined writing is great writing; undisciplined writing is usually garbage. Discipline, however, must be self-imposed, and every decision purposeful. All rules and formulas for creative writing must emanate from the writer and the particular story being written. Emulation of another writer is fine just so long as the emulation is done as per the original definition of the word, meaning striving to be equal to or as good as, but imitation, by any definition, is a sure-fire formula for mediocrity.

Every writer should have a sentence or more to serve as a model and an inspiration. For me that sentence has always been the opening of Hemingway's short story, "In Another Country": *In the fall the war was always there, but we did not go to it anymore.*

That sentence just might be the most brilliant one ever written in the English language. Look at the questions it raises for the reader: Which war? Where? What does it mean to "go" to a war? And why does the narrator no longer go to it?

The rest of that first paragraph is no less brilliant. From the profoundly ambiguous first sentence, the author shifts to exquisite detail, one after another:

> *It was cold in the fall in Milan and the dark came very early. Then the electric lights came on, and it was pleasant along the streets looking in the windows. There was much game hanging outside the shops, and the snow powdered in the fur of the foxes and the wind blew their tails. The deer hung stiff and heavy and*

empty, and small birds blew in the wind and the wind
turned their feathers. It was a cold fall and the wind
came down from the mountains.

Oh, the rhythm, the devious simplicity, the insinuations of that paragraph! Yet only by reading the rest of the story will we see the significance of those five lines. The cold, the dark, the dead animals, and even the little birds being pushed back by the wind from the mountains – every keenly observed detail is a symbol and a foreshadowing.

On those occasions when I am unsure of how to begin a story or novel, when the mood and tone have not yet come to me, when cadence is yet to be heard inside my head, I read that paragraph from Hemingway, and soon I am writing my own.

Most of my stories, like his, are all about the march toward death and the struggle to live the best life we can though we know that death is always there waiting for us. For that reason, no other piece of American literature has been as instructive and resonant for me as that first paragraph from Hemingway's story. Every writer should have such a model and inspiration of their own. Type it out and tape it to the wall above your desk. Memorize it. Absorb its beats and brilliance into your bloodstream, so that they will always be there for you when you need them.

A writer should never allow proper English grammar to get in the way of the visceral effect one is hoping to achieve. Just as background music and sound effects are employed to ratchet up the mood of a movie scene, syntax, diction, sentence structure and punctuation must be used in written fiction. Every important scene has its own soundtrack, its own melody, and the reader will not feel the effect of that melody if the prose is flat. Subject-verb-object is fine some of the time, but so is the occasional comma splice, the sentence fragment, the run-on sentence, and all of the other so-called grammatical errors that drive copyeditors crazy. Writers should think of punctuation and other grammatical conventions not as inviolable rules but as the hands, eyes, ears and baton with which they conduct the orchestra.

I write every day. Every single morning, seven days a week, year in, year out. If I have a novel in progress, I will work on it at least five mornings each week. But sometimes I will need a break from the novel, will need to think out a plot point or the right setting for a particular scene, and in those cases I might work on a story or essay or even another novel until I am ready to go back to my major project. But I never do not write on any given morning.

On weekends I might write only five hundred words instead of the usual fifteen hundred, because all work and no play makes Randall a little bit crazy. But not writing at all, even for a single morning, will also make Randall a little bit crazy. Randall walks a fine line between sane and crazy.

Not writing makes the whole day feel off-balance. I know from past experience, from back before I started waking up at four or four-thirty every morning, that to not write would make that entire day feel like a wasted day to me. And wasting a day is a sin that will bring me no pleasure but will, in fact, spoil any pleasurable activity I engage in that day. I am not OCD in all things but I am when it comes to my work. That is the discipline that works best for me. But it isn't for everybody.

I know of writers who will write only when inspired. Or will binge-write over the summer or on weekends or holidays only. They use their "primary" job, whether it is teaching or working in a call center or taking care of the family as a rationale for writing only when it is convenient to write. To me, these writers are hobbyists. Their creative output is generally pathetically small compared to that of a professional writer. There is not a thing wrong with this lifestyle, just so you don't hope to sustain a long and productive career as a writer. Hobbies are fun. Hobbies help us to relieve the daily tedium and stress of life. But in few cases will a hobby satisfy a deep psychological need, a driving ambition. Only hard, meaningful, disciplined work will do that, and getting up an hour or two earlier every day and going to bed an hour or so earlier seems a small price to pay for a long and productive career.

The demand made by some these days that a writer must not write about characters and situations outside his or her own culture, race, gender, lifestyle, or ethnicity is utter nonsense. It denigrates and attempts to nullify thousands of years of great society-shaping literature. Those who make such a demand are probably not even dedicated readers except of material that feeds their own narrow-minded viewpoints. Writers and their readers are among the most empathetic and sensitive representatives of our species and must never have their range of material and expression limited by a relative handful of bitter, myopic ideologues. To attempt to limit a writer's or anyone else's freedom of expression is the worst kind of censorship, and as every thinking individual knows, censorship is and always has been the strategy of cowards and petty tyrants. Muffling, handcuffing, and otherwise silencing diverse opinion is the first step taken by every would-be dictator. Tyranny cannot exist without the implementation of such censorship. I, for one, will continue to write about whatever I damn well want to write about, and I encourage all writers to do the same, and all publishers to have the spine to support those writers, and all readers to resist and actively rebel against every attempt to strangle their freedom to read whatever they damn well want to read.

Remember this: The moment you allow for other voices to be silenced is the moment you allow for your own voice to be silenced by others.

Recently I was tracking down the sources of some quotes I wanted to use in an essay titled "Ten Writers' Rules that Beg to Be Broken," and I was astonished once again by all the foolish things writers say about the process and profession of writing. What narcissists we can be! Unfortunately, many aspiring writers who yearn to join the profession will too easily embrace this foolishness as gospel. For example, if Stephen King finds starting a piece of work the scariest part, that's because of *his* personality and *his* fears, which are not necessarily the same as any other writer's. And if Saul Bellow believed that you never have to change anything you get up in the middle of the night to write down, that's because of *his* nocturnal thought processes; it is certainly not true for me or for thousands of other writers. And if Maya Angelou believes there is no greater agony than keeping an untold story to yourself, she doesn't know real suffering.

Writers exaggerate. Writers romanticize. Writers glorify. The writing profession, like every other walk of life, has its share of divas and drama queens and attention hounds. Every aspiring writer should be aware of that. The truth is that no writer can tell you what your writing journey will be like. Nor can you predict it for yourself. The only way to know it is to live it. And it is wise not to begin that journey steeped in the fears and exaggerations of others.

For a long time I used to have a notecard taped on the wall above my desk. Printed on that card was this quote from Ernest Hemingway: *All you have to do is write one true sentence. Write the truest sentence that you know.*

The use of the word *true* here often misleads those who read the quote. In this case, Hemingway, I'm certain, did not mean *true* as a synonym for *factual*, nor did he mean *honest*. He meant *true* as a carpenter would use it: to make everything level and plumb and square. In other words, a perfectly constructed and aligned sentence.

The full quote comes from Hemingway's *A Moveable Feast*, my all-time favorite memoir. The book is about Hem's early career living in Paris, and of how he taught himself to write, and about the many future literary luminaries he met along the way.

> *I would stand and look out over the roofs of Paris and think, "Do not worry. You have always written before and you will write now. All you have to do is write one true sentence. Write the truest sentence you know." So finally I would write one true sentence, and then go on from there.*

Writing can be hard. Sometimes the hardest part is getting started. I never sit down to write a piece, whether fiction or nonfiction, until I have the first sentence or two highly polished. This is all done in my head, not on paper. Often I do it while walking, but sometimes while on my motorcycle or lawn tractor or driving the car. Physical movement, in some magical way, helps to imbue the sentence with its own movement and momentum.

When the sentence is as perfect as I can make it, when it captures the voice of the entire unwritten piece and establishes the mood and telegraphs or foreshadows the drama to come, and when it virtually guarantees that a reader will want to keep reading, I sit down and begin to write. And all the time I was trying to perfect that first sentence, the fuller story was forming itself, setting up road signs for me to follow: this has to happen, then this, then this.

By taking the time to perfect the cadence, music, innuendo, and overall construction of that first sentence, you allow the bigger story to gestate. That's how important the first sentence is. Make it right, make it true, make it sing. And the rest of the sentences will follow. Most of them, anyway.

The key to immersive writing is details, specifically the small but significant details most people overlook, the kind that come with a subtext intact. To identify those telling details you must learn to be a good observer. Better than good. Some people are born with a natural and insatiable curiosity for the world, and consequently a gift for spotting telling details. Most times, these are introverts, a personality type that sees itself as an outlier to the rest of the world.

If you are an extrovert and want to be a good writer you might have to work a little harder, because extroverts tend to talk about and observe mostly themselves; they observe the world in relation to themselves rather than as something separate and distinct from their own lives. It is important to watch and listen and smell and touch what passes by you every day as if it doesn't even recognize your presence. The way a stranger walks. The facial gestures and what the eyes say and how a smile belies the truth of what a person is saying. The scent of the air through an open window on a bright winter morning. The scent and appearance of food served to a table adjacent to yours, and how the customers and server interact. The sound of an Amish buggy on pavement. The modulation in a woman's voice when she speaks to her child compared to when she speaks to someone else.

We must also pay close attention to what is close to us and what we know, but this is a second-class kind of observation; it is tainted by our presence and therefore risks generating a singular rather than universal reaction to it.

To notice the universal you must sink into the background and pay rapt attention to everyone and everything except for yourself. Don't judge what you see, just observe it with all your senses. If you see yourself at all in the situation it should be as an objective third party, outside of what is being observed and of no significance to it; i.e., if you did not exist, what you observe would be unchanged in every way.

The best writers are able to capture those universally authentic images and sensations that draw a reader into the story. They experience the thing observed, whatever it is, without ascribing an emotional or intellectual response to it. It is what it is. Extroverts *can* be keen observers too but they must first break the habit of viewing themselves as the center of the universe and learn to be an invisible spectator, a mere camera, but one endowed with all the sensory capabilities of a humble and curious human being.

It is only after what has been observed and recorded that the subjective self should contemplate it, dissect it, apply a meaning and significance to it. This split perspective can be tricky for some to achieve, though for others it comes naturally. Those who have undergone a near-death experience, for example, will often report how their astral body watched from the ceiling as their physical body lay on the operating table: the astral self felt no emotional connection to the body whatsoever; it was a curiosity, nothing more, though every detail of the operation was interesting. Later, of course, when the astral self returns to the body, then comes the application of meaning and emotion via the subjective self, which is driven by ego. For the writer, though, this return to ego should be to an ego striving for fairness and understanding; an ego striving to ignore itself.

Even the most distant and vague horizon, whether physical or nonphysical, such as becoming a published author, can be reached step by step as long as you never stop moving toward it. Writers who fail do so not for lack of talent but lack of discipline. The first and most important ingredient in the recipe for success is perseverance. Identify the horizon you wish to reach, and march toward it. Don't stop until you reach it. Then look around for the next horizon to pursue.

If you wish to be a writer whose work aspires to be more than entertainment, in other words to create work that touches the soul and lingers there a while, you must make friends with solitude. Only solitude and inner stillness in significant measure will allow the subconscious mind to speak its metaphorical language to the conscious mind, which can then copy the phrases and images onto a screen or paper. Daily meditation and a quiet work space can be instrumental in fostering the inner stillness that opens the door to the subconscious self, and will also, incidentally, mitigate the routine stresses of daily live. Creative work that merely entertains through scene after scene of action and violence and sex and other matters of the ego-driven consciousness can be composed by some in noisy coffee shops and other heavily trafficked venues, but to plumb the truth of the human spirit requires not hard, focused concentration – i.e. not thinking, as some might assume – but *wú niàn*, as Buddhists call it, no-thought, a relaxed receptivity to an inner knowledge that will not rise to the surface until the conscious mind is relatively calm and unperturbed by life's distractions. Most serious writers know this. Rilke knew it, Salinger knew it, May Sarton knew it, Annie Dillard knew it, Joan Didion knew it; the list is long and endlessly varied as to genre and style and subject. Writers whose need for approval and public adoration overwhelms their devotion to solitude almost always produce lesser works, if any at all, and often succumb to depression, alcohol, or drugs (i.e. Truman Capote, Tennessee Williams, Fitzgerald, Sylvia Plath, to name just a few). Some writers, such as Virginia Woolf, Hemingway, and others, allow a deep sense of loneliness and futility to penetrate their solitude, often with fatal results. But being alone is not the same as being lonely, and a serious writer must guard against that error in judgment. Solitude can be the most useful tool in the writer's toolbox. That is why productive writers (and artists of other mediums as well) find a way to sequester themselves for at least part of each working day. It is why some become lifelong recluses, because for them the art of creation is so fulfilling and intoxicating and self-liberating that the noisy and bellicose business of the world loses all meaning for them. It becomes mere backdrop – sometimes useful, often irritating, and frequently irrelevant to the larger business of rendering both the light and the dark of human existence in a meaningful, memorable way.

Rules are for accountants and architects, assembly line workers, mathematicians and neurosurgeons. In order to be successful in those professions, there are procedures that must always be followed, variations that must never be employed. The word creative, however, as in the phrase *creative writing*, demands, at the very least, an imaginative interpretation of the rules.

I have held well over fifty different jobs in my life, and it was always the rules that made me leave. Writing is the only profession that has never made me long to be doing something else.

Rules promote routine. Repetition. Redundancy. Imitation. Staleness. A lack of originality.

There are no rules that will guarantee success for a writer. There are no formulas, no closely guarded secrets. There is only what works and what doesn't work in every individual piece of writing. Does the writer manage to seize and hold and reward the reader's emotional, intellectual, and financial investment?

No writer living or dead has discovered a definitive method for producing successful fiction. None ever will. How can you discover what does not exist?

And for me, that is what makes the business and art of writing so exhilarating: working without a manual, without a map, and without a net. So shut off the GPS. Turn off the noise. Lock your door. Sit down and write.

Many years ago, author James Baldwin said, "The terrible thing about being a writer is that you don't decide to become one, you discover that you are one."

For me, discovering that I was a writer was one of the most wonderful things to ever happen, second only to the births of two sons.

It's all a matter of what you want from life and what you expect from the writing life. Yes, much of the writing life is filled with frustration and rejection and abysmally low reward for the time and effort required of writing a novel. But the first thing I wanted from the writing life was to be independent, to make my own choices, and to be able to work alone, just me and my imagination. I have done exactly that for the past forty years. Did I have to make sacrifices? Of course. Did I have to make a few compromises? Of course. Do I wish I had chosen a different profession? No way!

Writing has provided exactly what I wanted from it. I knew the road would be a difficult one, I knew it would sometimes be a lonely one, I knew it would often be a disparaged one. I knew all that from the beginning. But I love a good challenge, I couldn't care less what other people think about me, and I usually prefer to be alone. There could be no better choice of a profession for a person like me than that of writing.

It is not a good choice for those who seek immediate and consistent fame and fortune. Not a good choice for those who love crowds and being the center of attention. Not a good choice for those seeking praise and approval. Not a good choice for those who fear rejection and solitude and who lack the essential requisite of self-discipline.

Being a writer seems, to too many, a glamorous and exciting profession, and one that can be mastered in the classroom, and one in which success will be handed to you along with your MFA degree. None of that is true. In fact, those writers who allow themselves to be seduced by those myths are likely to be sorely disappointed. And those who allow themselves to be seduced by temporary glamor and celebrity usually end up composing substandard work afterward, or none at all.

So before you decide to become a writer, know what you want from it and know the odds against those desires being fulfilled. Know your own limitations and strengths. Know yourself, and to thine own self be true.

According to Margaret Atwood, "A good story may tease as long as this activity is foreplay and not used as an end in itself. If there's a promise held out, it must be honored."

So what did Ms. Atwood mean by the above quote?

Back when she and I were learning how to write, it was a given that every well-made story, long or short, was comprised of three parts: the beginning, the middle, and the end. Although the demarcations between these sections are nebulous, the beginning introduces the main character and conflict, the middle is where the protagonist confronts the conflict through escalating risk and dramatic tension, and the end is what follows the climactic confrontation. The end, in other words, is the story's resolution.

The "tease," as Atwood refers to it, might be an argument, a desire, a prominent hunting knife, a hurtful criticism, suspicious claw marks on the outside of the door – i.e. anything the writer injects into the story so as to imply imminent danger or risk or heightened conflict, whether physical or psychological. The teases occur in the middle of the story, or sometimes even in the first sentence. No tease should be arbitrary or superfluous. Every tease must lead inevitably to the resolution. They must be, in Atwood's words, "foreplay" to the resolution.

However, it would be an error to associate Atwood's statement with a similar-sounding one by Anton Chekhov: "If in the first act you have hung a pistol on the wall, then in the following one it should be fired. Otherwise don't put it there." That isn't what Atwood is saying, nor do many contemporary writers agree with Chekhov. Hanging a pistol on the wall in the first act *can* create an expectation in the audience, yes, but that is often the writer's goal, to establish a foreboding atmosphere. Tension will rise throughout the story because of the conspicuous presence of that gun, but it doesn't mean the gun has to go off. Every expectation created by the tease does not have to be fulfilled. The dramatic tension achieved at the climactic moment can be defused in a number of other ways.

What Atwood is advising is to avoid any elements, any teases, that do not have a clear relationship with the story arc. Take the suspicious claw marks on the front door, for example. If the claw marks are discovered by the protagonist at the beginning of the story, causing her to assess every impending threat in light of those claw marks, but then, later on, the resolution of the story comes without any pertinent explanation for the presence of those claw marks, the claw marks don't belong in the story. And it would be a cop-out at the end for somebody to explain, "Oh yeah, my neighbor's dog did that. He's always clawing at the door." I and lots of other writers consider that to be dishonest storytelling. To introduce a tantalizing detail into a story when it has no true relevance to the story is to deliberately mislead the reader, and that is the ploy of a lazy, dishonest storyteller. It is not our job as storytellers to trick the reader. Our job is to tell a compelling story, free of coincidence and cliché, with the *relevant* details intact.

Suffering is an inherent aspect of nearly every writer's life, just as it is for nearly every human being. But writers and other artists (and all individuals with an artistic temperament) tend to suffer more intensely than others. Some of this is because the work of writers and other artists is subject to criticism daily, but it is also because of our increased sensitivity to life, our heightened empathy and observational skills. (If you have not yet watched the Netflix documentary *Sensitive: The Untold Story*, I recommend that you do.)

But the question is not do we suffer, but how should we, as writers, respond to our suffering. We should not collapse into our beds, or bankrupt ourselves with expensive therapy, or squander our time by wallowing in depression, or numb ourselves with medication. We should put our misery to use.

Knowingly or unknowingly, we writers create characters to help us bear the burden. We shift a good portion of our misery onto those hapless characters and then allow them to work through their suffering. In so doing, their journey becomes our healing.

Although I have known far too many narcissistic writers, and numerous empathetic teachers and nurses and other non-writing persons, several studies indicate than writers and other artists generally score higher on sensitivity and empathy than the average human being. Therefore we are more prone to suffer from our own and others' misfortune. But we are also blessed, because our very talent and ambition as writers is the most effective remedy for misery that we can employ. Writers write.

And so far, Big Pharma hasn't found a way to synthesize and turn that remedy into a pill.

Sometimes we writers apply this remedy consciously, but more often, I think, subconsciously. We write because we are compelled to write. And out of the depths of our subconscious arise the stories and characters that give us purpose. So why in the world would any writer stop writing to allow herself to wallow in depression or hopelessness? To do so is to go off your most effective meds.

Every failure we experience, every love we lose, every triumph, every pleasure, every moment we live, is given to us for a reason: so that we might learn and grow. Writers very often grow through their characters, just as our readers frequently do by taking the same vicarious journey with us. Through our writing, we heal others as we heal ourselves. That connection, that shared empathy and commiseration, is what good, compelling writing is all about. And it might be just the medicine you need to stay healthy and strong and productive.

Too much affiliation is dangerous for a writer. Too much security breeds a fear that the security might one day be whisked away. This fear in turn engenders a complicity to the rules of the organization providing affiliation, an acquiescence to somebody else's (usually a committee's) parameters of thought and self-expression.

But a writer, in order to be a writer of worth, must be like the best of tennis players. He must be unpredictable as a server, fearless at the net, comfortable with every risk. He must play the lines. He must aim for the corners. He cannot be afraid of racing well behind the baseline to send a backhand blur across court in a slicing diagonal that will have his opponent screaming epithets at the linesman, who is sitting there rubbing his eyes.

A writer who is a team player, a corporate animal, tenured, politically correct, a writer who plays only the high-percentage shots, is little more than a marionette dancing to the tug of somebody else's hands, his movements determined by somebody else's song.

The song of commerce is imitation.

The song of society is conformity.

The song of art is originality.

Today during my very limited time for pleasure reading, I came across a passage that gave me pause. One character in the novel was assuring the other character, an unpublished poet, that she truly was a poet even if she wasn't yet published. And I thought to myself, *Only a non-writer or an unpublished one would think like that.*

For me, the noun *writer* has always been engendered with a certain dignity, a title of honor ascribed to those who provide entertainment, enlightenment, self-awareness, and/or information for strangers. Even as a small boy I held writers in high esteem – so high, in fact, that I never once considered aspiring to such a lofty perch until a couple of professors suggested I should consider it. So when the character in the novel I was reading today suggested that anybody could call herself a poet, or a writer or any kind, it struck me as absolutely false. It would be like me calling myself a surgeon because I had removed a splinter from my thumb.

When I was teaching full-time, I encountered numerous unpublished writers, especially those enrolled in MFA programs, who referred to themselves and their colleagues as *writers.* I admit that their doing so always made me wince a little. I would think *no, you're still an* aspiring *writer.* But it wasn't my place, and certainly never my intention, to throw shade on their enthusiasm. But after almost four decades of working in MFA programs, it has become fairly easy to distinguish those aspiring writers who have a real chance at dropping the adjective and those who never will or should. The latter category are the ones who toss around the title *writer* as if it were a trivial thing. *Oh, you wrote a scene today? I didn't know you were a writer!*

To treat the noun attributed to any profession so frivolously only demeans the entire profession. If anybody can be a writer, or a poet, or a playwright or essayist or screenwriter, what value do those distinctions have? My father was a steel worker not because he played with pieces of steel, but because he was paid to help create steel in its various evolutions inside a steel mill. He and the other steel workers produced a concrete product. A teacher does not become a bona fide teacher until she has been determined, by somebody willing to write her a check, that she is a verifiable teacher. Why should *writer* and *poet* be any different? A book is only a manuscript until it is published between covers.

It almost seemed, with some of the thousands of MFA students I have encountered, that claiming to be a writer was all the validation they needed. To them the profession did not require several years of close reading and even closer writing and editing; did not require several years of subjecting yourself to criticism and rejection; and did not require decades – no, a lifetime – of striving to be a better writer than you were. And it certainly did not require an agent or editor or other publishing professional to certify the presence of – not the potential for, but the actual presence of – writing talent. All it required was the desire, no matter how amorphous and undisciplined that desire might be. *I want to be a writer; therefore, I am a writer!*

There is no shame in referring to yourself as an aspiring or amateur writer. I did so for ten years before my first sale, and I was never embarrassed to do so. To me it was akin to saying, I'm studying to be a doctor. Or a lawyer. Or an engineer. Or a stock broker or hundreds of other professions. How many students in their junior year as an accounting major go around introducing themselves with, "Hi. I'm a financial analyst."

Would you allow your brain to be operated on by a young surgeon who, though he has read lots of books on the subject, has never successfully wielded a scalpel? I wouldn't. Can you buy a comb and a pair of scissors and announce that you are a barber? Maybe you could in the Old West, but not anymore. Even becoming a barber requires validation. Writing, of course, isn't the same as taking somebody else's life or hair into your hands. But it is the same as taking your own life into your own hands.

Only the arts allow an individual without any validating experience to claim to be an artist. What a ridiculously abused and overused word that is! *Artist* – what does it mean to be an artist? What it *should* mean is that the artist produces art. But what is art? Art is anything that is original, distinctive, and of an overtly higher quality than other examples of the same practice, whether that practice is visual art, dance, sculpture, or the many forms of creative writing. Unfortunately, that is still an amorphous criterion, and it is this very factor that allows aspiring artists to assume the mantle well before their own talent, if they actually have any, has been tested and proven worthy.

Every profession requires validation. Some are more demanding of this validation than others. Some require a history of demonstrated success before allowing the apprentice to drop the adjectives of *aspiring* or *amateur*. Brain surgeons, for example, actually slice into a few brains, and must do so successfully, before being turned loose upon an unsuspecting public. A barber, besides getting a certificate from a barber college after actually cutting lots of actual hair without scalping anybody, gains validation through his or her customers. Several somebodies must pay for a haircut, and then return six weeks later for another. Training, employment, pay, and reputation are how individuals in the trades are vetted. Without those three criteria in your pocket, you're still just an amateur, a wannabe.

The writing profession should be one such profession. Validation for a writer can come in only one way: in publication, and in most cases of a type not prefixed by the word *self.* Legitimate publishers take a significant financial risk when they sign a writer to a contract. *That* is when you become a real writer, how a writer gets her bona fides.

The only way a self-published writer can remove from herself and her work the stigma of vanity publishing is to sell beaucoup books. Nothing will make legit publishers and agents and potential readers sit up and take notice like $$$$. For many of us, this is a sad commentary on society, but today the size of an advance and the number of sales have supplanted quality as a standard for success. But they *are* standards, despite how crass we might think them.

Unfortunately, too many in the MFA in Creative Writing industry ignore this truth; they apply no standards other than being accepted into the program, no matter how unpublishable the enrollee's work might turn out to be. What a terrible disservice many of these programs have done, and still do to a once venerable profession by promulgating or even allowing this falsehood to continue. A few of the honest ones will post disclaimers on their websites, admitting that talent is a gift of birth and cannot be taught, but that the "nuts and bolts" of creative writing, such as story structure, can be learned. I only wish they would go further and also ask themselves if a keen ear for dialogue and a sharp eye for the telling detail can be taught. Can a sense of cadence and rhythm be taught? How about originality? How about self-discipline? And what of the detrimental effects of criticism by committee? Shouldn't that be included in the disclaimers too?

By the way, if you are a brilliantly original writer, the less talented members of the workshop will not recognize or appreciate your talent and will try to smother it with criticism, to the point that they will either succeed in homogenizing your prose or you will drop out of the program with even less confidence and self-esteem than when you entered it.

And maybe one final disclaimer would also be in order for some of the programs:

As you will see from our faculty's bios, none of them has published a book that sold more than five hundred copies, if indeed they have published any at all through a legitimate publisher. However, all faculty members do hold terminal degrees, which Human Resources has made a requisite for employment even though the degrees in no way indicate either a facility for writing marketable work or a facility for recognizing marketable talent in students, but which might, in fact, contraindicate the very same.

One of the best role models an aspiring writer can have is the homely caterpillar. Every writer faces failure, which comes in many forms at various stages of the career, all of which can be summed up by the word *rejection*. Whether your work is rejected by an agent, an editor, the critics, or the public, that is a kind of failure but it should never be viewed as a fatal one. That failure is simply the writer's larval stage. So do like the homely caterpillar: devour yourself, then rebuild from the few cells remaining. But don't rush the process; it cannot be hurried. When your butterfly self is finally complete, shed the husk and fly away. Don't look back. Don't bemoan the past. Just flap those wings and fly. Nobody rejects a butterfly.

I can't think of a single important thing I learned in a classroom. And it wasn't because I didn't pay attention. I entered every classroom rapt and open, craving knowledge and its appertaining skills. Yet eighteen years of formal instruction taught me not a single skill I currently employ. They did not teach me how to write, or how to make a living, or how to think critically, or how to love and be loved, or how to enjoy a song, a poem, a novel, a joke, or how to bring pleasure to others, or how to revere nature, or how to be a good human being, or how to connect with God. Those hundreds of classes did not teach me how to think outside the box; every class put me into a box and tried to keep me there. Formal instruction does the same for all students. Every bit of useful knowledge I possess, every practical or abstract skill, was gleaned from ignoring what I was told in the classroom while listening, watching, reading, and doing outside the classroom.

Some people might require formal instruction, and the more the better, but those with a fire in their bellies to learn what truly matters would be far better off if they were encouraged to break free from the mediocrity of public education at a very early age. Instead, those among us with the most elastic minds and most adventuresome spirits are often forced to struggle to free themselves, and only a relative handful of them are successful. Think what an exciting and glorious culture we might have if our society cultivated and celebrated originality instead of attempting to shape every mind into the same ordinary pot of conformity.

I have been teaching creative writing for nearly forty years, and, based on that experience, I can say with some authority that only one or two individuals in each of the hundreds of classes I instructed possessed the raw talent sufficient to becoming a writer. And of what does such talent consist? An innate understanding of story structure, an eye for detail, an ear for natural speech, a knack for subtext and understatement, a gift for the music of prose and the symphony of life. But raw talent is just the first requisite of the process. There must also be a driving ambition to become a better writer, and the self-discipline and perseverance to continue collecting rejection slips for at least five years and probably many more. This is where most talented writers fail. They fail because they don't want to put in the time and effort or they don't have the spine to face the rejection and criticism that is part and parcel of a writer's life. And that is why only 150,000 American writers will earn as much as $50,000 a year as a writer. The number 150,000 might seem like a lot, but it is only 0.089% of the 80% of adult Americans (according to the Bureau of Labor Statistics) who think they have what it takes to be a writer, and a mere 0.045% of the entire population of the country. So the next time somebody tells you that writing talent is common, don't believe it. Writing talent, like all true talents, is rare, and those talented individuals willing to endure the difficult work necessary to achieve success are even rarer.

I have never met a literary novel that would not have been improved by a little less navel gazing and a little more plot.

Those who grow up as I did – feeling, for whatever reason, like an only child, a stranger among strangers – learn quickly to rely on themselves. When you have no confidantes, no supporters, no champions – or when you believe that you don't – you learn to keep your feelings to yourself. You learn to keep you own counsel and to heed your own instincts.

When I reached the age of twenty and first learned that I had a talent for storytelling, I shared that discovery with no one. I knew no one who could help me become a writer. I knew no one who could show me how to write good fiction. I had no money to attend a university with a creative writing program, and besides, there were few in existence then. But even so, the notion of sitting around a table with ten or so other fledglings and discussing our work struck me as antithetical to real instruction. How can you learn from the criticism and praise of people who know as little about writing as you do? It made no sense to me. But, I told myself, since *you* know so little, how can you be sure you are right? So I tried a writers' workshop for a couple of weeks at a local college, but soon my suspicions were confirmed: creative writing shaped by a committee of neophytes is a farce. Writing is a solitary art.

If I wanted to be a better writer, a publishable writer – and I did want that more than anything in the world – I would have to do it alone. Consequently, I turned to the only teachers available, to the novels and stories I loved. Like centuries of writers before me, I embarked on a self-taught journey of close, analytical reading, the equivalent of a novel every other day for the next ten years or so. I drove librarians at three small-town libraries crazy with my inter-library loan requests. On occasion, I stole a book from a library just so I could hang onto it for as long as I wanted. For me it was like stealing a bag of apples; I was famished and would die without sustenance. I read all of Hemingway's work, all of Faulkner's, all of Stephen Crane's and Flannery O'Connor's and Hermann Hesse's and Camus's and Beckett's and Sartre's and García Márquez's and dozens and dozens of others'. I shaped my whole existence around that ambition for the next decade. Despite having two degrees, I took only manual labor or temporary jobs so as to keep writing and reading and learning, and, like Rimbaud and Hemingway and Kerouac before me, I crammed as many personal experiences into my life as I could. In so doing, I learned not how to write the way an instructor or a workshop consensus thought I should write, but to write the way the best examples of American and European and South American literature, all blended through my own instincts and desires and experiences, told me to write. My first success came the summer I turned thirty; four stories accepted in small literary journals. Three years later my first collection of stories won the Drue Heinz Literature Prize. Today, some fifty years and thirty books later, I still work that way. I write how and what I want to write, critics and trends and naysayers be damned. And I consider *that* the penultimate accomplishment of my life, second only to being the father of two brilliant, talented, and fiercely independent sons. With those accomplishments in my pocket, few as they are in number, I will leave this life knowing I leave it well-lived.

Albert Einstein, who believed that imagination is the highest faculty of man, also said this: "Imagination is more important than knowledge. For knowledge is limited to all we now know and understand, while imagination embraces the entire world, and all there ever will be to know and understand." If that is true, and I believe it is, then those engaged in creative pursuits, the finest of which depend almost wholly on one's imagination, are overdue for greater recognition and appreciation.

Among those who practice the creative arts, there are three distinctions, though they are seldom pointed out. The first are the artisans, who some call craftsmen and craftswomen. They take what has been done before and do it again, though with little originality or innovation. There is no fire in their prose, no startling surprises in their applications of color, no soul-wrenching tones in their melodies and harmonies. They command at least half of the available audience, and probably an additional ten or twenty percent.

Artists are those who take the conventions of the artisans and twist them here and there, or simply raise those conventions to a higher level of artistry. They represent the silver medalists of their discipline in that they do what artisans do but they do it better and with a little more originality. Theirs is a much smaller but more discerning audience.

Unfortunately, the distinction of artist is frequently usurped by practitioners who are mere artisans. For them, just to practice the discipline makes them, in their own self-definitions, artists. This is particularly true of the young, who have not yet learned enough or whose tastes are insufficiently refined to be able to distinguish between the first two distinctions, and among those who do not practice the art but are consumers of it.

Then there are the geniuses, they who disregard conventions altogether, who never learned them or chose to unlearn them, and in the sheer originality and ferocity of their visions produce awe and wonderment and great jealousy. They, in our current society, are adored by only a few and condemned by the rest.

Some geniuses find renown after death, when society's tastes become more elevated, or through the persistence of a handful of devoted admirers. But most do not. Edisons will always find greater acclaim than Teslas. Warhols will always outsell the work of Juan Gris and Anna Hyatt Huntington. Stephen King will always garner more praise than Robert Walser, Langston Hughes, Barbara Pym, James Salter, and John A. Williams combined.

If the value a society ascribes to its true artists and geniuses is an indication of the quality of the society itself, ours is not only in precipitous decline but is possibly not worth saving. Einstein also said, "Two things are infinite: The universe and human stupidity, and I'm not sure about the universe."

Throughout my life I have found only four enduring activities that make me feel truly alive and wanting to remain alive for as long as I can. The first, though the least important, was born in me at the age of twenty, after my two previous passions, athletics and music, quietly slipped into the pastime category of activities.

Had I been more confident of my abilities in those fields, I might have devoted long hours to driving myself up from a talented amateur to a professional, but I judged the likelihood of doing so as minimal. Fortunately, serendipity intervened to fill my ambition gap; I discovered, through two kindly professors, that I had a talent for creative writing. From that moment on I wanted nothing but to make my living as a writer, and to always be a better writer than I was. The fire of that ambition has been burning brightly inside me for the past fifty-plus years, and it rarely shows any signs of flickering out.

There have been many moments when the profession has felt like just that, work, such as when sifting through a copyeditor's tedious adherence to the rules of grammar or, a more recent development, a fawning obeisance to the nonsense called political correctness. But there were always the mornings, those sweet hours of sitting quietly in the low light and allowing ideas to come and grow and flourish in an atmosphere free of rules and conventions and discernible sources. Only during those hours, and only from time to time during those hours, do I feel truly free and alive. Those moments continue to be enough to keep me looking forward to sitting at my desk every morning.

For fifteen years or so, those moments were all I had to keep me from giving up on life. Oh, there were moments when the sudden red hot flare of romantic love made me think I'd found the necessary meaning and purpose to keep on breathing, but that too always soon became work, more constraining than freeing. But then another kind of love, a deep, all-pervading, inexplicable variety of love took hold of my soul and has never once released it. Becoming a father twice, and now a grandfather twice, imbued life with far more meaning and significance than any other activity available. All I need in order to fill myself again with a fervor for life is to spend a little time in the company of my sons or grandchildren. Just to be with them, just to watch and listen to them, just to laugh and be happy with them – I could live forever fed on that joy alone.

And along the way I discovered a fourth reason to be alive. If you have not discovered it too, you will not comprehend it, just as a nonparent will have difficulty comprehending the depth and breadth and scope of a parent's love. Unless you have personally experienced the sense of sacredness that can descend upon you and within you when you are alone with nature, with a piece of nature unspoiled by the noise and structures and corrupting habits of man, you will never understand the annealing effects of such communion.

In his essay "Nature," Ralph Waldo Emerson explains, far better than I can, how it feels to be alone with nature:

> *In the woods, we return to reason and faith. There I feel that nothing can befall me in life, – no disgrace, no calamity…which nature cannot repair. Standing on the bare ground, – my head bathed by the blithe air, and uplifted into infinite space, – all mean egotism vanishes. I become a transparent eye-ball; I am nothing; I see all; the currents of the Universal Being circulate through me; I am part or particle of God.*

Being alone with nature, without engaging in some diverting activity such as hunting that redirects one's focus back to the ego, is a form of communion with the unseen and unknowable. Just as laying a hand on my son's shoulder is a form of communion, just as rolling a ball back and forth to my toddler granddaughter is. Just as is quietly allowing ideas in the form of stories and characters to come to me, bidden and unbidden, and then rendering them into words and sentences and scenes that breathe and move and sing.

These three activities – being a writer, being a father and grandfather, being in nature – have saved my life. They have prolonged and filled my life. They give me hope and joy and a sense of purpose. Without them my life would be void of harmony, void of meaning.

Engaged in any of these activities, a quiet exultation will fill me, a sense of perfection, a knowledge that all is right with the universe and I am a part of that rightness. I could not live, nor would I want to, in the absence of these connections, these sacred, loving moments, these most holy of communions.

What many non-writers and a lot of aspiring writers fail to acknowledge is the capriciousness inherent to not just the business of creative writing but also to the craft itself. The market is capricious, individual critics are capricious, the book-buying public is capricious, the written word and its effect on readers is capricious. Numerous mediocre novels have caught the wave of a zeitgeist and ridden it to phenomenal success, but a far greater number of brilliant novels have decomposed in obscurity because they were written too soon or too late. Books that were spurned when first issued have been deemed masterpieces many years later.

What this means is that every novel is a uniquely new experiment. It's an experiment that will be conducted once and only once. It either succeeds or it fails. You could continue that one experiment most of your life if you wanted to, adding a gram of this here, turning up or lowering the heat a degree or two there, but you can never know for sure if the experiment fails or succeeds until the book is published.

Even then there will be no consensus. There will always be a critic, and in this culture of unrestrained and often pigheaded public criticism there will always be a multitude of critics because being a critic is the easiest thing in the world to be. It requires no real talent or intelligence and no risk at all unless you are criticizing a psychopathic writer who will search you out and torture you. Sometimes the experiment itself is not a failure at all but is so different from what readers have come to expect of the writer that those readers will reject the experiment. Sometimes a constipated critic will call a non-failing experiment a failure because his gut is crampy and he is sitting in a cloud of his own flatus, and then those readers who have been misled to believe that a single critic's opinion is of any value and who know nothing about the critic's flatulence will decide too that the experiment is a failure without even looking at it. Every individual who wants to be a writer must be ready to embrace this capriciousness in all facets of the craft. Be ready to accept a failure every now and then, especially when you know in your heart that the experiment did not fail. Be ready to walk away from that failure and start another experiment without looking back at the mess the last one made of itself. If you want to be a writer, a real writer, you must be ready and able to do this. In the end, completing a novel and making it the best book it can be is the only measure of success with which a writer should be concerned. All other measures are out of the writer's hands.

Too many teachers of creative writing, especially but not exclusively those who are not published authors themselves, don't really understand the nature of creative work, and so they build their pedagogies around tired academic chestnuts that have little to do with creativity, and which frequently curtail the very creativity the best writing strives to achieve. Understanding what is meant by such terms as beginning, middle, and end, genre tropes, cliffhanger, foreshadowing, and the like is all fine and dandy, but to turn these terms into dictums and absolute requirements is to *restrict* creativity, not promote it. These terms are fences for creative writers, fences put in place, most times, by teachers who are unsuccessful writers. The best writers bust down those fences and trample on them.

Creative writing as a process should be seen not as a craft but as something indefinable and even mystical, something a writer must search for with every new project, that perfect seashell that can be found only by scavenging mile after mile of beach, picking up one shell after another, tossing a thousand back into the sea and returning home with one or two that come closest to the searcher's ideal. Every piece of creative writing should be approached as an experiment with no rules, because every rule constricts and limits the experiment's dimensions.

This is not to say that the standard conventions must be ignored. Conventions such as good grammar and clear and precise word choice will always serve the writer well, if only because most readers do not appreciate having to struggle through a chaos of language. Beyond that, however, lies an infinitude of choices.

To access those choices, a writer must be willing to forget all the rules she was taught, all the admonitions about not going near the water. She must free herself to wander about the beach, to climb fences where fences exist, to ignore the No Trespassing signs. On the other side of the fences, beyond the warning signs, that's where discoveries exist – not on sand already trampled and scraped clean by tens of thousands of feet.

The best writers take chances. They tempt failure. They take risks with their work.

Unfortunately, few writers are willing to take such risks, and fewer editors and publishers willing to finance them. Still, there is a way to fool those editors and publishers, a way to slip over the fences without being seen. And that is to approach each story as a child would, not with one's pockets bulging with rules but with empty pockets to be stuffed with one unexpected wonder after another. Thomas Wolfe was that kind of writer, as were Samuel Beckett, James Joyce, William Faulkner, and numerous other unconventional writers who are now esteemed as literary masters.

Alas, they lived and wrote in a different world than ours has become. Ours is now a world of rules imposed by small, narrow minds. Does that mean that an aspiring author should conform to conventional opinions in order to get published? They should if their aspiration is to be just another conventional writer and human being.

Writing is, for the most part, a one-person business. You are the employer and the sole employee. Nobody is going to tell you what time to show up for work or what time to clock out. Nobody is going to dock your pay if you curl up in bed for six days and wallow in self-pity because your life isn't going the way you want it to. You can't blame your friends for insisting that you have a drink with them. You can't blame your spouse or children because they have lives too and want you to be a part of them. You and you alone must bear the burden and the blame when you are too lazy, too hung-over, too depressed or undisciplined or distracted to get the work done. You're the one who said, "I'm going to be a writer." You're the one who said, "I could write a better novel than that guy." You're the one who wasted two years and thousands of dollars taking classes no legitimate writer needs. It's all on you, every word you write and fail to write. So stop your whining and complaining and making excuses. Sit your ass down and write. Do the work. Or admit that you are already a failure, and find something else to do.

"You can't blame a writer for what the characters say," said Truman Capote, and probably every writer before and after him.

A situation nearly every writer faces is to be blamed not only for what his characters say but also for what they do. The more authentic a scene or character seems to the reader, the more tenaciously do some readers cling to the belief that they are reading not fiction but nonfiction. This can become particularly onerous when trying to absolve oneself to a parent or significant other. "It's fiction!" you exclaim for the third time in a row. "That's what I do. I sit in a chair and make things up!"

"Right," is the inevitable answer, accompanied always by a roll of the eyes.

Why do so many readers leap to this conclusion? It seems logical to assume that there is a higher per capita percentage of readers among introverts than among extroverts. Extroverts are usually too busy talking about themselves to open up a book. So when an extrovert is chasing about to find somebody to listen to him or her, an introvert is reading silently in a quiet room somewhere.

This tendency toward inwardness often results from a life of tedious routine. Lots and lots of extroverts also live lives of tedious routine, but they tend to break the monotony by going out to drink and be loud with their extrovert friends. Introverts, in other words, live inside their heads, especially in the fertile fields of imagination located in the right hemisphere of the brain, whereas extroverts live principally, I guess, through their mouths and egos, which take up nearly all of the empty space in the left brain.

This has all been scientifically proven, of course; I wouldn't make this stuff up, even though that is what I do for a living.

My point is this: introverted readers do not have exciting lives. They get their excitement vicariously. This causes them to look with admiration and gratitude on the creators of that vicarious excitement, which leads to an incorrect assumption that the author, and not just the character, did have a series of simmering affairs, and did participate in several criminal activities, and was a double-agent during World War II. How else to account for the authenticity of those scenes?

The truth is, the scenes in a novel or story that seem most authentic usually *do* come from the writer's life, sort of. Writers are extraordinarily adept at hindsight. For example, if a writer spent most of his adolescence gazing woefully across the room at a beauty he was too timid to approach, he can, through remembering that humiliation, recreate it as a scene of charming seduction by a character who just happens to bear a striking physical resemblance to whom the author would like to be.

In this way, most of what a writer writes *does* have an autobiographical component. I, for one, have never actually killed anybody (wink wink), but I've imagined doing so at least once a week, usually when my neighbor's neurotic dogs start their hours-long barkfest. We writers, then, spend a lot of time rewriting our own lives, which we deftly conceal behind made-up names and settings. And this is what readers do too; they live vicariously through our more flamboyant and successful and charming characters. Then they blame us for doing the kinds of things that, let's face it, most of us are afraid to do.

I am not suggesting here that writers live lives of unrelentingly tedious routine. I, for one, do not. Long ago I tore a page each from the lives of Rimbaud and Hemingway and James Dean, and now I am proud to say that I have done everything there is to do. Everything I've wanted to do, anyway. So yes, dear gentle introverted reader, I am my characters. My characters are me. In this one instance, at least, you can hold a writer solely responsible for everything his characters say and do. I've done it all, usually more than once. So go ahead and blame me. I deserve it. No lie. I'm not making this up.

I am always amused by the naïveté of young aspiring writers who assume that completing a book-length manuscript will magically herald their entrée into the writing profession. I suffered from the same naiveté as a young man, and perhaps the condition is a requisite if one is to sustain the necessary optimism for such a perilous undertaking. Unlike a 9-5 job, where simply showing up to work every day and performing to the supervisor's expectations without screwing up too frequently can guarantee a secure and stable career, the writing profession comes with no such warranty. In reality, unless you are independently wealthy or supported financially by someone else, you will most likely have to complete that manuscript and a few others while *simultaneously* working a fulltime job. This can continue for ten or more years and will require a great deal of self-sacrifice and ironclad discipline. And this is where 99% of aspiring writers will fall by the wayside.

There is also the belief among many that obtaining an MFA degree will pin the badge of *Writer* onto one's chest. But, as I have said many times, an MFA is of dubious value for a writer, and can even erode the talent of the most original writers. To some the degree might imply potential success but it seldom delivers upon that implication. And the completed manuscript that is often a condition of being awarded the degree is itself no seminal accomplishment. Instructors in MFA programs tend to be encouraging and supportive of student work even when it has no chance of ever being published. There are probably several hundreds of thousands of successful yet unpublishable thesis manuscripts moldering away in drawers or slowly corrupting on hard drives in this country alone.

The first real accomplishment an aspiring writer can hope for is to pique the interest and enthusiasm of a respected literary agent. This is the first real step to becoming a writer. Note that I am talking about traditional publishing here; self-publishing still carries, and justifiably so, the stigma of work that has failed to attract serious attention from a professional agent or editor. And let's be honest about it: anybody can self-publish. Doing so is no accomplishment, no affirmation of one's talents as a writer. Self-publishing remains, for the most part, the last resort of failed writers.

However, every rare now and then a self-published book can break the mold and acquire a significant audience. But this is usually the result not of the author's literary talents as much as a result of the author's talents as a marketer and self-promoter. Also, thanks to the always conservative nature of most publishers, many writers who have already achieved success will opt to self-publish because they are too prolific for their publisher's comfort, or have written something outside the genre the publisher prefers, or because they are fed up with earning less per book than everybody else in the publishing chain. These small groups of successful authors who self-publish are all that keeps self-publishing from being universally viewed as the garbage dump of literature.

Another fact that is not often emphasized in MFA programs is that even the most successful writers must stand naked before the public on a daily basis, enduring the slings and arrows of public criticism in the form of Amazon, Goodreads, and other reader reviews, a few of which are insightful and honest, but many of which are uninformed, unjustified, or written by readers who can't type a single paragraph without committing a dozen grammatical errors. Nine-to-fivers seldom have to face such abuse, but it is indigenous to every writer's life.

So why write at all? There is only one good reason to do so: because nothing else you do or can conceive of doing makes you as happy and fulfilled as a morning spent at your writing desk. The creative impulse is far more complicated than that, of course, but what it boils down to is simply that. You love doing it not because it promises fame, because it doesn't. And not because it promises riches, because it doesn't. And not because it promises some vague form of acceptance or admiration, because it doesn't. What the writing life promises is hard work, self-sacrifice, frustration, criticism, public rejection, despair, hunger, marital and relationship problems, overdrafts, too many meals of ramen noodles, missed opportunities, and just about every other tribulation known. But it also promises this: a profound sense of satisfaction when you push away from the desk each morning.

That sense of satisfaction is exhilarating in much the same way as skiing a black diamond slope when you are equipped with only novice skills; at the bottom of the hill you can't resist turning to gaze up at the mountain and laugh in wonder that you are still standing and yet unbroken.

I have had approximately 17,000 of those mornings thus far. I am hoping for a few thousand more before I hang up the skis.

Ever since the late sixties or so, since the boom in MFA programs and the consequent rise of minimalism, the art of writing has been increasingly commercialized and politicized. Sales numbers and advances are mentioned in nearly every writer's profile now; in fact, the only writers to be profiled in major media outlets are those whose sales and advances are high. And knotted together with these numbers, especially as they pertain to literary and mainstream writing, is the degree to which the author has addressed and embraced the political agenda of the day, which has been imposed upon us by what is popularly called the cancel culture. Cancel culture academics have taught the past three generations of writers and editors and agents, as well as those who became publicists and copyeditors. That's three generations of writing professionals who don't even realize how their indoctrination during high school and the college years has hamstrung and poisoned an industry that once was a bastion for free expression. It happened to education first, then journalism, then to the creative writing industry as a whole. The general effect of this subterfuge has been to turn the entire country into a propaganda state.

The question that every aspiring and current writer must ask themselves is this: do I want to conform or resist? Do I want to be a literary lamb or a literary lion? Do I want to live my own life or the life I am told by others to live?

Any novel written in imitation of any other novel is, by its nature, an inferior piece of work. The original is the product of magic – the magic of imagination – whereas its successors follow the template laid down by the original. They are mere copies then, and no matter how much they might improve upon the template, they are of lesser artistic value. This holds true whether the author is imitating another writer's work or his or her own previous work. And that is why I have always done my best to avoid writing and reading novels in a series. I agreed to write the Ryan DeMarco series only under the condition that I could make each book different, whether in structure or voice or character arc or through the manipulation of other elements of fiction.

Those differences might be too subtle for the fast reader to notice, but fast readers don't often care about an author's attempts at artistry. And the differences are not necessarily made *for* the reader, though I always hope that a handful of perceptive readers will notice the differences and appreciate them. I impose this challenge on myself so that I can respect the work, and so that I can respect myself as a writer.

For this reader, too much familiarity with a character and his situation breeds predictability, which in turn breeds contempt, not only for the character but also for the writer who is telling his story.

Fiction, like life, is composed of scenes. What readers remember of a book are the scenes that most affected them emotionally. So, too, what we remember of our lives. The difference between fiction and life is that a writer deliberately composes and structures the scenes in a book, whereas life seems to throw scenes at us willy-nilly. I say "seems to" because there is yet no concrete evidence one way or the other that those scenes have not also been composed, whether for entertainment or edification, by some unseen writer scribbling away in obscurity.

Conflict is the engine of every story, whether the story is one page long or four hundred. The conflict should begin very close to the beginning of the story – in the first sentence, if possible – and remain unresolved, the dramatic tension unreleased, until very near the end.

The objective of this conflict is to provoke change and growth in the main character. To produce "fiction that matters," as Hemingway called it, the main character must be put under near-constant pressure, always struggling with this decision or that, this or that obstacle. Throughout the course of the story, this pressure will provoke an internal change, so that the character, in the end, discovers and embraces a better version of herself.

In this way, fiction acts as a microcosm of real life. Just as every main character must evolve and improve to have a meaningful impact, so must every author, every reader, every human being. To my mind this requires a recognition that we are all connected to one another, and therefore, in a way, responsible for one another. I will not go as far as to say that we are all one while in this material life. The needs and desires of our selfish bodies prevent that recognition from all but a few individuals. But we can work toward that recognition in this life. Every laugh, every tear, every smile, every ache, every agony can and should be an epiphany of increased awareness. Else what good is fiction? And what good this life?

WHAT I'VE BEEN READING

For me the year 2019 *was not a good year* for reading in a quantitative sense, but qualitatively it was one of the best since I was young and discovering the masters of literature for the very first time. I spent most of the summer afternoons of 2019 avoiding the incessant barking from my inconsiderate neighbor's dogs' and the neighborhood's incessant mowing and hammering and other noise-making by piling up miles on one of my motorcycles, usually the sexy candy-apple red Honda CTX cruiser I call Candy. My neighborhood is a tiny little piece of suburbia consisting of six houses shoulder-to-shoulder alongside a private lake, and like all suburbs it is a hive of busy bees in slavish labor to their homes.

Me, I adhere to the theory of the survival of the fittest when it comes to landscaping, preferring to sit by quietly and watch nature taking care of itself. I also used up a good portion of 2019 by driving around five states in search of a home with quiet sun-filled days, star-filled nights, and no neighbors. I'm still looking.

And of course I used up a lot of time by writing and thinking about writing. On average, six to eight hours each day, every day. In total I composed two new novels and two new novellas, edited and revised an earlier novel, three story collections, and three collections of personal essays; I wrote three new short stories and six new essays and a handful of poems, and added approximately two hundred new pages to five novels in progress, and engaged in as much publicity and self-promotion as I could stomach. Overall it was a productive year creatively, but it did not leave more than thirty or so minutes of spare time each day for reading for pleasure. I still had a girlfriend in 2019, so any spare spare time was commandeered by her.

Of the forty or more books I started to read in 2019, I finished perhaps a third of them. The rest went into my *Give Away* stack. Of those books I finished, here are the five best, in no particular order. None of them are new or even recent works.

A. Scott Berg's excellent biography, *Max Perkins, Editor of Genius*, not only revealed the many undercurrents of uber editor Perkins but also the warts and wonders of his three most famous authors. Perkin's influence on Hemingway appeared to have been limited to getting Hem to delete many of his f-bombs, but the always hatted editor kept Fitzgerald writing and financially afloat, if not always sober. He even put Fitzgerald's daughter Scotty through college. In the meantime, Perkins virtually created author Thomas Wolfe, whose work, without his editor's tireless whittling and reshaping, might have remained a self-indulgent morass.

As I made my way slowly, savoringly, through Berg's portrait of the industry's most revered editor, I found my admiration *and* my annoyance steadily growing for Perkins. As an editor, his tolerance and generosity and support for his writers was unparalleled, but as a man outside of his office, he embraced life timidly, and in the meantime gave his own family the short end of the attention and affection stick.

Thanks to Berg's book, I found myself admiring Fitzgerald less, Thomas Wolfe about the same as always, and Hemingway more. In these pages there is a soft, effete, whiny quality to Fitzgerald, whereas Hemingway embodies the kind of disciplined, workmanlike writer I have always striven to be. I never learned to enjoy Thomas Wolfe's self-indulgent and self-obsessed autobiographical fiction, and the man who created that prose, despite Perkin's attempts to tame it, comes across as a kind of huge, impulsive, and pretentious child instead of as a journeyman writer – a diva who believed that every word he penned, and every thought he thought, was golden, and that his only job was to scribble it down so that lesser men, like Perkins, could whip it into a saleable product. If the portrait of Wolfe painted in this biography is accurate, he was probably bipolar.

Fitzgerald was said to be a perfectionist when it came to writing, but he allowed his personal life to peter out in an almost hysterical mess of posing and alcoholic self-pity. Hemingway certainly wasn't perfect as either a man or a writer, and many of his attitudes, when juxtaposed (unfairly) upon current social attitudes, have been condemned (as some of Max Perkins' would be), but Hemingway lived the life he consciously chose to live and he wrote the books he chose to write. I doubt that he ever referred to himself as an "artist," though Fitzgerald and Wolfe did so repeatedly and unashamedly, yet in my mind Hemingway stands alone among the three as an artist to admire and emulate.

For me it all comes down to the prose. Despite my repeated readings over the years, I am always moved by the subterranean quality of Hemingway's work. His use of understatement and subtext and insinuation, as well as his careful employment of cadence and rhythm, are nothing short of masterful. In fact, he was the master who subsequent generations tried to emulate. He is remembered by those who don't know his work well as a writer of short sentences, but he wrote plenty of long sentences too, descriptive phrase after descriptive phrase, laying on details like carefully calculated brushstrokes. As an innovator – even a revolutionary – in the matter of prose style, he remains unequaled – or, as he would say, undefeated – by any other American writer.

Fitzgerald's prose, on the other hand, though as clean and polished as prose can be, has none of Hemingway's depth. It moves along the surface like a clear but shallow stream, its bottom readily visible. Wolfe's prose, on the other hand, can be a twisted thicket of tangled vines, brambles, branches, and weeds. A reader can easily exhaust herself in trying to crawl through to the other side. And when she does manage to do so, what is the reward other than an assortment of pricks and scratches?

Still, reading is a subjective pleasure. In reading, as in life, it is the presence of mystery that most compels me. There is something numinous about Hemingway's prose that is missing in Fitzgerald's and Wolfe's. Hemingway understood what the other two writers did not – that the unsaid will always exert a greater hold on the reader than the overstated or even the simply said. To employ a mixed metaphor, Wolfe's prose was the bellow of a wounded bull, Fitzgerald's a polite dinner party tale trying to be risqué, and Hemingway's a hypnotic half-whisper delivered through a hole in the wall. Max Perkins, to his enduring credit, championed those three voices and many more. Although a lamb in his personal life, in his professional life he was a lion.

And now to the novels. There are a lot of great storytellers at work today, but only a rare few can couple that gift with an individualistic yet wholly accessible style. Out of the many novels I read in 2019, these three stand out as the most memorable: Charlie Smith's *Men in Miami Hotels*, Sebastian Barry's *Days without End*, and William Kent Krueger's *Iron Lake*. All three authors are, first and foremost, brilliant prose stylists. Add their deep characterization and compelling storylines and you have the perfect recipe for a novel to win my admiration and envy.

Smith's and Krueger's novels are both crime novels but of different sorts. Smith, best known as a literary novelist and poet, writes in the 2013 *Men in Miami Hotels* about a petty gangster on the run from just about everybody, and the tale leans only lightly on a plot, which consists of spur-of-the-moment decisions made by the unfortunate protagonist, and depends heavily on character development and personal relationships. The noir elements in this novel are strong, but don't come to Smith's novel looking for standard crime fare. There is music in his prose and pathos in his characters. I loved every page of this novel for its unpredictability and jewel-like sentences.

Krueger's *Iron Lake*, originally published in 1998, unfolds within the framework of the first book of a traditional mystery series, but his endearingly flawed protagonist, Cork O'Connor, the disgraced former sheriff of small-town Aurora, Minnesota, is the real focal point here. And Krueger's wonderful descriptions of O'Connor's milieu are clean, precise, and graceful – as bracing as a gulp of chilled whiskey. I will be starting 2020 by reading Krueger's *Ordinary Grace*, a stand-alone novel from 2013.

Sebastian Barry's *Days without End* is the most recent book on my list, published in 2016, the most original and individualistic, and the hardest of the three novels to describe. It's a kind of picaresque, I suppose, that follows two young men in the 1850s, one an Irish immigrant and the other an American black man, who fall in love and travel throughout the violent American landscape seeking not fortune but survival, trying on this profession and that, sometimes dressed as men and sometimes as women. The journey itself is mesmerizing, as is the Irish author's portrayal of America, but it was the often stream-of-consciousness voice of the protagonist that first captured my attention and never released it. Barry's countryman James Joyce wrote in a similar style, but I read Joyce's *Ulysses* and *Finnegan's Wake* with ambivalence and even resentment at times because of the prose's turgidity and undisciplined focus. Barry's prose, on the other hand, though equally dense with introspection and observation, is always clear and evocative and hypnotic, and generates nothing but attention and an enduring admiration.

The fifth book to leave a lasting impression on me is Joan Didion's memoir *The Year of Magical Thinking*. Another brilliant stylist (and one who claimed Hemingway as an influence on her own writing), Didion in this book turns her extraordinarily keen observational skills upon herself and death and grief and how to cope with it all.

Before reading this book, published in 2005, all I knew of Didion's work were individual essays such as "At the Dam," "The Santa Ana," and "On Keeping a Notebook," which I used as texts to teach my students the importance of close observation and of melding telling details with personal reflection on the deeper implication of those details. *The Year of Magical Thinking* should be a text for all of us who will someday experience the death of those we love and the grief that accompanies it.

None of these books were new releases, but I am so glad that I finally got around to reading these very talented authors. It means that I now have their other work to look forward to. If I am half as enthralled by their other books as I was by these first encounters, my *Give Away* stack will grow no taller, and 2020 will be yet another year of magical reading.

How many times have you come across a piece of writing that makes you have to stop, lean back, and catch your breath? I can count on one hand the writers who have caused that to happen. One of them is Pete Dexter. He does it to me with every book he writes. Fortunately I happened upon Dexter's work early in my own apprenticeship, and I've been turning to him ever since, every time I need to be reminded of how powerful the best writing can be.

Lately I've been re-reading his novel *Train*. Beautiful, distinctive prose, fascinating characters, and a storyline that grabs you by the throat and won't let go. His writing somehow manages to be both gritty and gentle, violent and tender. Anybody who wants to learn how to write can learn everything there is to know by reading *Paris Trout*, *The Paperboy*, *Train*, *Spooner*, and Dexter's other books. His talent, which includes a deep understanding of human nature, always takes my breath away.

Here is a brief excerpt from *Train*; the year is 1953, and two men (Arthur and the mulatto) have secretly boarded a sailboat in the early hours of morning, killed the captain and the owner, and brutally raped the owner's wife. They are still trying to get the boat's engines started when the police arrive:

> *A moment passed, and then the sergeant sighed and picked up the shotgun. He broke the breach to check the load, then closed it again. Arthur's eyes opened at the sound. He began to sit up, and the shot tore away his shoulder and the side of his neck. He was strangely still for a moment. A pink mist floated out behind him, and then gravity took his head sideways and down, in the direction of the missing part of his neck. There were tiny noises then as the bits and specks fell into the water.*
>
> *"Wait a minute," the mulatto said. "Wait a minute here. We had a misunderstanding, sir. All this situation need to be sorted out...." The sergeant nodded again, as if this were, in fact, something they would sort out, as if this were all ordinary Sunday-morning sailboat business, and then he turned himself a little and the shotgun turned with him.*

The next time you are looking for something to read, check out Pete Dexter. He's one of the best.

All month long I have been hopping back and forth between Tea Obreht's novel *The Tiger's Wife* and Harrison Scott Key's memoir *The World's Largest Man*. To me they epitomize the great divide in contemporary American literature and the dilemma it presents to writers. Obreht's novel, published in 2010, does a good job of portraying life in the Balkans following the end of war at the beginning of this century. But the novel is long on history and backstory and nearly void of actual story. I struggled through at least one hundred pages before getting the first meager glimpse of the title character, which leaves me feeling manipulated and a bit cheated. Since then I've been skimming, reading a sentence here and there in search of another thread of plot, or at least for a character I can relate to and care about. But this is literary fiction, fiction with an agenda, and, as such, plot is irrelevant.

Key's memoir, on the other hand, bristles with plot and relatable characters. Told in a series of short, hilarious personal essays about himself and his family, and with the cleverest use of exaggeration since Mark Twain, this book has me laughing out loud on every page. Every single page. He writes about nuisance neighbors, about his father trying to turn him into an avid hunter and football player, about teaching his toddler daughter how to use the toilet, and so forth. No, Key's prose is not as graceful as Obreht's, but it's also not as boring. In fact, it's not boring at all. And he writes about subjects that every parent can relate to. Each piece has momentum, starting with a conflict and then moving toward a resolution of that conflict. It's great fun to read even for the second time, as I am doing. Obreht's much praised book, however, is one I probably won't finish. If I do, it will go onto my *give away* stack of books. When a novel makes the reader work too hard to find the story, it isn't worth reading a second time, or even a first.

As someone who started out as a so-called literary writer in the midst of the doomed minimalist movement, I vowed never to abandon plot. The best fiction, I have always claimed and always will, is fiction that pays attention to *all* of its elements: character, plot, setting, point of view, style, dialogue, and tone. Writers such as Hemingway and Faulkner and Flannery O'Connor all did this, never forsaking plot. That's what the masses care about: interesting characters caught up in an interesting situation rife with conflict, and working hard to resolve that conflict, facing one obstacle after another. Unfortunately, contemporary literary fiction continues to suffer the weakness minimalism imposed upon it back in the 70s. And that's why today's audience for literary fiction is so much smaller than the audience for plotted fiction. And that's why my *give away* stack of books is so much higher than my *keep these* stack of books.

Jane Harper's The Lost Man is a very engaging story about a fragmented family living on a sprawling ranch in Australia. It's fascinating to watch how, with very little dramatic action, Harper keeps a vicelike grip on the reader's attention by delineating the uncertainty and misery of the characters, mainly through the character of the oldest son, Nathan. There is a single dramatic question that runs throughout the novel, and that is the question of how the middle son, Cameron, died. Was it an accident? Suicide? Murder? Nobody knows. But as the novel progresses, tiny bits of evidence gather as the secondary characters reveal themselves to Nathan in barely perceptible ways. Overall, the novel is a master class in how to hold a reader's attention with feelings and thoughts and suspicions rather than with explosions and car chases and seductions and such. Not that there aren't any seductions in *The Lost Man*. I mean, hey, the story takes place in the Australian Outback. Of course there's a seduction or two. But even those are understated. *The Lost Man* provides fine writing throughout, and fine storytelling.

I am sad to report that my pleasure reading this month did not provide much pleasure. Of the three books on my reading stack, I finished only one of them, and then only because I had nothing else new to read. I finally gave up on Tea Obreht's *The Tiger's Wife* (featured in a previous newsletter) around page 250 or so. Solid writing but way too much backstory and history, little if any narrative thrust.

John Updike's *My Father's Tears and other stories* was another disappointment. From my twenties to forties I had a literary crush on Updike. Loved his short stories and Rabbit Angstrom novels. But this final, posthumous collection, published in 2009, left me cold. I dipped into three or four of the stories but didn't finish a single one. His style strikes me now as more appropriate for an earlier era, back when every suburbanite couple honored the cocktail hour with martinis and desultory conversation. Readers had the time and patience back then for poring over minutiae about those superficially polite but inwardly scheming and devious lives. Today we're just too freaking busy to care.

The only book I actually finished, though often begrudgingly, was Jonathan Lethem's 2016 novel, *A Gambler's Anatomy*. I've really enjoyed some of Lethem's earlier work, especially the short stories but also novels such as *Motherless Brooklyn* and *As She Climbed Across the Table*, but this latest one failed to trip my engagement trigger. I didn't much like the main character, Alexander Bruno, nor could I find any common ground with him. Several of the novel's secondary characters, however, had more vibrancy and humanity, and generated more sympathy and interest than Bruno did. Unfortunately, those secondary characters came and went. And so will, in my memory, *A Gambler's Anatomy*.

In my last newsletter I mentioned that I had stumbled upon what might be the most compelling book I've read in a long time. As it turns out, I didn't. Terry Hayes's *I Am Pilgrim* starts out brilliantly, then quickly falls apart.

For the first four chapters of this massive 600-page novel, I was well and thoroughly hooked. A woman murdered in a hotel woman, her body slowly disintegrating in a tub full of acid. The investigator is a former agent with a black ops intelligence agency. Oh boy!

But with chapter five, this narrative line is abandoned in favor of flashback. I stay with it because it still rings of truth, a young man's recruitment into a secret government intelligence agency, how he rises through the ranks and proves himself better than the best. Yet I keep waiting for the author to return to the really compelling stuff, but as the pages unfurl I begin to suspect that the opening hook is not intended to be the real story, but only a hook that will be dispatched with quickly and easily in the final pages.

I think of that kind of bait-and-switch on the part of the author as a cheap trick and disrespectful of the reader. But I tell myself that as long as the flashback story remains interesting, I will stay with it and concede that the real story being told is the story of the narrator's life as a spy and assassin for the US government. That's an interesting story too, though it lacks the thrust and momentum of the murder mystery left behind on page 18.

Unfortunately, around chapter 14, the narrator turns his attention to a ruthless character known as the Saracen, and it is here that any illusion of verisimilitude begins to collapse. Though the story continues to be told in first person, with the narrator frequently referring to himself, he begins to delineate not only every big and tiny action the Saracen takes, but also every unspoken decision and observation and thought the Saracen thinks, as if the narrator is walking along beside the Saracen from his childhood to adulthood and has a direct feed of the Saracen's thoughts.

This, as every aspiring writer should learn early in his or her career, is an unpardonable sin for a first-person narrator. Only a third-person omniscient narrator has access to more than one of the characters' thoughts; a first-person narrator can voice only his/her own thoughts. A first person narrator can guess or imagine what other characters are thinking, but he certainly cannot detail the tiniest of actions and gestures and behaviors of another character unless physically sharing the scene with that character, nor can the narrator, under any circumstances, voice exactly what any other character is thinking. As John Gardner wrote in *The Art of Fiction*, "first person locks us in one character's mind, locks us to one kind of diction throughout, locks out the possibilities of going deeply into various characters' minds, and so forth."

Where, I had to ask myself, were the editor and copyeditors of *I Am Pilgrim* when this egregious mistake was being compounded again and again?

Soon the Saracen kidnaps a man, gouges his eyes out, and uses them to gain entry into a high-security building. Then, after a long series of improbable coincidences that allow the Saracen to accomplish his mission, he returns to the kidnap victim, half-chokes him with a seat-belt he has somehow made "as tight as any garrote," then drives off to a private place where he can prop the man against a Dumpster. The story has begun to read like a cartoon crime story.

It reaches another peak of ridiculosity when the kidnapped man, blinded, choked, and having "plunged into a twisted and psychedelic unconsciousness," is revived enough by a bit of fresh air that he can complement his kidnapper. "'You do good work with the garrote – one professional to another,' he said through his damaged larynx.'"

And I groaned through mine.

The narrator then sticks the man's eyeballs back into their sockets and binds them in place with a bandage, only to then put two bullets into the victim. And through all this, the first-person narrator treats us to a comprehensive recreation of both men's actions and innermost thoughts – little or none of which the narrator could possibly know.

With 430 pages left to read, I have lost all trust in the narrator, and in the author, and in his editor. The novel, by the way, was a *New York Times* bestseller. Oy. I am willing to wager, though, that far more readers bought this novel than actually read it the whole way through.

Allow me to insert a word of caution here, folks: If you spend your life not just reading but devouring the work of the literary masters, nothing but true prose mastery will ever satisfy you again, and merely mediocre writing will make you want to re-watch all four seasons of *Shameless*, and conspicuously flawed writing will make you want to peel off your own skin in an attempt to mask the pain of your soul crinkling up like scorched cellophane.

And now, back to *I Am Pilgrim*. I am so disappointed by how this story is being told that I pause in my reading for a bit of structural analysis. I first started engaging in this practice while in my early twenties, when trying to teach myself how to write by analyzing stories by Hemingway and Faulkner and dozens of other literary masters. I came up with the following partial breakdown for *I Am Pilgrim*:

Pages 1-18, the story, the hook, the reason my heart first leapt in anticipation of encountering a brilliant storyteller.

Pages 19-67, all the rest of Part I, is narrator backstory. As backstory goes, it's interesting, but there's way too much fat in it.

Pages 71-106, the beginning of the Saracen story, which happens several years before the action that started the novel. There's nothing wrong with telling two or more stories non-chronologically, but there is a lot wrong with telling those stories poorly.

Pages 107-138, more narrator backstory; and here, again, this first-person narrator commits the sin of describing others' actions and reactions and thoughts, their hopes and fears, as if he can read their minds. In other words, this first-person and wholly human narrator assumes a Godlike omniscience. Again, any good editor and knowledgeable reader would cringe.

Pages 139-167, back to the Saracen storyline, which is rife with literary misdemeanors. Take this short paragraph as just one among the multitude of crimes:

"Trying to hear, certain there was someone else in the cell, Tlass held himself perfectly still. The Saracen knew there would never be a better moment. Truly, he was blessed. He squeezed the trigger."

Remember, there are only two people in this scene. Tlass and his kidnapper, the Saracen. The narrator is thousands of miles from this action. No tape recorder is recording this scene. No security camera or iPhone. This is all between Tlass, the Saracen, and God. Yet the absent narrator reports exactly what Tlass is doing. That's crime #1. Then, in the same paragraph, he switches point of view – crime #2 – to report the Saracen's thoughts and actions, crime #3. Four sentences, three lapses of honest storytelling.

Long before this point in the story, looooooooooooooong before, the editor should have stepped in, should have said, "Look, you can't do this. It's cheating. It's dishonest storytelling. The narrator can't possibly know all these details. He can't possibly know 98% of this stuff. Ergo you can't have him passing it on to the reader, no matter how interesting you might think it is. These 179 pages, they gotta go. Use them for another story, something you write in third person. But they don't belong here. Here, you should give maybe three pages of summary, what the narrator could have known through his research, the broad strokes. You just can't leave these other pages in. If you do, you break the covenant a good writer has with his readers. And you make me, as your editor, complicit in that dishonesty. I can't let that happen to either one of us."

Obviously, however, Hayes's editor was out to lunch on editing day.

I am on the verge of relegating this hefty novel to one of the cartons containing my Give Away books when, miracle of miracles, the author returns to the storyline with which he opened the novel. And, since I have no other unread book to read, I decide to hang in there a while longer.

But, alas, the tale soon relapses back to the Saracen narrative. And even this, for what it is, holds some interest – the story of an Afghani boy and his journey to megalomaniacal terrorist. But just as I am settling in to what reads like a solid third-person, though overly-detailed narrative, the narrator throws in another I or me or mine, reminding me that I'm getting my information here from a narrator who can't possibly know even a fraction of these details, and which, for the hundredth time, thoroughly undercuts my trust in the author.

A few pages later, the author introduces not only a U.S. President but also several members of the intelligence community as they react to news that the country is on the brink of disaster. The narrator is nowhere to be seen in any of their activities, many of which are conducted in view of no one, but that doesn't stop our all-seeing, all-hearing first-person narrator from detailing every movement and thought, and consequently committing his primary literary sin again and again. The only thing that might absolve the author and all of his editors from their negligence is if the narrator announces at the end of the novel that he is, indeed, God.

I'm three hundred pages into this morbidly obese novel and it's impossible for me to pinpoint the primary storyline. Between the opening story about the hideous death of one female at the hands of another female, and the story about the Saracen's goal of destroying America, and the narrator's backstory, we jump from incident to incident meant to showcase the narrator's brilliance and, in contradictory fashion, his courage and compassion.

It's the kind of sloppy craft we wouldn't be surprised to see in an indie publication, but from one of the Big Five? In my fifty years of reading adult novels, this is the first time I have encountered such utter disregard from an established publisher for the long venerated conventions of honest storytelling.

I am aware that I have many times preached that rules are meant to be broken. But I do not consider honest storytelling a rule of good writing. I view it as a necessary courtesy to the reader – a virtue that every writer should possess.

In short, if I can't trust a writer to be honest with me, why should I read him? There is always a degree of manipulation at work in fiction, but there is a difference between honest and dishonest manipulation. Switching points of view in the same paragraph or even in the same scene, like having a first-person narrator describing another character's thoughts, is not only dishonest but lazy.

It is quite likely that most readers won't even notice these errors. Maybe most editors are unwilling to sacrifice sales for craftsmanship. Maybe our society's literary I.Q. has sunk so low that only a few lumbering dinosaurs like myself care a whit about the ethics of honest storytelling.

Honest storytelling aside, this novel would still contain more fat than a sumo wrestler. At half its current weight, and minus the narrator's many egregious literary blunders, the story could have been a page-turner, a book I would have read in one or two sittings. But even as I continue to skim my way through this bloated novel, another three hundred pages remain. Is all of this frustration and disappointment worth the effort?

Not for this dinosaur.

After ditching the book I wrote about in last month's newsletter, I went in search of another one. And an interesting thing happened. While perusing the shelves in my local discount book shop (where I also buy tools, cases of dark coffee in Keurig cups, cleaning supplies, rolls of linoleum flooring, wall decor, and office supplies), my eye fell upon Wilbur Smith's memoir, *On Leopard Rock*. And I thought, yeah, I think I read that already.

But the book kept calling to me; I would walk away, then return to it, walk away, return to it again. No other book on those shelves beckoned me.

The third time I picked up the memoir, I glanced at the price tag: $2.99. I had already enjoyed a couple of Smith's novels, and besides, what else would three dollars buy – a couple of Sheetz hot dogs, which my digestive tract definitely did not need. So I laid the book in my plastic basket along with a jar of banana pepper rings and a pair of ear buds, then headed for the checkout.

Next morning, a Sunday, the news crawl on my Start page informed me that Wilbur Smith, the internationally bestselling author of numerous "adventure" novels, had passed away at 88 years of age. He had died the previous day – the very same day I had felt compelled to buy his book. Had he been making the rounds of book sellers before retreating into the ether, hoping to boost his sales?

And yes, I had read the book before. That became clear with the first few pages. Yet I kept reading. Perhaps it was my knowledge of his recent death that made me see, this time, several ways in which he and I were similar. I won't go into all those ways here, but I will mention a couple, as exemplified by his own words.

From chapter 1: "I turn to my wife, and she looks at me and smiles, but sometimes I think there is pity in her eyes for this driven man, condemned to never-ending wandering, in pursuit of something he cannot define, that will probably always be beyond his grasp."

From chapter 4, in which he relates his first encounter with Hemingway's work, specifically the short story "The Short Happy Life of Francis Macomber": "I loved this story so much that I immediately tracked down *The Old Man and the Sea*... Hemingway became my literary god and writing seemed to be the occupation of the gods, the noblest calling, the highest aspiration, the tallest mountain to climb."

My initial reaction to Hemingway's work was nearly identical to Smith's, just as my self-perception mirrors his.

Yes, there is a lot of adventure in Wilbur Smith's novels, but there is also more. There is attention to rich, evocative description, and to the beauty and danger of nature, and to the development of characters committed to being better than they are.

Smith falls short of Hemingway's artistry through a sometimes careless cadence, a lack of subtext and understatement, and through a perhaps too-heavy hand on melodrama borne of his larger-than-life characters. And as far as memoirs go, Smith's is no *A Moveable Feast*. Still, I feel a kinship with Smith. There are not many writers left of the post-Hemingway generation, and too few who continue to admire the master's artistic accomplishments. Hemingway changed American literature forever, and his literature has influenced nearly every writer since, whether they are aware of that fact or not.

I keep thinking about Wilbur Smith's time of death and my purchase of his book for the second time. A mere coincidence? Or could it have been Wilbur who guided my eye and then my hand to his memoir? Could he have whispered to me, unheard, "Go ahead, buy it. Read it again. You missed a lot the first time around."

I will also mention here, as briefly as possible, another book I started to read this month. Roberto Bolano's *The Spirit of Science Fiction*. It's not much more than a novella, really, and would fall into the genre of experimental fiction, mainly because of some irregular punctuation and a lot of jumping around with the narrative.

After the first few pages, I was happy that the "novel" is a slender one. It's not an easy read. Most experimental fiction isn't.

And that's why I probably won't finish it. I don't have time to waste anymore on a writer's experiment.

As a young man, I wrote a lot of experimental fiction. None of it was ever published, nor should it be. The older I get, the less patience I have for the self-indulgence of egotistical writers and for the editors and literary critics who promote such indulgences.

Let's start from this premise, with which, I think, we can all agree: Writers need readers.

Therefore, it seems to follow that writers should keep the needs of the reader in mind when composing a novel. To make a novel too difficult, too demanding, too esoteric, too weird or complicated or confusing for the reader will prove to be a self-destructive act for the writer and his/her work.

Consequently, a writer who disregards the needs of the reader is indulging his/her own ego at the expense of the reader's pleasure.

Why would a writer who needs readers in order to be validated as a true writer and not just an aspiring one deliberately construct a novel that is hard to follow or difficult to read? "To be different" is not a valid answer. It's the answer of an egotist.

Even the biggest egotists in literature understood that their first obligation is to tell a good story. "Good" is a rather vague word, but in this case it should include the qualities of being compelling, engaging, and comprehensible. Bolano's is none of those, at least for this reader. According to the copyright page, my discount hardcover copy is from the second printing. This suggests that somewhere between five and seven thousand copies were sold before the book was remaindered. Literary critics adored it, but of course they don't care how few copies are sold. A writer, unless living off a trust fund or a wealthy spouse, must care.

My copy cost $1. No royalties are paid to the writer, or in this case to his estate, for remaindered copies. So from this copy, nobody made any money except for the discount store where I bought it, and their profit was maybe fifty cents at best. Which is pretty much the amount of pleasure I took from reading it.

And, very briefly, *The Melody* by Jim Crace, a novel about an aging singer/songwriter and his final, anticlimactic years. I picked this one because I had enjoyed Crace's earlier *Being Dead*, or at least I think I did, since I can't remember a single thing about it except the title. *The Melody* is very British, very genteel, very slow. Were it not for the grace of Crace's prose, I would have tossed this one too had I anything else to read. Instead, I accorded it the respect I could by skimming through the entire thing, all the way from the mildly interesting beginning to the anticlimactic climax.

In the end, I just couldn't connect with any of the characters in Bolano's or Crace's novels. Isn't that what good writing is all about, making a connection with the reader through one or more characters? Without that connection, the reader remains at a distance, outside the page instead of inside the story.

A question: I know that some of you are "in the biz," so to speak, and that the rest of you are avid readers, so I hope that at least a few of you will respond to this. In the last newsletter I raged about an author mixing first person pov and omniscient pov in the same scene. I bought a new novel yesterday, only to discover that this author – another *NY Times* bestselling author – *does the same fucking thing!* Did I miss a memo? When did it become okay to break this rule? Seriously, is this something new, or have I been out of touch for a long time? Or did I slip into a parallel universe with different literary standards? I honestly want to know.

Every novel is a risk, a gamble, a roll of the dice. There are many ways to fail as a writer and storyteller. Most of those ways result in a loss of reader engagement, or in failing to ever gain the reader's engagement. Lose the reader and your gamble has failed, you've blown your bet, you rolled snake eyes.

Your risk is increased, maybe even doubled, if your protagonist is an unsavory character, a criminal or hustler or sociopath. Such a protagonist might be an interesting character but is seldom likable. And when a reader doesn't like a character, doesn't really feel for him when he gets beaten to a pulp or gets his fingernails pulled out, when the reader, in other words, isn't emotionally invested in the protagonist's future, some other quality of the story has to take over within the reader as a substitute for likability. In most cases, that other quality is plot. If the plot is rife with action, the air thick with dramatic tension, a reader will stick with it even when the main character is destined to end up in jail or in an icy river or unmarked grave. This is the I-need-to-see-how-it-ends appeal. As readers, we're waiting for the payoff, the money shot. Then we can go back to living our own lives and forget all about that piece of fiction and its cardboard characters.

A writer of such fiction might, however, attach to the unsavory character a secondary yet highly relatable and sympathetic character – an autistic son, for example, or a dying parent or spouse – and make that character's survival integral to the unsavory character's success. In other words, the not-so-noble protagonist has a noble motivation for his not-so-noble actions. It's a tried-and-true variation on Victor Hugo's Jean Valjean, who went to prison for stealing bread to feed his sister's starving children.

Such a move can incite the reader to cheer, albeit guiltily, for the unsavory character's success. We've seen it all a hundred times. Many mediocre writers have made fortunes by employing this little trick. It is a way for the writer of unsavory characters to hedge his or her bets. Now the storyteller can let up on the breakneck action from time to time and show us a tender and relatable scene between the unsavory character and the sympathetic character. And, voila! We will now view all of the unsavory character's actions in light of the sympathetic character's dilemma.

Highly relatable and sympathetic characters – though with a very interesting quirk or two to distinguish them from the boring hoi polloi – can carry a story with much less physical action. These stories substitute emotional action and character development for plot. Such stories, if they are also well-written and hewn from carefully chosen prose, will fall under the rubrics of mainstream and literary fiction. But know that the less plot a story has, the smaller an audience it is likely to attract.

I have always tried to have a good deal of both going on in my novels. Sympathetic, relatable characters engaged in an obstacle and conflict-strewn pursuit of a better state of being. This combines the literary notion of a character arc with the pulp fiction dynamism of plot.

It's not a strategy I invented. I grew up with it. You can teach yourself to do it the same way I did: by reading the good stuff. *The Brothers Karamazov, For Whom the Bell Tolls, Don Quixote, Huckleberry Finn, Train, Provinces of the Night, Frankenstein, As I Lay Dying, Robinson Crusoe*, and maybe ten or twelve thousand other novels.

Plot, like character development and setting and style and voice et cetera, used to be considered an essential element in the best fiction. Sadly, that notion got kicked to the curb about fifty years ago, as did rhyme and meter and subtext in good poetry. But removing those essentials from the definition of good writing was like removing the target in an archery competition. Consequently, much contemporary fiction emphasizes either plot or character development but not both simultaneously. Much contemporary poetry reads like lackluster prose broken into arbitrary lines. I blame the insidious proliferation of MFA programs, but that's a rant for another time.

My point here is to delineate a way in which the high-risk gamble of novel writing can be tilted, just a bit, in favor of the writer. Include both sympathetic, relatable characters *and* plot (i.e. a sequence of events escalating in risk and dramatic tension) in your stories. Cause some damage, then fix it. Place your sympathetic protagonist in danger, physically or emotionally. Wreak some havoc, then put all the furniture back in place. Make the reader laugh, cry, think, remember, and wonder. Whenever and however you can, engage the reader's mind, heart, intellect, sympathy, curiosity, the desires for justice and revenge and redemption and truth, the baby and the bathwater. Provide the most comprehensive experience for readers that you can. Hit them from every angle. A little sex never hurts, either, especially in the boring parts.

So much for the writing tip aspect of this installment. I will now talk about the two books I am currently reading, and how the above material relates to those books. I started the month by reading Michael Ruhlman's collection of three literary novellas, *In Short Measure*. The first novella is narrated by a middle-aged, unmarried, and childless woman who unexpectedly has an encounter with her one true love, whom she hasn't seen in twenty-five years. He is now married and a father. Complications ensue.

It takes, however, over 150 pages for those complications to emerge and be resolved. Ninety-eight percent of the action is mental, i.e. cogitation and emotion. So yes, the narrative moves slowly. But the prose is graceful enough, though not particularly distinctive, that reading nearly every line of it isn't painful. Plus, I like the main character (her) and him too, though less. I can relate to her situation, her moral dilemma, just as I can relate to his. The characters are real, the main character's thoughts confessional and compelling. I want things to work out well for her. I care about her future. The human dynamics are complex and interesting.

But after that first novella, I doubted that I had the patience to wade through another one at such a sluggish rate, so I laid that book aside for one that promised a bit more physical action: Patrick Hoffman's *Every Man a Menace*. Written in a style that is more Elmore Leonard than Raymond Chandler, with sentences such as "The windows were down," and "Roberts didn't like it," and "She sighed and started over," this crime novel offered little probability that I would be enchanted by the prose. Also, I soon discovered that the story was populated solely by unsavory characters. Drug users, drug dealers, drug traffickers, thieves and liars, murderers and ex-felons – not a single character I could actually relate to.

What kept me reading was the protagonist of Part One, an interesting fellow, though not one you would want living in your neighborhood. Fresh from prison, he's trying to make it on the outside the only way he knows how. Since that way involves even more crime, I'm not cheering for him to succeed, but I am curious about how he will fend among the nest of rattlesnakes in which he finds himself. And it's one action scene after another. Even when that action is mere conversation, there is a tangible amount of tension in every encounter he has with every other unsavory character. And those interactions become more and more convoluted. My emotional engagement with these characters is nil, and this novel is likely to fade from my memory within days of finishing it, but it's fun to read. I don't have to work. It's something like a comic book without pictures. I will probably finish it before I return to *In Short Measures*.

So that's it. Two types of fiction, two different approaches, two different responses from this reader. The crime novel was a selection of the Book of the Month Club, which suggests that it sold very well. As for the literary collection, it appears to have landed on the remainder table after just one printing. But publishers indicate printings and editions in arcane and sometimes indecipherable ways, so my apologies to the author if I have surmised incorrectly. Still, it is a safe bet that the genre novel, by virtue of accentuating physical action over intellectual and emotional action, had a much larger audience than the literary book.

Because of Mother Nature's meteorological hissy fit this month, I did a lot more reading than usual. I will discuss one of the books at length and comment briefly on two others.

February opened with a novel set in the South. The back cover of Greg Iles' *Cemetery Road* is filled with effusive blurbs written by reviewers and other novelists who compare the author to Faulkner, and the contemporary setting to a modern version of Faulkner's fictitious Yoknapatawpha County. That's one of the reasons I bought the book. But after reading it, I didn't know whether to laugh or shake my head in despair over those blurbs. Okay, I laughed in despair, because this wasn't the first time, nor the second or fifth or tenth time, when under-educated reviewers compared a merely good writer to one of the few true masters of literature. The writer of this particular novel is a very good storyteller, but his work is several rungs below greatness, a level Faulkner certainly achieved.

We all understand that blurbs are mostly hyperbole, mostly incestuous exaggeration written for a friend or colleague, or, at best, are surgically excised from longer, less flattering reviews. Yet still I wonder if any of the aforementioned blurbers actually believe their hyperbole. Similarities in setting or subject matter are no measure of greatness in a writer. To be great as Faulkner and Hemingway and García Márquez and others were great is to be daring and innovative, to break new ground, to introduce readers to a whole new kind of fiction.

In most cases, this is a matter of style. Hemingway's amazing subtext and understatement coupled with a surface appearance of objectivity. Faulkner's endless sentences strung together with their perfectly placed commas, and the swampy, muggy, sweaty atmospheres he was able to generate from them. García Márquez introduced to North America a whole new genre of fiction without even trying to do so.

Dostoevsky, Virginia Woolf, Jane Austin, Tolstoy, Steinbeck, George Eliot, Chekhov, and a handful of others also told great stories, memorable stories, unforgettable stories. But good storytelling alone is, I repeat, no measure of greatness. *Jaws* is a good story. *Get Shorty* is a good story. *The Da Vinci Code* is a good story. *The Shining* is a good story. Even the woefully written *Twilight* novels tell good stories. But never, under any circumstances that matter, have those stories or anything else written by their authors achieved greatness. Nor will the novel I most recently read. It's a decent novel, a good story, and that's why I kept reading it – to see how the story would play out.

And who among the last half-century of writers, you might ask (as I often do), has achieved greatness? Certainly nobody who has written in imitation of the earlier masters. Imitation might be the sincerest form of flattery but it is a lazy strategy for a writer, and there is nothing original about it. As a general rule, I hesitate to bestow the appellation of greatness on those authors not yet or only recently deceased. But I will suggest that you read Pete Dexter's *Train*, or *Paris Trout*, or *Spooner*. Read William Gay's *Provinces of the Night*. Read Joan Didion's essays; many of which, with their graceful prose and astute, gut-wrenching reflections, touch greatness.

In the end, greatness, like beauty, depends upon one's ability to recognize it, which in turn depends, and this is especially so for literary greatness, on the refinement of one's literary palate. If all you read is Elmore Leonard or Stephen King or Stephenie Meyer or E. L. James, you will never be able to recognize the limitations of their work.

So to all of you blurbers out there, I make this request: Please; unless you truly comprehend what made the giants of literature true masters, please refrain from comparing merely good writers to those giants. It not only misleads potential readers, but it makes you look ill-informed.

And now to the novel itself. *Cemetery Road*, by Greg Iles. The prose is bland and unremarkable, yet the storyline did not fail to exert its power. This is the first contemporary novel in a very long time that I have looked forward to getting back to, just so I could watch how the mystery and tangled relationships are resolved. At nearly six hundred pages, the novel is too fat by a third. If editors did any actual editing these days, the book would have come in under four hundred pages and would have been fifty percent more compelling. It also could have done without its numerous sour political observations. In my opinion, a piece of popular fiction, as one of the blurbers refers to it, employing a modifier only slightly less disparaging than *escapist*, should avoid such feeble attempts at social change. Just tell the freaking story.

Still, we all do it. We can't seem to help ourselves from injecting personal viewpoints into our fiction, even though it is likely to alienate half our audience in this highly polarized culture. Again, this is where a good editor should have stepped in and said, "Listen, this is a valid opinion, but what are the consequences here? Everybody knows that the likelihood of changing some reader's opinion about this issue is less than zero, but exceedingly high for pissing off a lot of your audience. Is it worth it to keep this in? Does your ego really require it?"

Truth is, I can't read one of my own novels without wincing. Too much fat in this scene, an irrelevant opinion here, another one there. As much as I might have balked at the suggestion of a revision, I would have come around eventually, unless I felt that the editor was trying to force his/her political point of view down my throat.

Let a character be a character is my motto. But when that character is also the narrator, we tend to associate that narrator, fairly or not, with the author. And no reader wants to feel that she is being preached to. Unless you are a Dostoevsky or Ayn Rand, save the proselytizing for nonfiction (like this highly opinionated book review that includes very little book reviewing). In most cases you will still be singing to the choir, as nearly all of the current bestselling nonfiction does, but people generally read nonfiction because they are looking for factual information and/or personal points of view. They won't be sucker-punched by the author's opinions as they can be when reading fiction.

Fiction readers don't want our political opinions. They want stories about people and their relationships, about people mired in conflict and struggling to overcome it. They want, as Faulkner observed, "the problems of the human heart in conflict with itself...the old verities and truths of the heart, the old universal truths lacking which any story is ephemeral and doomed – love and honor and pity and pride and compassion and sacrifice."

Okay, I will wrap this up with my final diagnosis of Greg Isles' *Cemetery Road*. It's not amazing or extraordinary or spellbinding or anywhere close to being an equal to the work of Thomas Wolfe and William Faulkner, as some of the blurbers claim. It is a damn good story that will keep you reading, though you will probably wish it had been shorter and better edited.

Next I took a fly at Larry McMurtry's *Cadillac Jack*. I have always loved, no, lurved the visual adaptations of McMurtry's novels, such as *Lonesome Dove* and *The Last Picture Show*, but *Cadillac Jack* wore me out before I'd finished even fifty pages. In his preface McMurtry warns the reader that he doesn't much care for this novel, and I could see why. It was just one vignette after another, and nearly all of them were peopled by caricatures. And that's all I have to say about *Cadillac Jack*.

Which brings me to Barry Lopez's *Field Notes*. I didn't read the first two collections in his trilogy of nature-dominated short fictions, but no matter. Years ago I had read some of his stories in literary magazines and anthologies, and I liked them. I like *Field Notes* too, even though this is probably my third reading of it. (The book was first published in 1994 and is shelved with my collection of first editions.) But these aren't really stories as I think of stories. There's a beginning to them and sort of a middle, but seldom a discernible ending. In most of them Lopez paints a detailed portrait of a character's inner life, usually a melancholy life, with the inherent difficulty and miseries of human existence played against the beautiful indifference of nature.

So far, I have read eight of the twelve stories, though I declined the opportunity to finish two of them; they are little more than ideological rants disguised as fiction. Even though I embrace the same ideology (a reverence for nature), I don't need or appreciate a sermon on it.

It's probably safe to say that *Field Notes*, among all the books I have started and stopped reading this month, most closely parallels my own February mood. So I will keep reading it until either February or my current melancholy ends, which I predict will be on the next warm and sun-seared day.

Early this morning, before sitting down to write, and with The Moody Blues' *Days of Future Passed* album playing in the background, I picked up a small-press book titled *MFA in a Box* that had been sent to me by a colleague in the business we call writing. I wasn't eager to read it, simply because I consider most (but not all) MFA writers and their writing uninteresting, but, by the top of the second page, I found myself chuckling. The author is a funny guy. His humor is what used to be called droll back when people still used that word. So I'm thinking, *Okay, maybe he teaches in an MFA program but, like me, doesn't have the degree himself.* And by page five I realized that the book isn't at all about learning to write, it is one writer's attempts to understand why he or anybody else should want to write. (Lesson #1: Read the subtitle, if there is one. In this case, there was one: *A Why to Write Book.*)

A bit further along in *MFA in a Box*, the author, John Rember (Lesson #2: Don't choose a name that looks as if it's missing a couple of letters, and therefore makes the reader stumble a bit every time he reads it, and which, every time he types it, gets redlined by SpellCheck), brings up John Henry Abbot, the murderer Norman Mailer helped to get out of prison, and who then killed again. I gobbled up all of that info like a St. Bernard gobbling hamburger after coming off a five-day fast. Rember then segued smoothly to a travelogue of all of the places in the Northwest where the U.S. government, in its infinite lack of wisdom, has buried enough radioactive waste and deadly chemicals to exterminate every living thing on the planet. Again, I gobbled.

That's what writers do. We stuff ourselves with as much arcane and esoteric and useless information as we can, and not just so we can spew it back up someday in our own writing. Writers tend to be curious individuals who value knowledge for its own sake. A lot of readers are too.

That recognition, in turn, led to another. It seems sometimes that writers exist only to serve as a kind of Akashic Library, mostly for other writers but also for non-writers who just want to know stuff.

Knowing stuff, though, is a double-edged sword. Sure, it helps writers fill the pages, but the more we know, the more we suffer, and the more we suffer, the darker we write. How can you truly enjoy the beauty of America's fruited plains, its shining seas and mountain majesties if you know that buried beneath them are not only enough manufactured toxins to send us all into that last goodnight, but also that they hide secret multi-layered military installments, tens of thousands of miles of paved tunnels and bunkers, and maybe even, in places such as Utah's Uinta Basin and Mount Shasta, Mount Adams, and numerous other high and low places, bases for extraterrestrials and colonies of subterranean Earth-dwellers?   Even if you pooh-pooh the existence of these latter groups, who can deny that greed, deceit, and power-mongering among mere humans is what makes this world go around?

Ignorance is bliss, remember? That's not universally true, but when it comes to recognizing what good people are up against in this word, yeah, the truth sucks.

I have always collected knowledge for knowledge's sake, and have attempted in my own writing to address life's ugliness only in piecemeal fashion. In other words, I've created some bad characters who do bad things, but none whose actions affect the entire world. My bad guys almost always get their comeuppance. But when I started researching *The Deepest Black*, whew! As the epigraph for that books says, in the words of Graham Greene, "Human nature is not black and white, but black and grey." There is a good bit of white to human nature, maybe even more in total than the black, but gray, by far, is the dominant color.

Anyway, that's where my mind went upon reading about the chemical and radioactive dumps in Rember's book. I love it when a few lines in somebody else's book can set my mind to spinning. And I'm only sixteen pages into the book! Will I continue to be hooked?

I find myself not always understanding the point Rember is making, and when I do understand, I don't always agree with him. But I always appreciate the depth of his thought on the subject of writing and being a writer. Take this, for example: "You wouldn't want to write if you didn't have criminal tendencies. Writing is rebellion, a defiance of the order of the universe."

Man, those lines made me nod and smile. As a younger man, my lifestyle was founded upon rebellion. Against what? What d'ya got?

I also secretly wanted to be a cat burglar, a second story man. Not for the booty I might grab, but just for the thrill of doing it and getting away with it. As a teenager, I did a lot of poking around in places where I should not have been. Walking through a neighborhood, I would study the second-floor windows and figure out how I might climb inside one of them. Strangely, I never wondered how to get inside from the first floor; I liked the challenge of having to go higher. Ninety-nine percent of my cat burglaries took place only inside my own mind, but the proclivity for rebellion developed early in me. And it makes me happy to imagine, now that my knees are bad and my back couldn't survive a freefall of three feet let alone ten, that I can still rebel. And it's true: every story I write is a rebellion against the way things really are. My entire life continues to be a rebellion, not only against the conventions of middleclass propriety and the laws of science but, more recently, also against this new and highly idiotic expression-suppressing cancel-culture. And *The Deepest Black* is three hundred pages of rebellion against governmental secrecy and duplicity, and against truly evil individuals everywhere.

Despite the title, Rember's book is not a how-to-write book or even a why-to-write-book, as he claims it is. It's a lot of anecdotes about famous writers and about Rember himself. But who doesn't love anecdotes? The part that most closely satisfies Rember's description of the book consists of numerous concepts and philosophical attitudes about writing, which, though interesting, have nothing to do with the actual practice of creative writing. In fact, were one to think too much about these concepts and philosophies – which essentially say that life is a garbage can full of grief and misery and that writers need to climb into that can headfirst instead of writing about superficial, unrealistic stuff like love and happiness – one would probably never write a thing. That's the problem with being a philosopher. You spend so much of your time musing and reflecting and despairing and deconstructing human existence that you do very little of actually living, except for the eating, sleeping, and other bodily functions parts.

Here's where my thoughts about writing diverge from Rember's: Storytelling, which is the essence of being a creative writer, is a lot simpler than doing the kind of dumpster diving Rember advocates. The storyteller tells stories because he or she loves stories. Loves to hear and watch and listen to and tell them. The why of it, in my opinion, is irrelevant to the practice of it. The storyteller sits down and writes. Period. But if you sit or stand or lie around too long thinking about how or why to write, or about how miserable you are, how you have been used and abused, ignored or demeaned, not much storytelling gets done.

Despite Rember's claim that he is wary of metaphors, much of the book, including periodic lists of rules for writers (I hate rules! Rules are limitations. And there is nothing creative about limitations.), is highly metaphorical, and encourages writers to take one deep dive after another not only into life's sinkholes but also into their own murky unconscious minds (even though he acknowledges that the unconscious mind is not readily accessible to the conscious mind.)

I'm not opposed to academics analyzing and deconstructing writers' work in an attempt to understand not only the writing process but the writer's intentions; it gives the eggheads something to do. But for God's sake, don't attempt to teach creative writing that way; you will do far more harm than good to the potential storyteller.

I'm betting that's what happened to Hemingway and Plath and Camus, Jack London and Virginia Woolf, Anne Sexton, Yukio Mishima, David Foster Wallace, and a whole lot of other writers who punched their own tickets. They started doing more thinking and fretting and dissecting of their work and their lives than actually writing and living. Had I been in the room with them just as they were about to pull the trigger or crawl into the oven or start packing their pockets with rocks, I would have stepped up and given him/her a whack on the head and said, "Stop thinking! Write!"

Unless you are writing only for an audience of English professors with a double major in psychoanalysis, there is little benefit to be gained by ripping your own soul and psyche into little pieces that will fit under the lens of a microscope. A storyteller don't need no stinkin' exegesis of his or her subconscious mind. That subterranean mind is going to find its way into the writing whether we like it not, and that's the way it should get into the story, and where (between the lines) it should stay. If we actively dig that stuff up and lay it out in the sunshine, so to speak, meaning if we purposefully seed our stories with it, those stories will ring false and fabricated. In most cases, it is the subterranean material that carries the power of a story – the writer's unconscious mind whispering to the reader's unconscious mind. Give your unconscious mind a megaphone, and you might well be so dismayed by what it has to say that you lose the will to write.

My final thoughts re *MFA in a Box*: I liked it as often as I didn't like it. Rember and I disagree now and then. So what? For me the best parts were the Epilogue, a long personal essay about trying to find a travel story in Thailand, and sporadic personal anecdotes throughout the book, each a little story about his life in Idaho or elsewhere. He remembers, and fondly, so much more of his past than I remember of mine. As he should with a name like *Rember*. (I predict that fifty years or so from now, if our literacy and language continue to degrade as they have over the previous fifty years, students will be asking each other, "Rember when there was them book things people used to start fires with?")

I also finished Barry Lopez's *Field Notes* this month; I talked about this book of short stories in the February newsletter. Lopez is from the MFA-schooled minimalist movement of the 70s and 80s, so I like his nonfiction more than his fiction. He has a great reverence for nature and is very knowledgeable about the West; in particular, the history of place and those who share his reverence. A few of the stories in this collection manage to capture the sacred and almost magical aspect of the western landscape, but most of them are bland, the prose and the characters flat and distant, having what in psychology is called a flat affect display. Too much telling and not enough showing. I will stick with his nonfiction from now on.

It took much of March and all of this month for me to get through Paul Howarth's *Only Killers and Thieves*. In length it is only a few pages over 300, but it wasn't the kind of book I couldn't tear myself away from. I tore myself away frequently.

The story is set in Australia in 1885 and features two cattle farming families, one barely scraping by, the other highly successful. The rivalry and bitterness between the two families are shown through the eyes of the protagonist, a fourteen-year-old boy. The author also devotes a lot of time highlighting the very negative and inhumane attitudes most of the white settlers hold for the indigenous Australians. It's a bit unrelenting, in fact. That's one of the reasons I could read only a few pages each day.

Is *Only Killers and Thieves* the kind of book I will look forward to rereading a year or so down the line, the way I read and reread *A Movable Feast, As I Lay Dying, No One Writes to the Colonel, Train*, and several others? No. And why not? For two reasons. First, though Howarth's prose is solid, there is nothing distinctive about it. It holds no magic, or music, or whatever you want the call it. Maybe delight is the word I'm looking for. I need that sense of delight in prose, those startling images or metaphors or syntax that pop up regularly in each of the four other books I mentioned above.

The second reason I won't be re-reading *Only Killers and Thieves* is because an oppressive air of misery permeates every page of it, including the last page. I don't care how much misery fills the body of a novel, the last page or two must be uplifting. As has been said by many other writers before me, the first page pulls the reader in, the last page pulls the reader back. Back to more of that author's work. Howarth's novel failed for me in that regard too.

But he's still a very young writer, and young, serious writers who are sensitive to the world's inequities and cruelty tend toward the pessimistic. So I wish him the best. If there is a bookstore in my next life, I will give him another chance then.

I have two books on my coffee table right now and have been dipping into both of them since the beginning of the month. When I first picked up a copy of *On the Road with Saint Aquinas*, I was eager to get into it. I wanted it to be another *Blue Highways*, or *Zen and the Art of Motorcycle Maintenance*, or even a *Travels with Charley*. It is none of those. Nor is it, as I'd hoped, a narrative full of Aquinas's observations and powerful insights, as revealed through the author's revelatory experiences while on the road. Instead it is more of an academic deconstruction of the question of why so many of us are infected with a restlessness and a search for self. This topic speaks to me, in fact it defines me, and a book-length consideration of the subject could have been fascinating. This one ain't. Though I find academic deconstruction invariably tedious, especially when the author mixes contemporary trends and trivialities with Augustinian complexities, and switches arbitrarily from first to third to second person point of view so that it's sometimes difficult to know if the author is speaking for himself or paraphrasing Augustine, I continued to skim the book in hopes of mining a nugget or two from the mind of the saintly profligate himself, though I suspect that my time would be better spent by pulling up an online site dedicated to Augustinian writings and quotes.

The other book, *Forest Dark*, a novel, grows more interesting with every page. It starts out with thirty-seven wordy pages about the disappearance of a senior citizen by the name of Jules Epstein. There is very little dialogue in these pages, very little white space, so I seldom read more than a couple of pages in one sitting. But there's just enough mystery in those prolix pages to keep me interested in the third-person narrative, especially since I don't have any other unread books on my coffee table. But then page 39 of *Forest Dark* begins in the voice of a young female novelist, who tells us of a mystical experience that overcame her suddenly one day, and how it has affected her marriage and career, compelling her to leave her family in Brooklyn to begin a new book in and about the Tel Aviv Hilton.

The back cover copy implies that the writer's research is going to dovetail with Epstein's story to "unlock a dimension of reality" we can't possibly imagine. Oh boy!

This is literary fiction, which is to say that the story moves at a snail's pace inconsistent with the length of my attention span, but I plan to persevere long enough to generate either glee or regret for my decision to drop the book into my shopping basket. At this moment I am cautiously optimistic, but I've been sorely disappointed in the past by novels that started out well, and especially by those named to the *New York Times Book Review* list of 100 Notable Books.

On July 4th I started a novel titled *Idaho*, by Emily Ruskovich. Unfortunately, instead of a great first sentence that drew me into the story, *Idaho*'s first sentence got my radar beeping: *They never drove the truck, except once or twice a year to get firewood.* The next sentences establish that it's an old truck that sits outside in the snow and rain all year long. Upon reading those sentences, I thought, *The writer better not have somebody climb into that truck and start it right up.* A vehicle left unprotected in the elements for very long is going to need a jump start. If the outside temperature drops to freezing, a vehicle's battery loses 35% of its power. If the temp falls to zero, the battery loses 60% of its charge. Prolonged exposure to the cold will drain a battery dry of its charge. Freezing temperatures can permanently damage a battery. That's why every person over thirty who doesn't keep their vehicle in a garage, and many who, like me, who do, know to keep a pair of jumper cables in the vehicle. Many of us also carry a fully charged jump starter in our vehicle.

But even if the temperature outside is warm, the battery on an infrequently used vehicle will suffer what is called parasitic battery drain; every other electrical component in the vehicle, such as a clock or radio or the vehicle's computer system, will continue to drain power from the battery when the engine isn't running. Also, vehicles are not airtight; a battery might fail to start a vehicle simply because the battery terminals became corroded from being exposed to too much rain or dampness.

And that is why *Idaho*'s opening triggered my radar. But yep, on page three of the story, the whole family climbs into the truck – which is at least nine years old and has been sitting unused in high grass and rain and snow for half a year or more – and the father turns the key, the engine roars, and off they go. Right there, the writer lost my trust. My willingness to believe in the authenticity of the story and the writer's ability to tell it just went *pfft!* And this from a writer who, according to her bio, "grew up in the mountains of Idaho."

Even so, I continued to read, a few pages a day for the next several days, each page increasing my annoyance for yet another reason.

Have you ever been in a hurry to get to an appointment of some kind, but then a family member or maybe a neighbor outside waylays you by saying something like, "Did you hear what happened last night?" So you stop, hoping for a succinct summary of last night's events, but the story goes on and on and never gets any closer to answering the original question, and all the while you are getting more and more antsy and thinking how late you are going to be for your appointment. That's what it's like reading *Idaho*. Ruskovich creates two interesting characters, a sporadically insane man and his past-obsessed partner, but she withholds all explanation of the tragic occurrence that made them both that way, and where the man's former family has disappeared to.

Just about everything I know about writing was learned from reading the works of the literary masters of the early twentieth century. Good storytelling, they believed, was also honest storytelling, with the dramatic tension inherent to honest storytelling arising out of the gradual release of important details and clues. That release should follow the timeline of what the narrator or point-of-view character knows and learns; i.e. as the pov character learns, so does the reader. But if the pov character or first-person narrator already knows the whole story, but withholds what he/she knows so as to tease the reader – that's dishonest storytelling.

The effect on the reader of dishonest (or uninformed) storytelling is that the reader focuses on what she wants to learn rather than on the fuller story being told. It's like going to a stage play in which a ticking bomb is placed on a table in the opening minutes of the play. Then, for the next three acts, the characters go through their pedestrian lives without ever referring to or acknowledging the presence of the bomb. But the only thing the audience cares about is that damn ticking bomb. And when it finally goes off in the final minutes of the play, if it ever does, the audience mutters an "It's about effing time," then trudges out of the theater feeling cheated and manipulated by the playwright.

The prose is clear and unadorned though nicely phrased, but as I read I was nagged by an irksome annoyance caused by the author's heavy-handed use of the carrot-and-stick device. She maintains dramatic tension by failing to disclose information that should be readily available. The two major characters, Wade and Ann, never ask each other probing questions, and that, to me, is unrealistic for a married couple. In this way the author withholds important information from the reader and makes those characters seem mentally defective. It's an easy way out for a writer. It is so much more difficult, and so much more skillful, to hold a reader's attention while also providing the reader with knowledge as it accrues to the main characters.

As for my overall response to *Idaho*, I'm not even halfway through it and I'm already skimming. In fact, I started skimming around page 30 or so. For me, good fiction requires a skillful *compression of relevant events*, not a tedious recounting of daily minutiae. Not everybody agrees. My copy of the novel is preceded by three pages of glowing quotes, so it's safe to assume that many people enjoyed *Idaho*. Several of those reviewers get paid to read novels, however, while other endorsements are from writers whose praise was solicited by the author or publisher. In general, I discount the opinions of these readers. Amazon reader reviews are a far better indication of how the public has responded, and those for *Idaho* indicate that only 65% of those reviewers ranked the novel with four or five stars, which means that the book disappointed a full third of its readers. Count me in that third.

I understand the negative reviews, which praise the prose but complain that the novel lacks "story" or plot. How this novel is classified as a mystery or thriller is beyond my understanding; the only mystery is why one character was killed, and the withholding of that known information further speaks to the dishonest storytelling element in *Idaho*.

Will I continue to read it? Only until I can get my hands on something new. Please know that I am speaking only for myself in this critique and all others. As someone who has been reading and assessing literature for over sixty-five years and writing fiction for fifty, my opinion has been formed/influenced/jaundiced by the tens of thousands of books I have read. Unfortunately for me, this author, thanks to her own and her editor's and copyeditor's lack of basic knowledge about trucks left sitting out in a field for months at a time, and about honest versus dishonest storytelling, and about applying compression to the events rendered, is going to have to work very, very hard to win back my interest. I find small enjoyment in reading when my radar is scanning for the next error or when I'm feeling unfairly manipulated or just plain unengaged and bored.

I sense that there is a far more interesting story underlying the one Ruskovich is telling, but instead of telling that more interesting story as it happened, she uses it as a ticking time bomb to hold the audience in their seats. But I have places to go and things to do. Get to the point, writer, or I'm outta here.

Fortunately for Ruskovich, I am but one reader. Countless readers will never notice the truck battery error, but those who possess a basic understanding of car and truck batteries will. And those who know the difference between honest and dishonest storytelling, and who recognize the virtue of a compressed delineation of events, will probably get as annoyed with *Idaho* as I am.

For those of you who own a vehicle but have never given much thought to how the battery works and how essential a fully charged battery is, I offer the following suggestion. Buy a jump charger, make sure it is always fully charged, and keep it in your vehicle. I take mine with me in the Jeep wherever I go, and especially when making long trips during which, if the battery fails, I might have to sit and wait two hours for roadside assistance to show up. I bought mine at Walmart for about $50. It's worth every penny and more.

I bought Like Lions by Brian Panowich on the basis of its first page, and couldn't wait to get home to dive into it. The first chapter was compelling and very nicely written: it introduces a woman who was forced to leave her three sons behind as she fled from an abusive husband. A Sophie's choice moral dilemma. I was hooked!

Sadly, with chapter two the novel made an abrupt jump forward in time thirty or so years, when only one son is alive, and he the sheriff of a crime-ridden county in northern Georgia. Here the characters all talk and behave like hillbilly/biker gang/druggies/criminals. The novel's sudden shift from a mainstream/literary novel to a pulp crime novel was jarring and disappointing. There is some dramatic tension in the interaction of rival gangs and the sheriff's sometimes drunken struggle to be a "good" man, but as I read I felt like I was watching a kind of *Dukes of Hazard/The Godfather* synthesis. No, wait a minute. *The Godfather* is a splendid recreation of a certain kind of individual throughout a certain period of time, so that watching those films is like eavesdropping on a very real, very layered cultural phenomenon. Those people were *real*. The characters in *Like Lions*, with the exception of the first chapter, are cartoons.

I need to stop reading back cover blurbs. One fool compared this book to the work of Faulkner and Flannery O'Connor. But *Like Lions* has none of O'Connor's insightful descriptions, nor a scintilla of Faulkner's stylistic and thematic depth. *Like Lions* is a Keystone Cops version of southern crime. With a Faulkner novel, despite his too often prolix and convoluted prose, there is what critic Conrad Aiken observed: "always with a living *pulse* in it." I.e. verisimilitude, to borrow one of Faulkner's favorite words. I could watch an episode of *Moonshiners* and gather pithier and truer observations about humanity than are found in *Like Lions*.

And why do the pulp fiction bad guys always go after the token female in the novel to bring the hero to his knees?

In the end, I did finish the book, with a whole lot of skimming, but only to discover whether or not it ended as I expected. It did. A very predictable pulp fiction crime novel. Another novel for the Give Away box.

The Cook by Maylis de Kerangal is more easily described by what it isn't than what it is. It isn't a novel, though it claims to be. It isn't a novel because it has zero plot, zero character growth, zero denouement, zero dramatization, zero story, zero emotional payoff for the reader. It doesn't even fit the definition of a novel in terms of length. At a mere 100 pages and approximately 20,000 words, it barely qualifies as a novella. What it is is a tedious summary of the fifteen-year journey of an aimless young narcissist as he works in one restaurant after another. Unfortunately, the titular character isn't all that likable, though the unnamed and never identified narrator seems to adore him. (Which made me question the intelligence of the narrator.) Am I a bit ticked off by this book? Oh yeah.

The only reason I purchased this little hardcover, translated from the French, was to find out just how outrageous it was for Farrar, Strauss and Giroux to slap a $20.00 price on it. Pretty damn outrageous. I don't know; maybe that's the way novels are written these days in France. The French attitudes toward food and dining are certainly different than American attitudes, sometimes even elevating dining to a sacred event, and maybe that explains such financial banditry. I bought a remaindered copy for $1.25, and even at that I feel cheated.

One of the reasons I shop for books on the discount and remainder shelves – in fact the only reason I do – is because I know I will buy fifteen or twenty of them before I find one I like well enough to read from beginning to end. You might be inclined to think that by buying remaindered books I am more likely to buy a bad or uninteresting book. I disagree. Some of the best writers have very small audiences. The masses, I'm afraid, do not have the most refined literary palates. I have picked up remaindered copies of books by Camus, García Márquez, Mailer, Didion, Kingsolver, and numerous other highly esteemed writers in discount stores, precisely because publishers over-estimated the public appeal of that writer. Granted, there are fewer such writers on the remaindered shelves than there are mediocre writers, but no writer is immune to the ignominy of having a book remaindered.

I pay full price for a book only when I know I will not resort to skimming or jumping ahead through the pages, and this is usually determined by previous experience and the trust thereby engendered. For example, I will read from cover to cover anything written by William Gay, Sebastian Barry, or Pete Dexter. For my money, those three are incapable of writing a tedious sentence.

I was all over the place this month – reading-wise, that is. I started the month with the novel *The Astonishing Life of August March* by Aaron Jackson. I bought the book because I had enjoyed Saul Bellow's brilliant *The Adventures of Augie March* many years back and believed that this novel might be a kind of sequel to it. Alas, I was wrong. Still, it started out well: a pre-WWI actress gives birth to a baby boy between the end of Act 3 and her appearance at the post-performance fete at a local NYC restaurant. She places the newborn in a basket of dirty laundry for somebody to find. And somebody does: the aging laundress. It's a nice set-up. But then the story falls flat. By page twenty August is six years old; he has lived exclusively inside the theater where he was born and where his biological mother and numerous others have failed to see or interact with him. His only direct human contact is his adopted mother. That's where the author lost me. The biological mother has never wondered what happened to the baby she abandoned? She disappears from the novel after the opening pages. And a little boy can grow and mature unnoticed by pretending to be a wandering spirit in an old theater, and without any social interaction at all, without any exposure to or understanding of the world outside? Too far-fetched for my taste. That's when I read the author's back-flap bio: he's an actor and former cast member of Comedy Central. So that's why the storyline reads like farce. I read no further. Not a fan of farce.

Fortunately, while packing up my books and other things in hopes of moving out of Pennsylvania sometime this century, I came across two old copies of Francis Ford Coppola's literary magazine, *Zoetrope All Story*. Apparently I used to subscribe to it. Strangely, I had two copies each of Volume 1, Number 1, and Volume 1, Number 3.

I dipped into both issues and found several enjoyable pieces, including stories by Rick DeMarinis and Tennessee Williams and a short play by Sam Shepard and Joseph Chaiken.

Having sucked all the enjoyment I could out of those two magazines, I turned to one of my *Books to Keep* plastic totes and pulled out *20: The Best of the Drue Heinz Literature Prize*, edited by John Edgar Wideman. No, I did not bother to reread my own story, "The Luckiest Man in the World," but I tasted several others and have so far enjoyed rereading them in their entirety "Weeds" by Rick DeMarinis, "St. Teresa's College for Women" by Ellen Hunnicutt, Edith Pearlman's "Vaquita," Adria Bernardi's "Waiting for Giotto," and "Limbo River" by Rick Hillis. The remainders should last me through the first half of October.

I really don't understand why publishers disdain story collections and anthologies. I love them! If you start reading a novel and don't like it, you lose the whole book. But it's hard to not find something to like in a collection of short pieces.

I got to know Lewis Nordan, whom everyone called Buddy, at my Drue Heinz Literature Prize award dinner in 1984. He was the preliminary judge who forwarded my *Luckiest Man in the World* manuscript to the final judge, Joyce Carol Oates. Buddy died a few years back, but he was such a delightful man, mischievous and sweet and always so very kind. I love his work. Unfortunately, he wrote only four books. His storylines are funny and dark and poignant, and the language is rich and evocative. A totally beguiling voice. He and I became great fans of each other's work. Back when I was doing a lot of script work for Hollywood, I asked Buddy if I could adapt his novel *The Sharpshooter Blues* as a screenplay, and he gave me his effusive approval. Six or seven weeks later I sent a copy of the finished script to him, only to have him inform me that although he loved the screenplay and thought I had captured his novel perfectly, he had forgotten to let me know that he'd sold rights to the novel to writer and producer Sherman Alexi. With the rights to a novel, along go the rights to the characters. This meant that my LA agent could not market the screenplay I wrote. But Buddy was such a sweetheart that it was impossible to be upset with him.

All of Buddy's novels are kept in one of my KEEP THESE plastic totes. Desperate for something good to read this month, I pulled *Wolf Whistle* out of the tote. Buddy fashioned his novel from a true incident, the brutal murder of fourteen-year-old Emmett Till in 1955 for whistling at a white woman. From that horrific event he created a cast of the most piteous, deplorable, hilarious, lovable, or just plain quirkiest characters you will come across in American literature. He does for his fictional Arrow Catcher, Mississippi what William Faulkner did for Yoknapatawpha County, but with a wheelbarrow of more belly laughs and a five-gallon bucket of more tears.

At a store called Ollie's – their motto is GOOD STUFF CHEAP! – where I went to purchase an 80-cup box of Margaritaville Keurig coffee pods, I also purchased a hefty paperback copy of David Sedaris's 2017 publication *Theft by Finding*, 500+ pages of excerpts from his 1977-2002 diaries. I had read a little of Sedaris's work previously but never found it as funny as others do. So my expectations were low. But a reader's got to read, so the book came home with me.

Again, my sense of humor just didn't respond. Yet I kept reading. Why? The David Sedaris of his diaries was turning out to *not* be the David Sedaris I imagined him to be. I expected someone cocky, an arrogant New Yorker dripping with self-important sarcasm. How very wrong I was! With every new page, I empathized with him more. His life and his family's life – what a mess!

Sedaris grew up in Raleigh, North Carolina, the second of six children. After graduating from high school, he tried visual and performance art with little success, plus playwriting and stand-up comedy, and eked out a living by cleaning houses and doing other odd jobs in Raleigh, Chicago, and NYC while also trying out his comedy chops at various clubs' open mic nights. In short, his was a tenuous existence. He continued with the odd jobs even after being discovered in a club by Ira Glass of National Public Radio, where Sedaris was using excerpts from his diaries as material. Long story short, his subsequent books finally brought him acclaim and financial freedom.

Back to *Theft by Finding*. I kept reading, never as amused as I wanted to be, but, honestly, empathizing more and more with the young David and his struggles, which were not unlike my own throughout my apprenticeship. Then, unexpectedly, on page 253, I laughed out loud. And it was as if the pilot light on my sense of humor had suddenly flared on. I warmed not only to the book but also to its author.

I finished reading *Finding* yesterday after coasting through five or six diary entries a day, few of them as long as a full page. What I found frustrating were the many individuals identified only by a first name, without any information regarding who they were or in what context they were meeting. I had to research Sedaris to learn that five of the numerous names belonged to his siblings. But I steadily grew to like the guy. He had a rough time of it for a while, but he's doing okay now. Better than okay. And I'm happy for him. He's not a snobby New Yorker after all. He paid his dues and then some. He's as self-deprecating as he is sarcastic, even admitting, after he became a household name, that he feels guilty making so much money when so many better writers earn next to nothing. He's a keen observer of human nature whose unexpected reactions to banal events are often thought-provoking. It's true that I didn't laugh frequently at his material – much of it is too true and too sad to provoke a laugh – but I did smile frequently. (I wish I had had the good sense to keep a diary!) I look forward to reading more of his work.

I started the month by rereading Famous People I Have Known, an autobiography by Ed McClanahan. I bought the book the year it was published, 1985, the summer following the publication of my first book. At the Drue Heinz Literature Prize award ceremony, I had met the writer Chuck Kinder (best known for *Honeymooners*, his roman à clef about himself and Raymond Carver), who later invited me to his annual Writers' Rafting Ruckus, a two-day event in West Virginia that included a white-water raft trip down the New River followed by lots of beer and barbecue and anecdotes. McClanahan was one of the ten or so writers in attendance, and I found him to be a very funny man. So I bought his book and read it and enjoyed it very much. But on a second reading thirty-seven years later, I was less bewitched.

There's no question that McClanahan is a gifted stylist with a warped sense of humor (traits I admire) but this time around the subject matter, mostly about the drug-dipped West Coast literary scene of the late sixties, just didn't enthrall me. I was a little over halfway through the book when I returned it to the shelf.

December's reading list left me significantly more bad-tempered than filled with goodwill toward all writers. That said, I do not enjoy dissing other writers' work, just as I never enjoy critiquing students' work. So I want to preface the following critiques by stating that my opinion is only one of billions. My literary tastes have been shaped by my own experiences and education, just as all readers' are. And my tastes, admittedly, often go against the grain of popular opinion. I can speak only to what strikes *me* as good writing and what doesn't. Writers, I believe, have an obligation to their readers, just as educators have an obligation to their students. Both obligations include honesty. Giving a student false encouragement is as dishonest as praising a writer's work that fails to fulfill its obligation to the reader. In both cases, I always strive for total honesty, but always with the recognition that mine is just one man's truth.

I started the month with Valeria Luiselli's *Lost Children Archive*, but after twenty+ pages of dry details about an unnamed couple and their two children, referred to as "the boy" and "the girl," I'd had enough. Tedious and boring.

After putting that book in the appropriate plastic tote, I drove twenty minutes to an actual bookstore, the nearest one to my home. Bypassing the current bestseller shelves, I combed through the classics first, hoping for a copy of Salinger's collection *Nine Stories*, only to come up empty. Next I hit the two tables filled with older books, but still no Salinger except for *The Catcher in the Rye*, my least favorite of his books. However, I did walk away with five other books in hand.

The first one I tackled was Dennis Lehane's 1997 novel *Sacred*. Twenty or so years ago I read Lehane's *Mystic River* and it blew my ankle socks off. Such graceful prose and compelling storyline! Since then I have read three or four of his other novels but enjoyed none as much as *Mystic River*. Still, I had high hopes for *Sacred*, which was published three years prior to *Mystic River*.

It turned out to be a solid private detective novel, but one that left my socks firmly in place. A couple of things I disliked about it: #1, the narrator makes fun of other people, just normal people, not the bad guys, just individuals going about their own business. I'm sure Lehane was attempting to add a little humor to the story but I have always found sarcasm and insult to be the lowest form of humor, especially when it is directed at innocent strangers of whom you know nothing; #2, a pivotal point in the plot happens around page 200, but it occurs not as the result of good detective work but when the two detectives *just happen* to be dining al fresco when a gust of wind *just happens* to blow the case file off the table, and the passing server *just happens* to pick it up and *just happens* to recognize a photo in it that *just happens* to be of a man the detectives are searching for and whose mug shot *just happened* to be in the previous day's paper, a copy of which the server *just happens* to have. Deus ex machine pm steroids. A painfully conspicuous plot contrivance. Bad, Dennis, bad.

Something I liked: up until page 270 or so, the storyline is very conventional, even predictable, yet still moderately compelling. But then, out of nowhere, something happens that turns that storyline on its head. Suddenly nothing is as it appeared to be. All of the principal characters, except the two detectives, turn their personalities inside-out and now need to be viewed in a different light. Nice trick, Dennis. It left me unable to predict the ending with any certainty. And that's a very good thing.

Then came the wrap-up. The bad guys have been cornered. But ah, another disappointment. I hate it when the bad guys turn into chatterboxes all of a sudden and explain everything they did and why they did it. Let's leave a little to the reader's imagination, can we? It's just so unrealistic to have everything spelled out for the reader. Bad guys don't do that. They might spill the beans in exchange for a plea deal, but not for a couple of private detectives who have no real authority.

So *Sacred* was a bit of a roller coaster for me. I liked as much as I didn't like. But I still haven't figured out the relevance of the novel's title.

With a dozen days left in December, I moved on to George Saunders' story collection *Pastoralia*, published in 2000. Saunders has been a literary darling for quite some time now, a rarity for a writer who focuses principally on short stories rather than on novels. I have liked a few of his many stories, but most leave me cold. Like Donald Barthelme before him, Saunders writes deadpan satire that is usually set in suburban banality. Sometimes he ventures into futuristic or unlikely settings, but they are only minimally described and meant to serve as metaphors for suburban banality. For my money, Barthelme's humor was more on point and more relatable. There is a sterility to Saunders' work that just doesn't resonate with me. But I purchased this book for the same reason I purchased a couple of his earlier collections: to try to figure out why his work is so popular, and because I really do want to like his work. I really want to like every book I pick up.

At approximately halfway through the first story in Saunders' collection – the 68-page title story – I started questioning whether I wanted to keep reading or not. Saunders wasn't making it easy for me to be generous with praise for his work. The story focuses upon a man and woman, not married or even friends, who live in a cave and reenact caveman life for an occasional tourist. The reenactors can't leave the cave except to dump their Human Refuse and are not supposed to speak or do anything else that can be construed as modern. They are sometimes reprimanded for their behavior by a supervisor who communicates by fax. A promising set-up, yes, but with each additional page read, I became more frustrated. The prose is plain and the actions needlessly repetitive. The plot reminded me of old Saturday Night Live skits when, week after week, Belushi and Aykroyd and Chevy Chase repeat ad nauseam the same pointless shtick. I never found it funny after the first time, nor do I find any humor in Saunders' story. To be fair, I might have enjoyed the story better if this 68-page story were trimmed to ten pages. That's as much as the concept needs and deserves.

If this story is supposed to be a satire of corporate America…why? Do any of us need to be reminded how soulless such places can be? As satire, the story has the consistency of meringue atop a lemon pie. My mother made fabulous lemon meringue pies, but I used to scrape the meringue off and go straight for the tangy lemon curd. Unfortunately, there's no curd under Saunders' meringue.

When it comes to reading, if I want to read social satire, I will go to Sinclair Lewis, Theodore Dreiser, George Orwell, John Updike, Joseph Heller, Flannery O'Connor, or Kurt Vonnegut.

Among the fourteen reviews that introduce Saunders' collection, he is compared to some of the above writers. To me, there is no comparison to be made, except for the one from *Time Out New York*: "Saunders' universe is akin to the Simpsons' Springfield…." I agree. There is something very cartoonish here. But why in the world is that considered praiseworthy for what is allegedly a literary work?

So, let's see; what does this story, which comprises a full third of the book, have going for it? The writing style is bland and uninteresting. The story is repetitive and five times longer than it needs to be. The story is exceedingly unfunny. The characters are none too bright and make no attempt to improve their situation. They show little true regard for their families, whose lives are falling apart while the two main characters continue their passive, superficial lives. There is no character growth. There is not a single admirable character in the story, nor any who generate empathy in the reader. Entertainment value, zero. Educational value, zero. Emotional connection value, zero. Time wasted, 100%.

And yet this book received effusive reviews, was named a *New York Times* Notable Book, and one of *Entertainment Weekly*'s ten best fiction books of 2000.

What am I missing here?

As for why Saunders' work is so popular, I can only guess it is because America's educational system long ago dropped Great Books programs and instead adopted the study of graphic novels and comic books. At the same time, educators have done their best to remove all conflict from their students' lives, to never challenge their adolescent preconceptions in any way, and to console and placate them at every turn. In doing so, those educators have thrown away the body of the pie, the reason for the pie's existence, and now serve students only the fluff and air.

According to the US Census Bureau, nearly half of all American young adults (18-29) still live with their parents. Could it be that by extending adolescence by an additional ten years society has also slowed the maturation of the neocortex? I wonder how many of the reviewers of *Pastoralia* are among those growth-stunted adolescents. How many of them have ever read a word of Lewis, Dreiser, O'Connor, and the other masters of deft, adroit, and illuminating satire?

I have read all of *Pastoralia* I intend to read. To wash the bitter taste out of my mouth, I will now switch to Jane Harper's *The Survivors*. I absolutely lurved two of her previous novels, *The Dry* and *The Lost Man*. With luck, *The Survivors* will prove to me that true literature, at least as it is still practiced in Australia, finely crafted and structured, is not yet dead.

There was a time in my life when I spent a large portion of my meager wages on subscriptions to *The New Yorker*, *The Writer*, *Writer's Digest*, *The Paris Review*, *Zoetrope*, and a handful of other writerly journals, all with the aim of teaching myself how to write. The realization that I wasn't really learning anything useful from those publications came at about the same time as the realization of how costly diapers and baby food are. Since then, I no longer peruse other writers' articles on how-to-write, no longer read reviews, no longer waste good money on reading stories that, nine out of ten times, fail to enthrall me.

I still read daily, but nothing that purports to be instructive. Reading a lot of good novels and stories, and starting but not finishing numerous bad ones, is the best instruction a fiction writer can obtain.

This month I read some of each type. Last month I returned from a bookstore with five novels in my arms. The first I read was Dennis Lehane's *Sacred* and George Saunder's *Pastoralia*, both of which I talked about in the previous newsletter. I started 2023 with Jane Harper's *The Survivors*.

The novel didn't grab me right out of the gate the way Harper's *The Dry* and *The Lost Man* did. Too many characters, none of whom really came alive for me. In fact I was three-fourths of the way through the book before I fully understood who was who. Also, from beginning to end, the novel moves very slooooooooowly. I would like to say it's a slow burn, but there is no sense of anything burning. I attribute the slowness to the fact that there is no gradual unraveling of clues in the story to generate in the reader some expectation or speculation as to how the center tragedy of the novel was brought about. The appeal of mystery novels is, for the reader, in going along on the investigation, gathering pieces of the puzzle and red herrings and trying to predict who did what and why. There are two conspicuous red herrings in this novel, but the story doesn't accumulate any evidence against either one of them, so this reader quickly pushed those characters aside for what they were. But that was all the dramatic tension I could feel as I read. Even after 250 pages in a 370-page book, no clues were dropped.

Also, just as I hate the easy tactic of ending a book with the murderer's detailed confession, it is equally frustrating when characters who are related to or close to the victims of the crime are so close-mouthed with each other. It simply isn't realistic. In real life those individuals tend to be just the opposite, always speculating, always trying to piece the puzzle together, deconstructing and reimagining. Maybe this happened, maybe that happened. What about this person, what about that person. Providing those scenes is a good way to keep the momentum going, to keep it fresh for the reader, because the reader is probably having that same conversation with herself. A writer can use such conversations to drop in a clue here and there, and with luck even surprise the reader with something she hadn't yet considered.

Many of the characters in this novel know a lot more than they are saying, but they keep it all to themselves. There is an annoying lack of deductive reasoning, whether in the interior thoughts of the characters or in their dialogue. Consequently, for all but the last few pages of the novel, I detected no forward movement in the story, no drive, no escalating tension. Reading this novel made me feel like I was shoveling out the driveway during a blizzard; I just wasn't getting anywhere.

The Survivors was published two years after *The Lost Man* and four years after *The Dry*. Could it be that, having already written two terrific books that became international bestsellers, the author or her editors took their foot off the pedal?

After finishing *The Survivors*, I needed something a bit more uplifting. So why not some hardboiled PI prose, especially when it is rendered in the startling similes and metaphors and observations made by Raymond Chandler's protagonist, Philip Marlowe. *The Little Sister*, first published in 1949, filled that ticket nicely. Chandler is also great with description, whether describing a setting or a person, as in this passage:

> *She didn't have to open her mouth for me to know who she was.... She was a small, neat, rather prissy-looking girl with primly smooth brown hair and rimless glasses. She was wearing a brown tailor-made and from a strap over her shoulder hung one of those awkward-looking square bags that make you think of a Sister of Mercy taking first aid to the wounded. On the smooth brown hair was a hat that had been taken from its mother too soon.*

Chandler makes every scene and every important character visual and memorable. Yes, the tough guy dialogue sounds a bit stylized these days, and nearly every female character throws herself into Marlowe's arms, but it's still great fun to read. And every scene does what *The Survivors* failed to do; it moves the plot forward. We are right there with Marlowe as he questions the woman, the doctor, the hotel manager, the actress, the security guard, the agent. We get the information at the same time he does, which allows the reader to assess not only the information but the characters' honesty. It is small wonder that Chandler is considered a master, if not *the* master, of the genre.

Despite the fact that I started James Lee Burke's *Heaven's Prisoners* in January (and mentioned it in the January newsletter), then stopped when I recognized that I had read it many years ago and did not wish to experience a particularly heart-wrenching scene again, I picked the book up again early in February, but not before reading several chapters of E.L. Doctorow's *City of God* and then giving up on that novel too. My tolerance for books that are not riveting grows shorter every day. As English poet and playwright Henry James Byron wrote, "Life's too short for chess." (Some attribute the quote to American writer Henry James, but he plagiarized it.) The same philosophy applies to cold weather, leftover food, relationship drama, lumpy mattresses, and books that don't keep me captivated. I'm done with all that.

Even Burke's beautiful prose lost its grip on me about halfway through the book. From there on I skimmed, jumping over long descriptive passages, and hurried to the end, which I found to be anticlimactic. But Burke's stories, to his credit, though often gritty, are never melodramatic or sensationalistic. February held me in more of a Hemingway mood, I guess; I wanted descriptive but concise.

And so ended the stack of five books I brought home in January. I needed to feed the beast again, and so found the mammoth novel *A Brief History of Seven Killings* by Marlon James shelved in a discount store's nonfiction section. The book was published in 2014 and won the 2015 Man Booker Prize as well as other literary awards.

Upon checking the book out, I informed the cashier that the novel had been incorrectly shelved in the nonfiction section. He said. "How do you know that if you haven't read it yet?"

I pointed to the announcement on the book's cover. "It won the Man Booker Prize."

He blinked once. "Yeah. So?"

I said, "That's an annual prize for fiction."

He blinked at me a couple of times, then said, "Are you buying it or not?"

As of today, the last day of the month, I am still in the shallows of this 686-page behemoth. The writer's gift for prose is very promising, but already I can foresee myself doing a lot of skimming. As with most plotless novels, and especially those written in first-person, the narrator tends to go on way too long. When there are no plot points to act as destination goals for the writer, he/she has a tendency to wander around aimlessly and take the reader along for what soon becomes a tedious ride.

It is too early for me to say for sure if that is what will happen in this novel. I can only say that the first ten pages could have been five pages without doing the novel any harm. And so on throughout the rest of the novel.

Anybody who has read or attempted to read James Joyce's *Ulysses* can admire the novel's innovation and verbal brilliance but still come away from it thinking, *I don't know what the fuck is happening in that book.* That is exactly how I felt while continuing to read Marlon Jones's *A Brief History of Seven Killings*, which I wrote about in last month's newsletter. The novel won the 2015 Man Booker Prize and elicited effusive reviews.

Nearly all literary awards handed out in this century are to books espousing the prevailing political slant of the academic elite, a slant that seldom mirrors that of the masses. *Seven Killings* falls into that category too.

In a 2019 issue of *The Guardian*, columnist Kenan Malik discussed the work of Harold Bloom, a very influential US literary critic. Bloom, Malik said, insisted "that the work should be judged purely aesthetically," and not based on its adherence to the current political zeitgeist, whether it be the "'Feminists, Afrocentrists, Marxists, Foucault-inspired New Historicists, or Deconstructors" who were not interested in literature but only wanted to 'advance their programs for social change'." In other words, said Malik, Bloom insisted that the "quality of a poem or novel or play must be judged in its own terms; social or political concerns were irrelevant in such judgment."

I side with Bloom. Novels and other forms of fiction should be about the telling of individual stories, and for making a poignant connection between those characters and the reader. Politics and social commentary should be left to the essayists. To tell a good story, a compelling and fulfilling story, there must be a beginning, middle, and end. To this point in *Seven Killings*, all I have encountered are individual anecdotes.

The only unifying thread between the seven killings and the many voices employed is a historical incident: seven gunmen burst into singer Bob Marley's house and shot the place up. However, I had to go back to the front of the book and read the gushing blurbs to learn that fact, because it hadn't yet been made clear in the narrative.

I have been dipping into this novel since February and am only on page 75. I think I will shelve the book for now and save it for when the Four Horsemen of the Apocalypse send humanity back to the Stone Age. I will have a lot more time to read then.

Have you ever purchased a cherry pie for eight dollars, took it home, cut into it, and found that the filling contained only one cherry? Neither have I. But that's how I felt after reading Don Delillo's *The Silence*. I felt like demanding my money back for false advertising. And would have done so had I not picked the "novel" up at a discount store for a mere $1.25.

Delillo's anorexic "novel" is about five people who, on Super Bowl Sunday, suffer a grid-down event together. It's an interesting premise that whines and whimpers and then crawls off to expire in a dusty corner of the room. For a story called *The Silence*, the main characters just can't shut up.

Truth be told, I bought the match-thin *The Silence* so as to find out how a once estimable publisher such as Scribner's could dare to call fewer than 15,000 words "A Novel" and sell it for $22 ($29 in Canada). If you like Delillo's work and postmodernism in general, you will love this one. I don't and didn't. But it's good to know that if I subscribe to Scribner's notion as to what constitutes a novel, I have written not twenty-five of them but nearly fifty. Max Perkins must be rolling over in his grave right now.

An average page of *Seven Killings* has 650 words; an average page of *The Silence* has fewer than 150. *The Silence* has 114 pages; *Seven Killings* has 686. *Seven Killings* has 76 characters; *The Silence* has five. Guess which one is a bona fide novel and which one is a bogus novel.

I read a few pages in each of two other novels as well, but there is nothing to be gained by lambasting them here.

This month I started reading but soon gave up on two novels and one story collection that will remain unnamed. Right now I am slowly working my way through *The Pier Falls and Other Stories* by English author Mark Haddon, who is probably best known here in the States for his short novel *The Curious Incident of the Dog in the Night*, which I enjoyed many years ago. The collection starts with the title story, which appears to be a fictional recreation of a true incident, the collapse of a popular pier along the shore of a touristy seaside town on the English coast.

I read the full story but was never truly engaged by it, and the reason for that is simple: it reads like the literary equivalent of a newsreel shot from middle distance. We see a pier collapse, see nearly a hundred people drown, we see others being saved. The story is little more than a summary that jumps from one faceless character to another. Reading it reminded me of the famous footage showing the Hindenburg airship going down in a ball of flames. We see human figures, some of them on fire, staggering or running out of the flames, but we don't know those people, not their names, their faces, their histories. It's a horrifying few minutes but our horror and our compassion are generalized. All those poor, unfortunate people. But we don't *know* them. We feel no personal sense of loss or grief. And that's what the story "The Pier Falls" is missing too. For my money, the story could have been so much more compelling and affecting had the author told it through the point of view of a single victim. Stories shot close up rather than from a distance are always the most successful ones, whether on the page or the screen. As writer John Hersey observed, "Journalism allows its readers to witness history; fiction gives its readers an opportunity to live it." Unfortunately, "The Pier Falls," except for one or two very short passages, reads like journalism.

Story #2, "The Island," was more successful because it focuses on a single person, a princess who sacrifices her own family for a criminal who then betrays her. I was hoping for at least a glimmer of redemption for her at the end of the story, but none came. The story died with a whimper.

Story #3, "Bunny," has the same problem. A morbidly obese man falls in love with a lonely spinster who feeds him the sugary sweets that are killing him. Again, no glimmer of redemption at the end of the story.

Story #4, "Wodwo," took me to the very brink of frustration. It opens with fourteen pages of unnecessary and tedious history of each member of a large family who are gathering together for Christmas dinner. Then, on the fifteenth page, just as I was about to toss the book aside forever, something happens. (It should have happened no later than page 3.) A large, bearlike stranger appears. With a shotgun under his coat. Then the twist: He lays the shotgun on the table and asks for someone to kill him. Someone does, but accidentally. Blood and guts everywhere. The family is stunned, then argues. And now I'm thinking, darn, this story is about to descend into a murky pool of soul searching. But wait! The man eviscerated by a double-barreled shotgun blast opens his eyes, stands, and thanks the shooter. Then says, "I will see you all again next Christmas. Then it will be my turn." What a hook! Who could stop reading now? Not me.

Unfortunately, after sinking the hook into the reader, the author gives us another twenty-five pages wherein the activities of the next year are delineated, not just for the shooter but for all members of the disintegrating family. What a waste of ink and wood pulp! A simple jump cut or even a one-paragraph summary of the year would have served the reader better. The final few pages wrap up the story. And it isn't a bad story. Parts are compelling. The other parts, at least half of the 68-page story, are totally unnecessary.

I will finish reading this book, however. I now know what to expect from the remaining five stories: interesting characters, interesting plots, but too many skimmable pages. It's like a prime rib steak: burn off all the fat and there will be several tasty bites to enjoy. On the other hand, some people like fat in their meat and in their prose. I don't.

William J. Mann's massive biography The Contender: The Life of Marlon Brando is the only book I picked up this month. And I don't mean the only book I purchased, I mean the only one I literally picked up.

Brando was always a hypnotic figure to me, ever since I first saw him in *On the Waterfront*. His acting work was powerful and pained. He kept me mesmerized even in bad movies such as *The Island of Dr. Moreau*. I remember reading the novel *Blood Meridian*, and when I wasn't yawning over Cormac McCarthy's self-indulgent prose, I was envisioning Brando as the character Judge Holden, a man McCarthy described as "a massive, hairless, albino man."

And Brando as the Godfather, wow. I was spellbound, even though I was well aware of the prosthetic mouthpiece stuffed in his cheeks. (No, not cotton balls, as the myth goes, though he did use cotton balls for his screen test.) Very few actors have had that effect on me. As an actor (a profession he disparaged), Brando rose above the profession.

As for Mann's biography, though I think the author spends too much time on Brando's apprenticeship as an actor, and maybe a little too much time psychoanalyzing Brando's motives, I enjoyed the book very much. When I read biographies, I don't look for original images, stylistic distinction, and a compelling storyline but for interesting anecdotes that reveal the subject's inner self, and there is a lot to discover about Brando in this book, a lot I would not have assumed before reading this very interesting and illuminating biography.

A few days after finishing the book, I was lucky enough to catch an airing of *On the Waterfront* on the TMC Channel. And yes, the man was mesmerizing. Anyone who has suffered in life could not help but see the suffering in Brando's expression, even as a young man. Having read the biography, I now know that the suffering was very real and relentless throughout his entire life.

Introspective, self-critical, daring, rebellious, and contemptuous of America's celebrity culture, Brando remains the greatest actor this country has yet produced. *The Contender* captures every one of those facets and does so with the empathy and admiration they deserve.

Long before I discovered and was bewitched by the prose of Hemingway and Faulkner and García Márquez, there were two other important influences on what would become my writing style. In fact, Hemingway and the others were not caught in my headlights until *after* I had decided to become a writer, which happened in my 21st year. Only then did I embark upon a self-teaching program that had me analyzing dozens of authors in an effort to determine what made their work so compelling and successful.

Throughout my teens, Ray Bradbury was my favorite writer. I especially liked his story collection *October Country*; his science fiction, on the other hand, did not excite me. I found the characters and settings of *October Country* familiar and therefore compelling. I *knew* those characters and settings. I understood them. I lived among them. And I was enamored of his characters' strangeness, just as I was enamored of my uncles' and neighbors' strangeness. But it wasn't Bradbury's prose style that enchanted me; I don't remember looking closely at it or studying its effect on me the way I later did with other authors.

Before Bradbury, beginning in the early sixties and still to this day, there was another writer – and probably the biggest influence on my writing – and that was singer/ songwriter Paul Simon. I was enthralled and in awe of his songs, though it wasn't the harmonies with Art Garfunkel that hypnotized me, and it wasn't even the melodies – although, as an aspiring songwriter myself, I did pay close attention to the melodies. It was the lyrics. Those poetic, understated, sensorial lyrics. Simon's lyrics spoke to my soul. "I Am a Rock." "The Sounds of Silence." "A Hazy

Shade of Winter." "The Boxer." And on and on and on. As I struggled through my teens, attempting without much success to build a self-image, Paul Simon was writing the soundtrack to my life. Simon gave voice to my misery and loneliness and fear and self-doubt.

When I would listen to "The Only Living Boy in New York," it didn't matter that I had never been to New York; I was the only living boy in Sandy Hollow, Pennsylvania. And Paul Simon was singing my life. He understood it. He, like no other person in the universe, understood me. Else how could he describe to perfection, in the song "America," the condition I tried to hide from everybody: "I'm empty and aching and I don't know why"?

And I don't know why! If any phrase absolutely nailed my life back then, and still does from time to time, it is that phrase. And that's how I knew that Paul Simon was my brother. Though he was seven or eight years older than me, I ached to know him. I wanted to hang out with him. I wanted to talk with him about music and songwriting and life and how to navigate it all. I wanted him to be the supportive and loving and instructive big brother I never had.

I would have followed him around like a puppy, hanging on his every word. But I was too shy and self-loathing to even send a fan letter. So I listened to his songs. I learned to play them on the piano. And I did my best to absorb every bit of songwriting wisdom those songs had to offer.

I devoured the poetry in his songs. I lived on it. The poetry and emotion, both so crystalline and piercing. I liked the Beatles' work too, especially McCartney's story songs, "Eleanor Rigby," "She's Leaving Home," and so forth. But the Beatles' tragic flaw, in my eyes, once I got used to those otherworldly and almost dissonant harmonies, was that most of their songs sounded the same. They all came with the signature Beatles' sound.

Paul Simon, on the other hand, seldom repeated himself. He struck me as a musical pioneer. He was my Nikola Tesla, always experimenting, always trying new things. I told myself, "He's just like me. He has a low tolerance for repetition. He wants to do what is unknown. What has never been done before, especially by himself."

Whether I caught that bug from Simon or, more likely, was born with it, his influence resonates throughout my writing. If I have succeeded in doing something different with every novel, every story, a lot of the credit goes to Paul Simon for the affirmation of that objective imparted to me by his own brilliant and always exciting work.

So when an ad for an audio book titled *Miracles and Wonder: A Conversation with Paul Simon* popped up on my screen, I didn't, for maybe the first time in history, curse at the offending ad and those who perpetuate the plague. I hit the BUY button so fast and hard that I knocked the phone out of my hand.

It's a wonderful book, full of music and conversations between Simon and the two authors. Simon talks about his methods, his motives, his successes and failures. It is the most engaging book I have encountered for a very long time, and the only audio book I have listened to the whole way through. I am now listening to it for the second time.

Trent Dalton's Boy Swallows Universe makes *The Adventures of Huckleberry Finn* read like a middle grade novel.

I have read so many books over the years that it is almost impossible for me to come across an original storyline, and that is why I have excoriated or simply failed to finish so many books. Sheer boredom. But the characters and storyline of *Boy Swallows Universe* are not only unlike any I have ever encountered before, but something I never could have conceived of myself. This combination of masterful prose style and the small cast of wholly unique yet credible and sympathetic characters make this, in my eyes, a huge book. I am insanely jealous of what Trent Dalton has accomplished here, but jealous in a kind and pleased and forgiving way. This is the best novel I have read in a very long time. It's better than most of the best of all the other novels I've talked about in this newsletter, with the exception of Pete Dexter's *Train*. They are totally different books set in totally different worlds, but they are equally fine.

Set in Brisbane, Australia, *Boy Swallows Universe* is the story of Eli Bell and his older brother August. Both are autistic. The prose style is lovely and distinctive, which is difficult to pull off in first-person point of view, but the young narrator, Eli Bell, is very – as he tells us – special. But he is special in a wholly believable way. His father is an alcoholic, his mother is in prison, his brother August refuses to talk, his stepfather is a heroin dealer, and his best friend, other than his brother, is a notorious felon who is best known as the national champion of prison escapes. The plot of this compelling novel is survival: how will two autistic boys negotiate gangs and poverty and drugs and the mean streets that surround them long enough to save their parents yet retain their own inherent goodness and very special qualities?

The story is gangbusters, but it's the way Dalton tells it that makes this novel special.

> *I'm thirteen years old and like any self-respecting Queensland teenager with a deeper voice and bigger balls, I want to experience new things, like spending this next month with Lyle on his heroin runs. I subtly remind Mum about August's and my burning fascination with burning things whenever we don't have adult supervision. Why, just the other day, I mention, I'd watched August set fire to a petrol-covered globe we found dumped beside a Lifeline charity bin in Oxley. "Gonna set the world on fire!" I hollered as August held his magnifying glass over Australia and a hot apocalyptic dot of magnified sunlight descended over the city of Brisbane.*

Dalton also possesses that rare proclivity I first came across in García Márquez's short stories – the ability to say something pedestrian in a singularly stunning way. Here is just one of many examples of what I mean:

> *She's only thirty years old and she only drinks Scotch whisky on ice and she freezes the ice cubes for her drinks by staring at them.*

These little gems of description run all through the novel. In fact, *Boy Swallows Universe* has a lot in common with García Márquez's masterpiece *A Hundred Years of Solitude*. *BSU* is not just an excellent novel, it is an important novel. Right now there are probably fledgling writers all over seven continents struggling to write like Trent Dalton.

Throughout the entire novel, I encountered only one flaw – SPOILER ALERT! SKIP THIS PARAGRAGH IF YOU INTEND TO READ THE NOVEL – and that was the climactic scene. It struck me as too melodramatic, too B-movie-ish. And unnecessarily so; the first person voice is a clear signal that what a reader might fear worst is not going to happen. Otherwise, the novel never stumbles.

There is so much to like in this novel, especially the author's loquacious narrator Eli Bell, whose depiction brings back sweet memories of my own childhood through the boy's litany of misdeeds and flights of fancy. Eli also loves words and wants to be a writer when he grows up, a journalist.

Turns out that author Trent Dalton himself is an award-winning journalist and filmmaker, yet despite his talent and his youthful good looks and the enormous success his first novel has achieved, I can't wait to read his next novel. Fortunately, he is a much younger man than I am, so he is likely to outlive me by three or four decades. I pray that he keeps writing novels like *Boy*

Swallows Universe, that he drops everything else and does nothing but write more novels like this one. According to Amazon, he has written at least one other novel, *All Our Shimmering Skies*. I plan to get my greedy hands on a copy ASAP. If I can read just one novel a year the equal of *Boy Swallows Universe*, I will die a reasonably happy man.

A Temporary Conclusion

A study conducted a few years ago by University of Toronto researchers Djikic, Oatley, and Moldovenau found that habitual readers of fictional literature are better at "processing information generally, including those of creativity." Their concluding statement deserves repeating here: "In ancient Greece, all students, no matter their future profession, had to know Homer by heart. The method may seem outdated, yet one may still wonder how such an immersion in literature may have contributed to the education of philosophers, mathematicians, and writers who, although separated from present time by two-and-a-half millennia, developed minds whose supple and agile turns are still admired."

Although I write both fiction and nonfiction in various genres, fiction is my principle métier. And, as I have watched the literary sophistication of college students and my adult acquaintances deteriorate over the past fifty years, I fear that more and more people in this country are growing up without ever experiencing the magic of good fiction.

I am tempted to use the words *soul* and *spirit* in a definition of that magic, but such terms make many readers scoff and might only reinforce their disbelief in the power of something as insubstantial as, in their minds, the child's play of imagination. But I have felt that magic a thousand times. As a person, it has sustained me. As a writer, I have been graced by readers with expressions of gratitude for that magic. Let me relate to you one of the clearest expressions I've received of a magic that is so difficult to articulate:

Several years back, I was having lunch with a woman, her husband, and the woman's ninety-one-year-old father, as I had done in the past maybe four or five times, whenever they were in the area. I don't know this family well, but well enough to enjoy a couple hours of conversation and good food. The woman, whom I will call Melissa, told me that she had recently read my novel, *The Boy Who Shoots Crows*. "After I finished it," she said with her husband at her side, "I felt so lonely that I carried the book with me wherever I went. For at least a week afterward. I missed your voice so much."

I was startled by her words and afraid that her husband might resent them, but he was smiling and nodding. His wife wasn't flirting with me, and she wasn't saying she had missed *me*. She had missed the voice of the story. She had turned the last page, closed the book, and that voice fell silent.

What does this mean? How does this speak to the magic of story?

The sadness Melissa felt when the story ended is not a bad thing. It is a life-affirming sadness. It is the sadness that comes after many hours of deep connection with the characters of a story, with many hours of walking by their side and watching their turmoil and *feeling* it deep in one's self. It is a profound and lasting empathy for characters who have become as real to the reader as her own family.

One of the main characters of that novel is a woman drowning in guilt and remorse; the other is a man drowning in loneliness. Both are inherently good people trying to do their best with the limited amount of understanding available to them as human beings. There are no real villains in this story – which is just one of the ways in which stories with a serious intent often differ from stories that only aim to titillate and entertain. The villain here is life itself, its unpredictable and uncontrollable nature, and the unbridgeable gulf that life inserts between every person and every other person.

A writer can receive no greater compliment than the one Melissa gave me: *I missed your voice so much.* She was telling me that the story had filled her with empathy for its characters and that she had not wanted to leave the company of those characters, that she had come to love them and care about them and was saddened to have to tell them goodbye at the end of the novel.

Our lives are filled with such moments of life-affirming sadness, especially for those of us fortunate enough to be parents. The day we drop our child off at school for the first day of kindergarten…the day that child moves into her dorm room…the day we walk that child down the aisle or watch him standing at the altar awaiting his bride. The day we hold our parent's hand in the hospital room, and whisper that it is okay to let go now…the day we comfort a friend at graveside.

Most of us cannot read each other's minds or hearts. We can never truly experience what another person is experiencing. The only tool we have available to help us narrow the gulf between ourselves and another person is the emotion of empathy, a form of love the Greeks called *philos*, a love that requires virtue and a sense of equality.

This is the power and the magic inherent to story. Story articulates and gives form to and evokes our empathic response to one another. Story takes us inside another's heart and soul and allows us to understand again that we are all the same creature inside a myriad of different skins.

Words have power, and when thousands of those words are strung together in service to a story, magic happens. Good stories have saved millions, perhaps billions of lives. I know that they saved mine. I wish a never-ending supply of good stories for all of you.

Randall Silvis is the multi-genre author of numerous critically acclaimed novels, story collections, and books of creative nonfiction. He was the first Pennsylvanian to win the prestigious Drue Heinz Literature Prize (1984), and was chosen for that award by author Joyce Carol Oates. His work is available in twenty countries in over two hundred editions and several languages.

Praised as "an author's author" (*Book Reporter*), "a wordsmith extraordinaire" (*Booklist*), a "masterful storyteller" (*New York Times Book Review*), and as an author whose writing "leaves the reader breathless with the force of its beauty" (*Erie Times News*), Silvis is also a prize-winning playwright, a produced screenwriter, and a prolific essayist. His work has appeared on Best of the Year lists from the *New York Times*, the Toronto *Globe & Mail*, *Strand* magazine, the International Association of Crime Writers, and several other review sources.

Among his many literary awards are two National Endowment for the Arts Literature fellowships, a Fulbright Senior Scholar Research Award, six writing fellowships from the Pennsylvania Council on the Arts for his fiction, drama, screenwriting, and creative nonfiction, and a Doctor of Letters degree awarded in recognition of "a sustained career of distinguished literary achievement."

A Note from the Author about
The Legacy Collection

A couple of decades ago, with a dozen novels and several literary awards under my belt, I decided that the time and energy spent in marketing short pieces was no longer cost effective. Yet I enjoyed writing them and continued to do so, but then filed them away for future consideration along with all the stories, novellas, and personal essays that had already been published. And the years passed – far, far too quickly.

Circa 2020. On a slow winter's afternoon, it occurred to me that I might have written enough short pieces over the years to fill a few genre-based collections. Imagine my surprise when I finished curating my best pieces and discovered that I had, in fact, enough short stories and novellas for five collections and enough personal essays for another five collections.

Fully aware that story and essay collections are notoriously difficult to market, I discussed the situation with my literary agent. She reminded me that publishers are not fond of sharing their authors with other publishers, and that most publishers will put out only one book a year from an author. So, rather than wait ten years or more for traditional publication of my books, maybe I should become a hybrid author with one foot in the traditional publishing world and the other in the indie world, with the hope and expectation that both audiences would merge into a larger audience.

I found her suggestion highly appealing, but not principally because of potential audience enhancement. My sons will eventually inherit my literary estate, and the notion of them sitting in my basement trying to piece together multiple drafts of manuscripts from twenty or so plastic totes and file cabinets and scattered over numerous files and folders on my hard drive did not present a pleasant image. But if all my best work were already curated, copyrighted, and between covers for them, their chore of maintaining my literary estate would be much less difficult.

Hence Two Suns Books and The Legacy Collection. Some of the books in this collection have already been released. The rest will be forthcoming shortly. All are listed with my previous publications in the front matter.

Other possible titles might include a re-issue of my Drue Heinz Literature Prize-winning collection, *The Luckiest Man in the World*, a collection of my produced plays and optioned screenplays, and a book of my favorite poems and song lyrics.

All these books, including my traditionally published books, will be my legacy to my beloved sons, and to you, my cherished readers. I couldn't have survived this thing called Life without you.

With my love and gratitude,

RANDALL SILVIS ON SOCIAL MEDIA
https://www.randallsilvis.com
https://www.facebook.com/AuthorRandallSilvis
https://twitter.com/randall_silvis
https://www.instagram.com/randall.silvis
Author Randall Silvis - YouTube

FOR ADDITIONAL INFORMATION
Book Wyrm Literary Agency: Ms. Sandy Lu
sandy@bookwyrmlit.com
For book-to-film inquiries: Jim Strader
jstrader@quattromedia.com
For a speaking engagement inquiry:
authorssocmedmgmt@gmail.com

SIGN UP FOR
RANDALL'S FREE MONTHLY NEWSLETTER
at www.randallsilvis.com
and subscribe to his YouTube Channel at
Author Randall Silvis - YouTube

Made in the USA
Coppell, TX
13 February 2024

28967661R00213